MAKE ROOM FOR DREAMS

**Recent Titles in
Contributions in Philosophy**

Physician–Patient Decision-Making: A Study in Medical Ethics
Douglas N. Walton

Rethinking How We Age: A New View of the Aging World
C. G. Prado

Rationality in Thought and Action
Martin Tamny and K. D. Irani, editors

The Logic of Liberty
G. B. Madison

Coercion and Autonomy: Philosophical Foundations, Issues, and Practices
Alan S. Rosenbaum

Einstein and the Humanities
Dennis P. Ryan, editor

From Science to Subjectivity: An Interpretation of Descartes' *Meditations*
Walter Soffer

José Ortega y Gasset: Proceedings of the *Espectador universal* International
    Interdisciplinary Conference
Nora de Marval-McNair, editor

The Dynamics of Knowledge: A Contemporary View
David Z. Rich

Dilthey Today: A Critical Appraisal of the Contemporary Relevance of His Work
H. P. Rickman

The Structure and Confirmation of Evolutionary Theory
Elisabeth A. Lloyd

MAKE ROOM FOR DREAMS

Spiritual Challenges to Zionism

Haim Gordon

Foreword by Shulamit Aloni

Contributions in Philosophy, Number 39

Greenwood Press

New York · Westport, Connecticut · London

Library of Congress Cataloging-in-Publication Data

Gordon, Hayim.
    Make room for dreams.

    (Contributions in philosophy, ISSN 0084-926X ; no. 39)
    Bibliography: p.
    Includes index.
    1. Zionism—Philosophy. 2. Israel—Politics and
government—Philosophy. 3. National characteristics,
Israeli. I. Title. II. Series.
DS149.G5854   1989   956.94'001   88-34716
ISBN 0-313-26054-0 (lib. bdg. : alk. paper)

British Library Cataloguing in Publication Data is available.

Library of Congress Catalog Card Number: 88-34716
ISBN: 0-313-26054-0
ISSN: 0084-926X

First published in 1989

Greenwood Press, Inc.
88 Post Road West, Westport, Connecticut 06881

Printed in the United States of America

The paper used in this book complies with the
Permanent Paper Standard issued by the National
Information Standards Organization (Z39.48–1984).

10 9 8 7 6 5 4 3 2 1

For Myra and Harold Shapiro
who have often helped me make room for dreams

Contents

Foreword   ix

Introduction: Making Room for Dreams   1

    The problem: No room for dreams   1
    Vision, seeing, dreaming   7
    Political action and vision   13

Part I: Philosophical Background

1 Existentialism and Political Thought   23
    Space and freedom   23
    Freedom and thinking   33
    Civil courage and existentialist philosophy   41
    Daily engagements   53
2 The Reading of the Bible and Zionism   64

Part II: Challenges

3 Introduction   83
4 Justice and the Demise of the Kibbutz Myth   85
5 Faith Versus a Religious Obstruction of Belief   105
6 Peace Versus the Idolizing of the Israel Defense Force   121
7 Dialogue: Men and Women as Free Partners   136
8 Art: A Gateway to Freedom and Dreaming   144

Summary

Accepting the Challenges   159
Room for a New Vision   165

Selected Bibliography   167
Index   173

Foreword

by Shulamit Aloni

Israel is a country of contradictions and contrasts, not only in the structure of its population, or in the faiths and religious beliefs of its peoples, or in the structure of its political body, but also in its legal system, its judiciary, and its approach to justice.

Although the Zionist movement evolved and flourished in late nineteenth-century Europe by emancipating itself from the ghetto and embracing liberal ideas of progress and justice, although this movement, as a political body, promised in Israel's Declaration of Independence a constitution, freedom for all citizens of Israel, equality, laws without bias toward a member of any nationality, race, religion, or sex—despite all this, we are witnessing today in Israel a forceful trend of religious, tribal, and ethnic isolationism coupled with a devastating rise in prejudices stemming from religious and ethnic beliefs. We are also witnessing much confusion and no little ignorance as to the universal meaning of justice and government by law. Let me add that these contrasts and contradictions, these biases, this ignorance as to the meaning of democracy and government by law are not only in relation to Israel's acts in the occupied territories, which is a painfully severe and complex problem, but primarily relate to the State of Israel, that is, the area where its laws, institutions, and judiciary reign.

Historical reasons, such as the Second World War and the Holocaust, facilitated the establishment of the State of Israel and determined the character of its people. The population of 600,000 Jews who resided in Israel when the State was established was trebled within a decade. Most of the Jews who came during this decade were not from Western Europe or from the United States; they were spiritually broken refugees from Eastern Europe and Jews from Islamic countries around the Mediterranean Sea and from Yemen and Iraq. It has been said that Jews arrived from 102 different cultures; but it has rarely been mentioned that the large majority of these cultures were without a democratic tradition, and that these Jews had no experience in civic responsibility or participation in self-government. Before coming to Israel, almost all of these Jews had lived a closed, communal, congregational way of life. In order to survive, they distanced themselves from the government and from the majority of the population in the country; they developed an ideal of Jewish segregation, segregation from government, from the Goyim, and from responsibility and participation in the problems of the land, be it transportation, health, security, taxes, culture—yes, especially education and culture.

David Ben Gurion, who was a great and courageous leader, was not nurtured in the Western democratic tradition. He seems to have been fascinated by the bureaucratic centralization constructed by a national party, a fascination influenced by Bolshevik structures. Hence instead of drafting a constitution for the peoples that flocked to Israel, so as to hold representatives, government, and citizens accountable, instead of spelling out what is permitted and what is forbidden in a democratic state, instead of establishing a system of checks and balances, Ben Gurion decided that democracy means majority rule and there is no need for a constitution that would allow the minority to curb the ruling majority.

Thus after the first Knesset election Ben Gurion set up a government with the religious parties, which until then had had little political influence. He placidly bowed to their demands, which until today allow rabbis to rule each Jew's most personal life from the moment of birth until death, including their determining the status of marriage, divorce, and so on. Ben Gurion never understood how civil rights are thus distorted, and he tabled the proposal to draft a constitution or to legislate a bill of rights, although both were promised in the Declaration of Independence. Instead, he adopted the Ottoman law from medieval times, according to which every citizen in Israel is born into a religious group, which can judge his or her personal life.

In the identification card that each Israeli must carry, his religious–ethnic affiliation is inscribed, not his citizenship; we are thus identified as Jews, not Israelis. This card is a basis for segregation between the Jewish majority and the Arab minority; it often nurtures the traumatic hatred of the Goyim that many Jews brought with them from their diaspora life. On this strong basis, by slowly broadening religious coerciveness and tyranny and by enhancing the power of religious parties, it is not difficult to develop a nationalism that borders upon racism. When such occurs—and it is currently occurring—there will be spokesmen who will adorn ethnic isolationism with national and religious myths such as a "Chosen people" or a "Promised Land." They will add to this the ancient commandments to demolish the peoples of Canaan and to capture the entire land.

Jewish civil rights have also totally deteriorated under these ancient debilitated laws. One should note especially the degraded status of women, of minors, and of other groups upon which the orthodox religious establishment can vent its decrees after having attained political, governmental, and economic power.

Thus we live in a dual and confused system. The Declaration of Independence with its enlightened promises is an accepted ideal; many Jews, because of their past and their status in liberal movements, dream of setting up here an ideal state; the supreme court attempts and at times succeeds, by legislating through court decrees, in imbuing our life with the values of equality, in ensuring freedom of speech and of the press. But, on the other hand, the reality of the power of the government and its willingness to surrender principles of freedom for narrow political gains and to allow religious persecution and compulsion of Jews by Jews make our life into a strange system of enlightened revelations and dark oppression, bolstered by shameful bigoted persecution stemming from a religious ethnic background.

It is with this complex situation in mind that one should read Haim Gordon's book. Since Israel occupied the West Bank and Gaza in 1967, and especially in the last few years, the justification of persecution, of violence, and of not legislating a bill of rights has grown. On the other hand, these developments have aroused those Jews who wish to live in a constitutional republic, who believe in the words of the prophet: "Zion shall be redeemed with justice" (Isaiah 1). Like Haim Gordon, these people are struggling and dreaming, because they fear that if we do not realize an enlightened regime that promises equality for all, the Zionist revolution will be squandered and we will return to live in a closed tribal ghetto. I believe that their statements, like this book, will not fall upon deaf ears.

I also believe that through such struggling and writing our vitality will be strengthened; we will be able to make peace with our neighbors, and we will establish an open society, dynamical and just. We will recall that the Jewish heritage did not only designate a certain land holy, in which one should be buried, but also includes the ethical commands of the prophets and the belief in the value of each personal life. We will learn to put aside our traumatic fears, which lead us to antidemocratic manipulations, and to relinquish our anxieties, which until now are not quieted by our having the strongest army in the Middle East and our being a majority in our country, with a government, a police force, a legislative body, and a judiciary. I believe that such writing as this book will contribute substantially to the process of a renewed Zionism; it will help us make room for dreams and find ways to realize them.

MAKE ROOM FOR DREAMS

Introduction:
Making Room for Dreams

And they said one to another:
Behold, this dreamer cometh,
Come now, therefore, and let
us slay him and cast him into
one of the pits.
                              Genesis 37, 19–20

THE PROBLEM: NO ROOM FOR DREAMS

There is a story that at a labor party meeting in the early 1970s, the writer
Amos Oz addressed a question to Golda Meir, who was then prime minister
of Israel. "When you came to Israel in the early 1920s, half a century ago,"
Oz asked, "you dreamed of establishing a Jewish State based on justice and
equality, you dreamed of living peacefully with our Arab neighbors, you
dreamed of renewing our relationship to our Jewish heritage in an enhancing
manner. What do you dream of now?" Golda responded firmly: "The ringing
of the telephone every night about official business leaves me no room for
dreams."

For some years I perceived this story as a testimony to the lack of vision of
Israeli leaders, to their being politicians and not statesmen, to their not
understanding that in politics one should pursue justice, equality, fraternity.
I took these leaders to task because they merely sought power and were not
concerned with questions such as: How should one use power justly? In
short, I used the story as a battering ram in order to storm "the bastion
constructed by those myopic politicians who govern Israel." Lately, my
attitude toward the story has changed.

1

It is not that the politicians have become less myopic. They haven't. It was that I began to understand that Amos Oz's position as questioner (if the story is true) is no less an expression of what Golda Meir called no room for dreams. Otherwise, somewhere in his writings in the past fifteen years, Oz would have expressed his seeking for a dream. He hasn't, but of that later. Thus Oz's question, which I embraced, was not only in bad faith. It was a manner of lying to myself, an attempt to use a question in order to evade coping with my existential state. It was an attempt to cheat ontology of its due desert. Put differently, on the superficial level I used this story to deny responsibility for what occurs in Israel. On a deeper level, I used the story to justify my cowardly mode of being-in-the-world. I did not have the courage to dream, the relations I built with others were rarely ontic, and left no room for dreaming, so I shifted the burden onto Golda Meir. I was cunning and dishonest, but also unsatisfied, bored by my shallow criticism of others.

This book is an attempt to be less cunning and more honest. In seeking an honest response to our situation today in Israel, I shall be guided by two philosophical approaches which, to the best of my knowledge, have never been blended. Thoughts of existentialist writers from Kierkegaard and Dostoyevski to Buber and Sartre will underlie both my description of the manner of being-in-the-world of Jews and Arabs today in Israel, and my intuitive personal response to Biblical texts. The political writings of Hannah Arendt, which are based on classical political thinking, will allow me to describe how this being-in-the-world relates to political developments. The blending is important because any dream concerning human existence which a person wishes to pursue must have a political component. Most existentialists ignored this political component. Hence, the weakness of Nietzsche's vision of the superman, or of Buber's vision of a community guided by I-Thou attitudes—both visions lack the political component that would allow the reader to comprehend how such a goal may be realized.[1] Put differently, to realize a dream, one must enter the realm of politics; there its mettle is tested.

But there was an element of truth in Oz's question—it pointed to a patent lack of spiritual goals which characterizes contemporary Zionist thought and action. Since the 1970s when the question was asked, matters have not changed. Realities, exigencies, contingencies seem to block out all possibilities for dreaming about such goals. I suspect that many, if not most, Jews grasp Zionism as I did for many years, as a way of enlisting political or economic support for Israel or for contemporary Jews who are suffering. They no longer believe that the Zionist movement should seek ways to realize humane or spiritual goals. In short, Zionism is merely a label which many a Jew affixes to one's way of life; usually it has no influence on the way a person lives his or her life.

Yet perhaps I am posing a pseudo-question. National movements tend to disappear once national independence has been attained. Now that the State of Israel has been established, why discuss what occurs in Israel or among the Jews in terms of Zionism? Is it not more appropriate to discuss the political or economic goals of Israeli society or of the Jews in the diaspora? A full answer to this question will emerge in the course of this book. Here I shall only indicate the direction of my personal answer.

Learning from Buber,[2] I believe that to be true to Jewish history, Zionism should base its realization on the rejuvenation of a covenant between a people, a specific land, and God. (I submit that this view was rarely held by more than a minority of Zionists; still, I believe it to be the only manner of being true to the Biblical encounter with God.) This covenant is not limited to the attaining of national independence by the Jews in the Promised Land. As the Hebrew prophets repeatedly stressed, the covenant demands of each Jew that he or she pursue a just and holy way of life on that land. Thus the realization of a true Zionism must lead to a way of life that will encourage each Jew to live in accordance with the Decalogue and the spirit of the encounter with God. Hence, to take a simple narrow example, if many Israelis tend to steal from their government—and at present it does not interest us if it is the rule of the bureaucracy or mere greed that leads to such a stealing—those Jews who participate in such a stealing are not only breaking Israeli law, they are also rejecting the covenant with God and eroding the basic goals of Zionism.

Put differently, Zionism, or the return of the Jewish people to the land of Israel, will only be a true return if it is accompanied by a changing of certain basic attitudes concerning the Jew's manner of being-in-the-world. On the initial level such a change entails the realization of national aspirations. On a more profound level this manner of being-in-the-world means accepting the responsibility of trying to live in the spirit of the encounter between the Jewish people and God.

Buber repeatedly stressed that the spirit of Judaism can only be expressed in concrete daily actions.[3] In the Bible the encounter with God occurred in the concrete everyday reality of work and action, of loving and killing, of eating and dreaming. It had little to do with following many of the dogmas developed by Jews in the diaspora or with a life dedicated to the solitude of study. Therefore, a return to the land of Israel which attempts to live in the spirit of the Godly encounter must learn primarily from the Biblical period, during which Israel lived on the land, and, at times, fulfilled the covenant with God; it must honor the sages of the diaspora, but it must learn from them only to the extent that their teachings help one live one's freedom creatively and spiritually when facing current exigencies. Put differently, the Bible reveals that living in the Promised Land in the spirit of the Godly encounter demands more than obedience and thinking, it demands one's freedom, one's entire being. It also demands being involved in political developments. Some early Zionist pioneers, among them Golda Meir, sensed the difference intuitively. And as givers of their life and freedom to the renewal of Jewish life on the land of their forefathers, they permitted themselves to dream.

One can dream of a better future for humankind when one trusts in oneself and in other persons, when one strives to live a life of passion, not of lust, when one is willing to be guided by principles and by love, not only by success and by power. The ontology of the dreamer differs from that of the mediocre person who dares not dream. Of course, there will always be economic, political, or other exigencies that may hinder one's dreaming; but when they stifle the dreaming entirely, they are also stifling the spirit. Since the mood in Israel is guided primarily by pragmatic or fanatical goals, the possibility of dreaming is reduced to these goals and one dreams nightmares or stupidities. As brief examples, which will be expanded later in the book, I shall consider two prevailing attitudes: the Jew's relationship to the land of Israel and to the growth of the Israel Defense Force.

In Israel, as thoughout the world, soil is slowly being eroded, polluted; salinity is growing, land is being destroyed as a partner to human existence. Three decades ago Israeli farmers practiced rotation of crops so as to preserve the fertility of the soil. Today cash crops dominate. There is almost no rotation of crops. Farmers use chemical fertilizers and pesticides without reflecting at all about the long-term devastation they may bring. Pollution of the land with industrial and personal waste grows daily, as is reported almost weekly in the press. For many Israelis the land itself seems to have become a commodity which one can use and discard.

The attitude that prevails in most kibbutzim and moshavim in Israel is to relate to agriculture as an industry; the result is alienation from the land. In Marx's terms, the farmer has become mainly a provider of commodities. Sartre has shown that deep alienation may lead to fantasies and nightmares; it will not encourage visions or dreams.[4] Theodore Herzl was a case in point. As long as he was deeply alienated from his fellow Jews, he nurtured fantasies of leading the Jewish people to a mass baptism and conversion to Christianity led by the pope. But when he transcended this alienation and embraced the plight of Alfred Dreyfus, he could write The Jewish State and dream of Zionist goals.[5]

Alienation between the Jew and the Promised Land is evident in the insipid manner Israelis relate to the three Biblical agricultural holidays: Passover, Shavuoth, Sukkoth. Each of these holidays has both a historical and an agricultural source. In Biblical times, when the people of Israel worked the land, those holidays were a culmination of a period of waiting and praying for successful crops. The farmer thanked God for creating conditions that allowed the land to produce its bounty. The holiday also initiated the new period of waiting and hoping for the next crops, thus partaking in the cyclic mystery which binds human beings to the land from which they must draw their sustenance and to which, at death, one's remains will return. Almost nothing of this personal relationship to the land is evident today. Orthodox Jews, even if they cultivate the land—which few do—relate primarily to the historical aspects and to the ritual of these holidays which was developed in the diaspora. And farmers, many of whom are secular Jews, utilize the holidays for fairs, shows of achievements as in many kibbutzim, or family get-togethers. For city dwellers these holidays have almost no agricultural significance. In short, even during the traditional agricultural holidays, the relationship of most Jews living in Israel to the Promised Land is devoid of concrete spiritual acts.

If one is an alienated person one lives in a dialectic whereby one is unable to establish meaningful, trustful, or creative relations with other persons, or with that section of the world which one daily meets. Often, as Marx has shown, in such situations one is so steeped in producing and consuming commodities as to relate to oneself as a commodity. Yet, as many existentialists stressed, if one lives without relations of trust and creativity one learns to not trust oneself, and to not assume responsibility for that portion of the world in which one finds oneself. One may attempt to escape this dialectic by creating fantasies—often Kafkaesque fantasies—yet these fantasies only deepen one's alienation from the persons and the world that one encounters. As long as the dialectic of alienation rules one's being, such fantasies can never become dreams of a spiritual future. Hence, when through social and economic decisions the Jews in Israel are slowly alienating themselves from the Promised Land, they are stifling their personal ability to have visions of a spiritual future and to live in their light.

The Israel Defense Force was born out of the need for Jews to defend themselves while realizing Zionist goals, which included peace with our Arab neighbors. Slowly it has become, in the mind of many Jews, the most important symbol of Israel. It is admired and extolled, worshiped and fetishized. Many economic and social developments have contributed to such attitudes. For instance, every fifth Jew in Israel is either directly or indirectly employed by the Ministry of Defense. Many of these employees have a vested interest in the continued development of the military–industrial complex. Even after the peace treaty was signed with Egypt—until then our most dangerous foe—Israel continued to invest an enormous portion of its budget in the military. In Sartre's terms, the Israeli Defense Force and the military–industrial complex have become a practico-inert force that molds Israeli attitudes and Israeli society in its image.

But dreaming of a better future must essentially be a dream of peace, and one cannot dream of peace while worshiping a military machine. Put differently, since the growth of the military–industrial complex has become an end in itself in Israel, it has contributed to the blotting out of many Israelis' ability to dream; we are daily disregarding the warning of the Hebrew prophets that dreaming of a better future must include the hammering down of swords into ploughshares. Yet why is peace so central to a person's ability to dream, to visualize a better future?

Dreaming of a more spiritual future can only flourish in an ontology of innocence and trust toward one's fellow human beings. Such innocence and trust are the basis of peaceful relations between people. Peace not built on trust is merely the absence of war, it is a world built on the assumptions that Hobbes developed in *Leviathan*. Today the justification for the tremendous buildup of the Israeli military machine is: We mistrust our neighbors. The reality in which each Jewish child is nurtured includes the tenet: Never trust those Arabs. This ontology both sustains the military machine and is sustained by it. In short, the military–industrial complex in Israel is a powerful force in promoting mistrust of our Arab neighbors; as such it stifles the ability of many Jews to dream of peace, and of a better world.

I agree that my criticism of Israeli agriculture and of the Israeli military machine is rather simplistic. There is a story behind the developments in Israeli agriculture and the evolution of the Israeli military establishment which should not be overlooked if one wishes to be true to history. But, on the other hand, one must not succumb to complexities. Or as Golda seemed to indicate in the story, living in a world of complexities will often block one's ability to dream.

Since frequently I shall be suggesting rather simple approaches, one may ask: In our complex world how can one present simple approaches to complex problems? For instance, a person's relationship to the land is today governed, partially at least, by economic developments that are beyond one's power to alter. A farmer who will not use pesticides and chemical fertilizers is courting bankruptcy. What substance will embody this farmer's dreams if he or she follows the above principles but does not survive as a farmer?

The problem with complexity is that it is often used as a tactic to justify one's not assuming personal responsibility. Franz Kafka's novels repeatedly reveal that fascination with complexity can slowly erode the possibility of even discussing what one's personal responsibility in today's world can and should be. Dostoyevski wrote a hundred years ago in *The Brothers Karamazov*: "masses, masses of the most original Russians do nothing but talk of the eternal questions."[6] Today, unfortunately, the masses disregard eternal questions; they talk of the complexity of the world. Worse, the eternal questions have all but disappeared. The reason, I suspect, is a cowardly pragmatism; persons sense that to talk of the eternal questions may lead them to assume responsibility for something they wish to evade, so they evade the question. And one good excuse for such evasion is the complexity of the situation that confronts them.

Of course, one may call my response merely an unmasking of those who may criticize me for my simplistic approaches. Hence, the question still remains: Why should one respond "simplisticly" to a complex situation such as the disappearance of a Zionist vision? The answer, which achieved sublime eloquence in the sayings of the Hebrew prophets, is: The only way to indicate a direction for positive development is by *simply* pointing in that direction. They also simply pointed to the evil that Israelites had done. The prophets knew that such a pointing does not solve the complex issues one may encounter while striving to attain the desired developments. These need to be faced when the appropriate moment arises. But without such a pointing one will be overcome by the whirlpool of complexities that characterizes many a situation. Thus in pointing out that it is wrong to worship the Israel Defense Force, I am not denying the complexity of the situation in which we find ourselves, as Jews isolated in an ocean of hostile Islam. I am suggesting that there is a direction for development which will not include such a worshiping, despite the acknowledged complexity of our situation.

Hence, the goals of Zionism are simple goals, much as the Decalogue is written in simple, concise language. Not losing sight of these goals in the vortex of complexities which engulf one is a difficult task. Yet how does one learn to see simple goals? How does one learn to find room for dreams?

VISION, SEEING, DREAMING

While seeing and dreaming usually relate to private experiences, vision is a term which often defines a communal or political wish. In Hebrew the distinction is upheld by language; one cannot use the Hebrew word for vision, *hazon*, in order to speak of a personal dream, say, if a person wishes to become president of Israel. *Hazon* can be used to name only a communal or a political wish. What angered me in the story of the encounter between Amos Oz and Golda Meir is that while he used the word dream to ask about her vision of Zionism, she evaded the question by responding on the personal, private level of dreaming. Often, in order for a person to be able to strive to realize a vision, he or she must perceive, albeit vaguely, a direction of development. Thus, by transferring the question to the private realm of dreaming, Golda Meir, the prime minister of Israel, evaded seeking a direction of development.

In order to perceive a direction of development, one must often see everyday reality differently. How does one acquire such an ability to see? I shall present Buber's partial response to this question, which emerges in his discussion of the Patriarch Abraham.[7] It resembles responses of other existentialists, for instance Nietzsche in *Thus Spake Zarathustra* or Sartre in *Nausea*.

Buber points out that the first of the seven revelations of the Patriarch Abraham is God's command: "Get thee out of my country, and from thy kindred, and from thy father's house, unto the land that I will show thee" (Genesis 12, 1). The last of these revelations begins with the command: "Take now thy son, thine only son, who thou lovest, even Isaac, and get thee to the land of Moriah; and offer him there for a burnt-offering upon one of the mountains which I will tell thee of" (Genesis 22, 2). Both commands include the Hebrew words *Lech Lecha* (Go thee) which appear together only in these two places in the Bible. According to Buber, these words indicate that in order to become a seer, Abraham must first be able to cut himself off from his past, and finally he must be able to cut off his future, which includes sacrificing the bearer of God's promise of succession and immortality, his son, Isaac. One can learn from these terrifying ordeals, even if one cannot and dare not emulate them. To undertake such learning one must consider the existential situation in which Abraham finds himself.

What does it mean to cut oneself off from one's past? Clearly it is not equivalent with becoming alienated to one's past. The expression "to cut off" indicates that there exists a physical attachment before the act of cutting off; in the case of living beings, the attachment provides sustenance for the limb which may be cut off. The cutting of the umbilical cord, which initiates a new independent life, is perhaps the most vivid example of a person being cut off from one's past. Such a cutting off need not lead to alienation: most children are not alienated from their mother after birth. Alienation is a relationship of indifference, aversion, or estrangement, where one grasps oneself as an object. An alienated person will usually not strive to establish new relations with the object of his or her alienation. In contrast, Abraham, who cut himself off from his family and land of birth, grasped himself as a subject and sought to reestablish his relationship with his kin. He commanded his servant, Eliezer: "thou shalt go unto my country, and to my kindred, and take a wife for my son, for Isaac" (Genesis 24, 4).

Cutting oneself off from one's past is a manner of asserting independence, which often allows a person to see the encompassing reality with greater depth or to see a new direction. On the basis of such seeing one may establish a new relationship with one's past. In contrast, becoming alienated to one's past is an active passivity. By "active passivity" I mean that one passively accepts all major developments in one's life and acts only in response to these developments. One does not initiate. Hence, an alienated person's view rarely penetrates beyond the surface of events. Nor does such a person assume new responsibilities. (In rare cases, though, it may occur that one will become alienated toward a specific realm because one has assumed responsibility in another realm. Many of the pioneers who returned to Israel at the turn of the century assumed the responsibility of living a new Jewish life in Israel, while alienating themselves from diaspora Judaism.) A grotesque, yet vivid description of the link between active passivity and alienation emerges in the plight of K. in Kafka's *The Castle*. K. slowly alienates himself from his entire milieu by always acting passively, by never cutting himself off and asserting his independence. Hence his gaze always skims upon the surface of events; he never sees a direction of development, or a way out of his gross predicament.

The story of Abraham suggests that cutting oneself off from one's past is often a necessary condition for being able to see a new way of life. It is not a suffient condition. There is no sufficient condition since the guiding of one's life in the direction of a vision is an act of freedom, and as existentialists from Kierkegaard and Dostoyevski to Sartre and Buber indicated there are no sufficient conditions for acts of freedom. In other words, when one is seeking a new way of life, the cutting of oneself off from certain aspects of one's past can help one learn to see. But in accordance with Abraham's example, such a cutting off must be an existential decision which affects one's entire life; it is not a psychological method, or trick. For instance, if we Jews wish to see ourselves as living in peace with our Arab neighbors, we must learn to cut ourselves off from the Masada syndrome[8] and from our Holocaust fears. Of course, there is historical justification for this syndrome and these fears. Still, as long as this syndrome and these fears, justified though they may be, influence our being-in-the-world, they will hinder our attempts to actively guide our lives in the direction of peace, they will not allow us to see new possibilities in the encompassing reality. Unfortunately, today, quite a few years after the signing of the 1979 peace treaty with Egypt, many Jews still grasp their being-in-the-world as a sitting atop the Masada fortress surrounded by enemy legions.

In short, I am suggesting that cutting oneself off from the complexities of the past may allow new visions to emerge. Initially these are simple visions. But that is their power. When one today reads *The Jewish State*, one is surprised at the simplicity of the ideas that Herzl presented and how little they draw on Jewish history. We know that, as a person, Herzl was cut off from traditional Judaism. But it seems that he also sensed intuitively that the simple, the naive, often leads persons to see new possibilities that an acknowledging of complexities conceal.

Cutting oneself off from the future may be much more problematic, especially for a contemporary person whose being-in-the-world is often a continual planning ahead. Here the distinction between courage and daring is significant, because cutting oneself off from one's future may lead to seeing if it is an act of courage. I doubt that one may learn to see through acts of daring. The *Random House Dictionary* defines "daring" as adventurous courage or boldness. I am unhappy with this definition since it does not take into account that in an act of courage one often takes full responsibility for one's actions. Such does not occur in an act of daring. Dostoyevski described the difference between daring and courage vividly in *The Brothers Karamazov*. Both Father Zosima and Dimitri Karamazov begin their adult life with escapades of daring; but through a profound existential encounter they become converted to a life of courage and responsibility. Note that in both cases there is a cutting of oneself off from one's future at the moment of conversion.

Daring is influenced by and can lead to fantasy, while courage may lead to vision. The two major prose writers of early Zionism, Agnon and Brenner,[9] describe many of the Jewish pioners who, following their fantasies, came to Israel in the early twentieth century; for them, coming to Israel was an act of daring. Only when these pioneers began assuming responsibility for each other and for their dreams and deeds did they begin to act courageously—and some of them also began to guide their lives in accordance with a vision.

In all acts of courage there is a cutting of oneself off from the future. One decides to do something because it is the right thing to do at this specific moment, without one's being influenced by how this action may affect one's future. Abraham's willingness to sacrifice Isaac is perhaps the most terrifying of such acts of courage. Buber links this deed to Abraham's becoming a "Seer." He thus suggests that one may learn to see the present differently if one is able to stop one's constant flight into a planned future.

Seeing as described by existentialist writers is more of a worldly involvement than the act of contemplation and the striving to see objectively which appear in Greek philosophy. In Plato's *The Republic* the philosopher, who emerges from the allegorical cave in order to contemplate the Reality of ideas, is detached from both the shadowy existence in the cave and from the Reality of ideas. Historians of science suggest that a similar detaching of oneself—including the detaching of the appearances one is examining from teleology and from Godly intervention—characterizes the quest for objective knowledge and the rise of modern science. These detachings are manners of cutting oneself off from the past and from the future which help the philosopher and the scientist see the world differently than the ordinary person. Yet such seeing does not encourage one to act in the world. The contemplating philosopher returns reluctantly from the realm of truth and reason to the darkness of the cave and hesitantly becomes involved in the affairs of the shadowy world of appearances. And most scientists perceive their work as being divorced from their personal way of life. In contrast, the learning to see that existentialist writers have described can bring about a changing of one's manner of being-in-the-world; it is a learning to see through involvement and which leads to involvement.

Such a seeing through involvement characterizes the Biblical prophets. While being involved in the world of appearances, the Hebrew prophet presented a vision and demanded of his or her listeners that they change their way of life. Hosea was instructed by God: "Go take unto thee a wife of harlotry and children of harlotry, for the land doth commit great harlotry, departing from the Lord" (Hosea 1, 2). After this experience Hosea spoke out against Israel's betrayal of God. After struggling in his corrupt milieu, Elijah fled to the desert, but was instructed by God to return to the milieu which he had abandoned and to struggle *there* for the fulfillment of God's ethical and religious commands. Jonah fled God, his past, and his mission; he rebelled against God's mercy toward the inhabitants of Nineveh; by going through these bitter experiences he learned to comprehend the world differently, and to see God's manner of involving Himself in the world. In short, the Biblical personage who learns to see does so through involvement in the world of appearances that Plato disparaged.

Of course there are difficulties in such an involvement. Franz Kafka succinctly described one major difficulty in a parable:

He has two antagonists: The first presses him from behind, from the origin. The second blocks the road ahead. He gives battle to both. To be sure, the first supports him in his fight with the second, for he wants to push him forward, and in the same way the second supports him in his fight with the first, since he drives him back. But it is only theoretically so. For it is not only the two antagonists who are there, but he himself as well, and who really knows his intentions? His dream, though, is that at some time in an unguarded moment—and this would require a night darker than any night that has ever been yet—he will jump out of the fighting line and be promoted, on account of his experience in fighting, to the position of umpire over his antagonists in their fight with each other.[10]

The man that Kafka describes exists between a past that is pushing him forward and a future that is pushing him backward. Such a struggle characterizes many a person's life. One way of escaping this situation, Hannah Arendt suggested, is by living in the realm of thinking, of ideas.[11] The Hebrew Bible describes another way of overcoming this struggle: One gives oneself to the matter at hand as a whole being; thus one lives fully in the present and the struggle between past and future disappears.

Existentialists also described and discussed instances of living fully in the present. Dostoyevski believed that active love can lead one to moments of living fully in the present. Buber held that such occurs in moments of genuine dialogue. Nietzsche indicated that dancing is a manner of living fully in the present, and when one gives one's entire being to a melody in dance the struggle that Kafka depicted vanishes.

Living fully in the present is usually linked to an act of relating. The dancer relates to the melody and to his or her partner or partners in dance; in genuine dialogue one relates to the *Other*, be it nature, or another person, or a spiritual being; active love is to another person or to a living being in the world. Such relations of dance, dialogue, and love allow a knowledge of the other person to emerge, a knowledge that cannot be analyzed, only lived. In the Bible sexual intercourse is called knowing, perhaps because in sexual intercourse the struggle between past and future that Kafka describes may fade; one may live fully in the present. And after sexual intercourse, especially if it was an act of love, a new knowledge of the other person emerges. Following Dostoyevski, one might add that this knowledge is an expanding knowledge: one loves life and the world through one's loving and knowing the other person.

Kafka's parable also describes the loneliness of one's attempt to assert oneself while struggling with one's past and with one's future. This loneliness is deepened when the person who is at the center of the struggle lacks a direction for development. This lack prompts the man described in the parable to wish to become an umpire over his antagonists. Such a manner of escape is cowardly; it is a fleeing of involvement in the world into a new loneliness, the loneliness of merely judging what is happening. Here one can point to the difference between loneliness and solitude. When one is undergoing a period of solitude, having cut oneself off from one's past and future, one is often developing in a specific direction. Such rarely happens—if at all—during periods of lonliness. The Hebrew prophets often underwent periods of solitude—Moses tending his sheep in the Sinai desert comes to mind—during which they developed so as to be able to become bringers of God's message.

There is still one point to be made. The cutting off from the past and from the future can best be described by telling a story. Only a story tells us *who* a person is; an abstract description merely tells us *what* a person is—a teacher, an accountant, a sailor.[12] And since both the act of cutting off and the seeking of a vision are profound personal experiences, one should describe them as accompanying the exigencies and daily decisions of a person's life.

This point helps illuminate the situation in Israel today: There are few meaningful or courageous stories to tell. One reason is that there is little vision in Israel and there are few—very few—courageous persons. In many areas mediocrity reigns unchallenged. Contemporary Israeli literature describes this mediocrity and also contributes to its perpetuation. This is a literature in which almost no courageous persons are described; hence there is no place for vision. Furthermore, most authors do not even know how to tell a good story. Or to cite a thought from Isak Dinesin—who knew how to tell stories and knew the significance of such a telling—a good story-teller knows that when the story ends the silence must speak out. This silence accompanys the reader or the listener during his or her daily endeavors, challenging him or her as a person. But if a story is merely polished chatter, as occurs in almost all of Israeli contemporary literature and will be discussed in the chapter on art, when the story ends the memory of the clever insipid chatter rapidly fades.

Hence, a good story is more than mere entertainment, it is more than a mode of artistic expression. Because it describes the life or the lives of specific persons, it can be a challenge to the reader or the listener to relate spiritually. Such is perhaps easier if the story describes a striving to live one's freedom courageously, creatingly, lovingly. But one can also learn from stories that describe the perversion of freedom, if these stories hint as to how one could have lived otherwise.

To convey the spirit of my approach, I will be interspersing stories into the text of this book. I have gleaned these stories from personal experiences, from friends, and from other texts. The following story taught me much about cutting oneself off from the past and learning to see.

At the turn of the century the chief orthodox rabbi of Hungary had a devout son who became involved in Zionist activities. A mutual trust existed between father and son; hence, when the father asked: "Why do you spend your time with these strayers from the path of Judaism?" the son responded: "Father, come to a Zionist congress, and you will understand." The father decided to come.

They traveled together to the next Zionist congress in Basel. The son was a delegate and sat in the chamber. The father, an old bearded man with silver hair and sidelocks, sat quietly in the balcony. When the son questioned him a few times as to his impressions, the father was silent. Thus he sat four full days, listening.

When the congress ended, the father suggested: "Since we have come this far, let us travel a bit further to Frankfurt, to visit the rabbi there who is a close friend." On the train the father continued to be reticent.

The chief rabbi of Hungary was treated with great honor when the train arrived in Frankfurt. After he had been put up in the house of the local rabbi, and he and his son had rested a bit, they entered the study to spend some time with their host.

"What brings you to our area?" asked the rabbi of Frankfurt.

"We were in Basel," responded the old man.

"And what was your purpose in visiting Basel?"

"We went to the Zionist Congress, my son as a delegate, and I merely to listen."

"What?! You went to the Zionist Congress! You, the chief rabbi of Hungary! How could you? That Herzl is a nonbeliever. Don't you know that he doesn't eat kosher, that he doesn't pray regularly, that he parades himself without a skullcap, that he doesn't read Hebrew or study the Talmud?! How could you go there to listen to such a sinner, to such a perverter of Judaism?"

At last the rabbi from Hungary was compelled to state his impressions. "You are right, Herzl is not an observant Jew," the old man said quietly. "And I thank God for that. I thank God that Herzl doesn't keep kosher and that he doesn't wear a skullcap or pray. Because if he did, if he was an observant Jew, I would have to climb up to the roof of your house, stand there and proclaim and yell so that all the Jews could hear: The Messiah has come!"[13]

POLITICAL ACTION AND VISION

The rise of the Zionist movement at the end of the nineteenth century was accompanied by the belief that any vision of Jewish national life, which is to be realized in this world, must be based on political action. Such was a breakthrough, since Jewish history according to Arendt

offers the extraordinary spectacle of a people ... which began its history with a
well-defined concept of history and an almost conscious resolution to achieve a
well-circumscribed plan on earth and then, without giving up this concept, avoided
political action for two thousand years.[14]

Becoming a Zionist meant cutting oneself off from one's past of avoiding
political action, it meant beginning to act in the realm of politics. A person
who acts politically endeavors through words and deeds to influence the
direction of development of his or her society, people, government, regime.
By such endeavors one also, albeit indirectly, assumes responsibility for what
occurs in the world. Jews did not assume such a responsibility, and as a
result they lacked political ability and judgement; such was "caused by the
very nature of Jewish history, the history of a people without a government,
without a country, and without a language."[15]

Here, perhaps is Herzl's most significant contribution to Judaism and to
Zionism. At the turn of the century he demanded of the Jews that they relate
to themselves as persons capable of political action—what is perhaps truer to
history is that Herzl took it for granted that Jews *must* initiate political action.
He knew that only such action could lead to the realization of his vision. His
success, which was only partial, was still astounding, because the Jews he
was addressing were the descendants of a people who during at least eighteen
hundred years in the diaspora had almost always refrained from such action.

The fact that for eighteen centuries the Jews lacked a country, a state, a
government, and a language of political interaction often distorted their
understanding of political action and its relation to vision. For instance,
during the centuries that the Jews lacked a country and were barred from
owning land and tilling it in the countries where they resided, the Promised
Land became a mythical abstraction. The Jew read in the Bible about the
Promised Land, prayed for its flourishing and dreamed of its being rebuilt as
a homeland for all Jews; but for almost two millennia Jews made only very
few and limited attempts to return to that land in order to make it flourish or
to rebuild it. For some Jews the Promised Land was a dream, for others it
was a concept, an abstraction—for most it was definitely not a land in which
one resides. The diaspora Jews did not feel its soil under foot or smell the
fragrance of its air after the first fall rain. They were not burned by its sun in
the summer, nor did they rejoice when flowers covered its slopes in spring.
The Jew did not live in this land or from this land; it had nothing to do with
one's day-to-day existence, with one's livelihood, or calling, or career, or
immediate past or future. When the Messiah will come, the Jew believed,
this Promised Land would be the place of homecoming for all Jews.

This abstract relationship to the Promised Land, coupled with the feeling
that the land in which one resided was not one's country, contributed to the
fact that few Jews were interested, until the Jewish Enlightenment, in the

making and learning of history. Such was expressed by Moses Mendelssohn in a letter to a Christian friend who had decided to write a history of mankind: "Until now I regarded history more as a science of the citizen than of man. I was of the opinion that a man who has no country could not expect any advantage from history."[16] Mendelssohn asks his friend how to commence his study of history. Prior to that letter, Mendelssohn, as a Jew, a man without a country, had little inclination to study history, or to involve himself intellectually in understanding political developments. He seems to have had no qualms about his being barred from participating in the political realm. He does not seem to have recognized that accepting his situation was a flight from the freedom and the responsibility that one assumes by acting in the realm of politics.

Even the influential Jewish bankers, who helped many European politicians, were not at all concerned with acting in the political realm. They served whoever was in power.

The history of the relationship between Jews and governments is rich in examples of how quickly Jewish bankers switched their allegiance from one government to the next even after revolutionary changes. It took the French Rothschilds in 1848 hardly twenty-four hours to transfer their services from the government of Louis Philippe to the new short-lived French Republic and again to Napoleon III.[17]

Arendt gives many additional examples in which Jewish bankers grasped themselves as servants of those in power, not as persons capable of political action.

In Israel one finds no few remnants of these diaspora approaches. For instance, many Jews relate to the land of Israel abstractly: Very few Jews consider the land, or a portion of it, as a partner in their quest for sustenance; few Israelis are concerned that what they call "The Holy Land" is becoming polluted, and that industrial waste is contaminating the land, the water, and the air; there are very few parks where one can relate to nature, and these few parks are often cluttered with garbage—the shore line park around Lake Kineret (Tiberius) is a case in point; and most Israeli architects, when they design buildings, or high-rise complexes, or towns, do *not* design them so a person can relate to the land or to nature. In short, many a Jew does not live as if this specific land is his or her own land—with its garbage in the parks, its polluted Jordan River, its smog in Tel Aviv—and he or she is responsible for its degradation, for the way it looks and smells. This abstract manner of relating to the land can lead to a distorted vision of Zionism. Here is an example.

Around forty percent of Jewish Israelis believe that the West Bank and the Gaza Strip should be annexed to Israel. To understand the chauvinism and the abstractness of such an approach some demographic information is necessary. Three million six hundred thousand Jews and seven hundred thousand Arabs reside in Israel and are Israeli citizens. On the West Bank and in the Gaza Strip live more than a million and a quarter Palestinian Arabs. Thus, annexing the West Bank and the Gaza Strip will result in Jews being around sixty percent of the enlarged State of Israel. Given the fact that Arab population growth is much greater than Jewish population growth, the Jews could become a minority in their own country in less than half a century. Hence, the wish to annex the West Bank and the Gaza Strip is, aside from being immoral, anti-Zionistic in that it threatens the tenet that the State of Israel should be predominantly Jewish. And yet, large numbers of Jews in Israel, among them many who have never worked the land and do not plan to do so, are vehement and, at times, fanatic about annexing the Arab populated West Bank and Gaza Strip. Why?

The answer is that these Jews relate to the Land of Israel abstractly, greedily, not as partners, but as exploiters. To substantiate these charges, two more facts merit attention. First, the polls reveal that a large majority of the Jews who support annexing the West Bank and the Gaza Strip originated in countries where political freedom was harshly suppressed, such as the Soviet Union and Arab countries. Second, there is currently no lack of land for Jews who live in Israel, nor is there a lack of land to cultivate. During the past two decades Jews were offered high government subsidies if they would settle in the Galilee or in the Southern Negev. Few did. Furthermore, during the ten years (1977–1987) of right wing and unity governments which supported settling on the West Bank, and which organized a propaganda blitz to do so, and poured hundreds of millions of dollars into building settlements on the West Bank—during these years only forty thousand Jews transferred their residence to these settlements. Another thirty thousand settled in new suburbs of Jerusalem on the West Bank, but these can hardly be called settlers. (Most of these settlers do not work the land. They merely reside in these settlements, and work in Tel Aviv or Jerusalem.) Thus, neither a lack of land, nor a wish to cultivate the land, nor an assuming of political responsibility for one's deeds underlies the wish to annex the Gaza Strip and the West Bank.

There seem to be two and only two ways of relating to nature and to the land which sustains us. Either the land is there to grab and to exploit, or we human beings, as sojourners on this land, must relate to it as a partner to our human endeavors. The Patriarch Abraham's relation to the Promised Land was that of a sojourner. The land was a partner to the covenant between Abraham and God—this specific land upon which Abraham tended his flocks and from which he wandered to Egypt when drought ruined all pasture; this specific land whose inhabitants he honored, whose glens and ravines he traversed; this land from whose bounty he lived as he slowly crossed it from north to south and then back north again. Of course, one can argue that Abraham's manner of relating to the land was exceptional. He shared wells with other inhabitants; when his shepherd's feuded with Lot's shepherds he allowed Lot to choose the better pastures. King Solomon, for instance, did not relate to the Promised Land as an earthly sojourner—he exploited the land and the People of Israel who inhabited it. Still, today, when the Jews have a land of their own, additional territory will not help us learn to relate to this land as a partner to our earthly endeavors.

Yet what does relating as a sojourner to the land have to do with acting in the political realm, or with being able to pursue a vision? Put briefly, a person relates as a sojourner on (and a partner to) the land when he or she is aware of the moral implications of his or her own mortality. As a mortal, a person passes through the land for a period of years; he or she can draw sustenance from this land, but must not defile or destroy it; others need to come after this person and pass through the land as he or she did. Undertaking political action so as to realize a vision is also based on an awareness of one's being mortal.

Men and women, unlike animals and plants, are identified as persons and not merely as instances of a species; hence each person's birth and death are significant events. And since each person knows that he or she is mortal, that one's life is limited, the manner of one's existing together with other human beings is an issue that may be addressed. In order to address this issue, as the Greeks of antiquity insisted, a space must be created wherein persons will discuss and determine their manner of existing together. This space is the political realm. In it persons, as free unique human beings, can discuss and define the just way of life, and in light of this discussion can discuss and determine their future manner of living together. According to the Greeks, those persons who lived in tribes or communities without a political realm were less than human—barbarians the Greeks called them. These barbarians identified themselves as members of a tribe, not as free responsibile persons capable of discussing and determining their manner of existence. (The totalitarian regimes of the twentieth century which were established by movements that abolish and annihilate the political realm and strive to attain tribal unity are, even in the Greek sense, barbarian.) Barbarians were also less than human because in the political realm one can participate in the making of history. Thus, when a political realm exists, those persons whose words and deeds will be remembered and not pass into oblivion—these few persons will achieve immortality, in the face of their own mortality.[18]

By political action one assumes responsibility for the ethical character of one's country, milieu, and state. When political action is possible, a person can act and speak in order to bring change for the better in face of what one encounters, even if one doubts the results of one's deeds and knows that they might be influential only after one's death. (Think of Socrates, or of Brutus.) Such a person knows that despite one's being mortal, despite the frivolousness of many participants in the realm of politics, and despite the fact that most (if not all) of a person's acts and words (unlike works of art) will disappear from human comprehension once their relevance has passed—despite one's awareness of these facts, such a person also knows that political action is the only way one can express one's freedom while striving to attain ethical (and, perhaps, religious) goals.

Unfortunately, as this book will reveal, many Jews in Israel retain remnants of a way of life that avoids political action. This avoidance limits their possibility to make room for dreams.

A central tenet of Plato's philosophy, which is so clear to Plato that he sees no need to prove it, is that only a free person can seek a vision and attempt to realize it. (In the parable of the cave, those who are unfree sit chained to their place, seeing only shadows.) As Hannah Arendt pointed out, freedom for the Greeks was the ability to interact in the polis, that is to discuss and determine together with one's peers the future of the polis. Women, or slaves, or laborers, or craftsmen, or artists, who could not dedicate their life to such a challenging task, were not free. Free persons were not tied down to the tasks of laboring or fabricating, hence they could discuss various topics at leisure, for as long as the discussion required. Persuasion was central to their mode of interaction, and they perceived as worthy endeavors discussions of the character of justice, or the significance of love, or the best way of life a man should pursue. In short, Plato's dialogues depict aspects of the life of freedom in the polis; they are not only a literary genre.

The structure of Biblical society after the Children of Israel settled in the Promised Land was tribal, and later monarchal. There was no polis where free persons could congregate and influence each other by persuasion; few persons enjoyed leisure; political action does not seem to have been a goal on the horizon of most persons' possibilities. Still, prophets arose who strove to persuade their contemporaries that their way of life was unjust and that they had betrayed God. They described the abandonment and destruction that would reign if persons and rulers would continue to betray God and His demands for justice and faith. They also presented visions of a better life, when peace, justice, and true faith in God would prevail.

In this book I shall often indicate what I personally learned about freedom, political action, and making room for dreams from my reading of the Bible. My reading is personal, perhaps naive, definitely not scholarly. I am trying to hear the Biblical messages as a simple reader can hear it. Of course my reading of Buber has helped me, but it is not overpowering—I may disagree with Buber's interpretations. My manner of reading was suggested by Buber, who pointed out that the Hebrew prophets spoke to the whole being of their listeners. They did so even while responding to particular acts of evil, because pursuing the justice and living the faith that they demanded required that a person unite one's entire being. This ability to relate to the whole being of their listener is one reason their pronouncements still resound. Through such a relating, they could indicate the challenge that each person must face in striving to realize the vision that they presented. As I shall show in the chapter on reading the Bible, I have tried to read the Bible with my whole being.

Before turning to the philosophical approach that I believe can serve as a basis for new challenges to Zionism, one more point needs to be made. The dreaming, and seeking of a vision, and learning to see, and acting in the political realm, and reading the Bible as a whole being which I have briefly described can be joyful acts. They can be a passionately giving of oneself to the world, they can be attempts to live with other persons in freedom and communion. They are also acts of courage.

NOTES

1. Nietzsche was not a political philosopher. In Walter Kaufmann's *Nietzsche: Philosopher, Psychologist, Antichrist* (Princeton, N.J.: Princeton University Press, 1950) the word politics is not even indexed. I have shown that Buber disparaged the political realm in Haim Gordon, "Existential Guilt and Buber's Social and Political Thought," in Haim Gordon and Jochanan Bloch (editors), *Martin Buber, A Centenary Volume* (New York: Ktav, 1984), pp. 215–232. I disagree with those scholars who have described Buber as a politically active person. See, for instance, Haim Gordon, "The Sheltered Aesthete: A New Appraisal of Martin Buber's Life," in Gordon and Bloch, *Martin Buber, A Centenary Volume*, pp. 25–39. Also, Haim Gordon, *The Other Martin Buber: Recollections of His Contemporaries* (Athens, Ohio: Ohio University Press, 1988).

2. See, for instance Martin Buber, *On Zion* (New York: Schocken, 1973).

3. See, for instance Martin Buber, *Israel and the World* (New York: Schocken, 1948).

4. Two of Sartre's plays show this explicitly: "No Exit" and "The Flies." One can also sense it in his novel *Nausea*.

5. Alex Bein, *Theodore Herzl: A Biography* (Philadelphia, Pa.: Jewish Publication Society of America, 1940); Amos Elon, *Herzl* (New York: Schocken, 1966).

6. Fyodor Dostoyevsky, *The Brothers Karamazov* (New York: New American Library, 1957), p. 216.

7. Martin Buber, "Abraham the Seer," in *On the Bible: Eighteen Studies* (New York: Schocken, 1968), pp. 22–43.

8. Masada was a fortress in the Judean desert west of the Dead Sea in which Jewish zealots fought against the Romans at the end of the Jewish rebellion in AD 73. When the Jews perceived that the Romans would soon scale the cliffs and overcome them, they preferred to take their own lives. The plight of Masada is described in the last pages of Josephus' *The Jewish War*. The Masada syndrome is the existential manner of grasping oneself that many Jews express, that "the whole world is against us, out to kill us, and we are living on this fortress in the middle of the desert, alone." I disagree that the Masada syndrome is merely a myth, as described in Charles S. Liebman and Eliezer Don-Yehiya, *Civil Religion in Israel* (Berkeley, Calif.: University of California Press, 1983). Later in the book I explain at length why the sociological approach, developed by these and other authors, is superficial and will not suffice to relate to Israel's spiritual challenges.

9. Josef Hayyim Brenner (1881–1921) who was killed by Arabs is considered the first major Hebrew and Zionist prose writer. Few of his writings have been translated into English. See, for instance, *Breakdown and Bereavement* (Ithica, N.Y.: Cornell University Press, 1971). Shmuel Yosef Agnon (1888–1970) was encouraged to publish his writings by Brenner. He received the Nobel Prize for Literature in 1966. Few of his writings have been translated into English. See, for instance, *In the Heart of the Seas* (New York: Schocken, 1948) and books listed in the Bibliography.

10. This parable by Kafka and Arendt's discussion of it appear in Hannah Arendt, *Between Past and Future* (Harmondsworth, England: Penguin, 1977), p. 7. Arendt admits to having altered the prevailing translation.

11. Hannah Arendt, *The Life of the Mind: Thinking* (New York: Harcourt, Brace Jovanovich), especially Chapter 20.

12. Hannah Arendt, *The Human Condition* (Chicago, Ill.: University of Chicago Press, 1958). See p. 10, but Arendt discusses this distinction throughout the book.

13. I heard this story from Jochanan Bloch in an interview on Buber. See Haim Gordon, *The Other Martin Buber: Recollections of His Contemporaries* (Athens, Ohio: Ohio University Press, 1988).

14. Hannah Arendt, *The Origins of Totalitarianism* (New York: Harcourt Brace Jovanovich, 1951), p. 8.

15. Ibid.

16. Quoted from Alexander Altmann, *Moses Mendelssohn, A Biographical Study* (Tuscaloosa, Ala.: University of Alabama Press, 1973), p. 107.

17. Arendt, *The Origins of Totalitarianism*, p. 24.

18. Arendt, *The Human Condition*, esp. Chapters 1–3.

PART I

PHILOSOPHICAL BACKGROUND

1

Existentialism
and Political Thought

SPACE AND FREEDOM

If one examines the relationship between space and freedom as it has been
discussed by some contemporary philosophers, one finds that each thinker
viewed this relationship from a specific perspective. I believe that much can
be learned from an integrating approach, and in what follows I shall show
how the thinking of Buber and Arendt on this theme can be partially
integrated, while learning from other existentialists. This integration will
allow me to elaborate upon deficiencies in political and personal life in Israel
today. It will also provide a foundation for spiritual challenges for Zionism.

Since this is a book on the need for a vision and what may be done to seek
and pursue vision, it may, at times, include what no few detractors of
existentialism have called "existential musings." Put differently, I will not be
presenting a *full* historical, sociological, political, or any other argumentative
analysis of the faults and failings of Israeli society that I shall be attacking.
Although such a full argumentative analysis is important, it rarely—if
ever—leads to a new vision; in contrast, "existential musings," such as
Nietzsche's, may lead to vision. After briefly explaining two spatial
concepts—one central to Buber's thought, the other to Arendt's writing—
and describing the sad situation in Israel, I shall be indicating that if we
Israelis will learn from Arendt and Buber, and from other existentialists,
there is a way of transcending this situation toward a more just, and worthy,
existence.

A basic tenet of all Arendt's writing is that "the prequisite of all freedom
which is simply the capacity of motion ... cannot exist without space".[1]

Discussing the Greek polis she points out:

The *polis*, properly speaking is not the city-state in its physical location; it is the organization of the people as it arises out of acting and speaking together, and its true space lies between people living together for this purpose, no matter where they happen to be.[2]

Not being able to enter the space of the *polis*, either because one was a slave, or a woman, or an artisan or artist who spent one's entire day working, also meant that one did not have political freedom, that is, the freedom to act and speak on political principles and to influence political developments. The slave, the woman, and the worker were confined to their social tasks, much as when a person is jailed he or she is confined to a limited space and cannot interact freely with other persons. In short, a life of freedom can only come into being when there is a public space between persons in which through acting and speaking they can live that freedom.

Although the fact that persons need a space in which they can engage in acts of freedom was first formulated and discussed in the Greek *polis*, this is not remote from the Biblical experience. In order to be able to relate to God freely, without arousing the wrath of his family and society, Abraham had to go forth to a new land, a space where he would be free to build altars to God wherever he saw fit. In order for the Hebrew tribes who left Egypt with Moses to become the people of Israel, they had to acquire a land of their own, a space where members of a nation could worship God as free persons. Of course one can also worship God in the desert, as the Hebrew tribes did; but the establishment of a life on the land—that is, the acquiring of a place where a people may constitute a political entity, and persons can undertake political action and can discuss political principles—enhances personal freedom. Put differently, for the God of Abraham to be not only a tribal God, but a God who relates to the freedom of each individual, that individual must have the space to live his or her freedom.

Even when one has a land of one's own, there are many manners by which the space for living one's freedom may be limited. It is clear that dictatorial states, such as Uruguay and Syria, or states on the verge of totalitarianism, such as North Korea and the Soviet Union, limit the space for living one's freedom. It is not only that one cannot travel freely in these countries, or out of these countries, or that one cannot question the workings and the principles of the regime, but also that one is never free from the look of the Other, which, to borrow a phrase from Sartre, creates a hemorrhage in one's freedom. That look, which can always mean that one may be reported to the secret police, limits the public space in which persons can freely express themselves, be it on political or personal matters or in the arts and sciences. In democratic regimes, of course, the look of the Other may also limit one's freedom, but it has no direct connection to violent means of oppression.

The manners of limiting the space of one's freedom in democratic regimes are much more subtle. But before giving a few examples of how this is done in Israel, I shall present my understanding of the concept of The Chosen People.[3]

I submit that the only manner in which I can relate to Biblical concepts is to view them as respecting human freedom. Without such respect certain Biblical passages can be cited and have been cited to support bloodshed, to condone rapacious regimes, to accept unjust actions. The Bible is the story of the encounter between Abraham and his progeny and God; it is a spiritual encounter in which Abraham and his descendants strove to live a life of freedom in which they could pursue justice and a true faith. The Bible describes these descendants often failing to realize the spiritual demands of God; but their prophets and judges repeatedly renewed the demand for such a realization. Inherent to these demands was that the people of Israel live as free, responsible persons, which is the first step toward living a life of spirit. These demands guide my understanding of the concept of The Chosen People: If we Jews have been chosen, it is to live our freedom responsibly and to encourage other people to live their freedom responsibly in our mutual world. Put otherwise, as an Israeli, striving to live a life of justice and faith, I firmly reject the idea that Jews were chosen merely to revere the written word of the law and to embrace a priestly dogma. Furthermore, I angrily condemn the chauvinistic use of The Chosen People to sanction crimes against Arabs, as some rabbis in Israel, and not only Meir Kahane, have been doing lately.

Someone may argue that Kahane and other fanatics are merely a marginal phenomenon. I read the political developments in Israel differently. I see racism as a growing phenomenon. But even if racism is marginal, there are other manners of using the concept of The Chosen People to slowly diminish the space for freedom. One manner is linked to a myth that has been prominent in Israel for years, and that gave birth to a popular song: "The Whole World Is Against Us." One doesn't have to be an astute dialectician to grasp that having the whole world against one is a manner of being chosen. The truth, of course, is that most of the world is indifferent to what is happening in Israel or between Israel and its Arab neighbors—the hundreds of millions of peasants in India or China, the impoverished multitudes in Africa or South America; even many educated Europeans and Americans are hardly concerned about the existence of Israel. They simply don't care, much as they probably don't care about the existence of Iceland, or Sri Lanka, or the Fiji Islands. But the myth is used by Israeli politicians of both right- and left-wing parties to boost the importance of the military, to convince their constituents that Israel must develop a huge military–industrial complex, and to limit the topics linked to security which are publicly discussed.

Someone may suggest that the myth is a remnant of diaspora life, in which "The Jews' political ignorance ... which blinded them to the political dangers of antisemitism, caused them to be oversensitive to all forms of social discrimination."[4] Such may be true, but it evades the point. It is an explaining of a situation which I refuse to accept. What perturbs me is that viewing ourselves as The Chosen People, without assuming the responsibility to live freely and to pursue spiritual goals that such a chosenness implies, allows for a dangerous jingoism to emerge. The Israeli begins to believe that one's being chosen implies that one is more worthy or more virtuous than other inhabitants of the world. In many realms of Israeli society one meets the attitude that the Israeli does not have to strive to excel; it is enough that one is Jewish, or that one belongs to "our group" within the Jewish people, be it our kibbutz, our political party, our industrial venture, or our bureaucracy. Needless to say in such a system personal accountability disappears and the public space, where, as Arendt stressed, human excellence can appear, is greatly diminished.

The lack of appreciation of a public space seems to have originated with the Zionist movement. Herzl, Weitzman, Ben Gurion, and many of the early Zionists did not grasp that having a space, a land, in which the Jew would be free is a necessary, but definitely not a sufficient, condition for Jews to espouse political freedom, to undertake political action, and to pursue a spiritual existence on the land. In short, these visionaries overlooked the importance of creating a public space where persons could discuss political principles and act in accordance with them. A main reason for their myopia may have been the lack of experience of the Jewish people in political matters, mentioned above. But there also seems to have been a willingness to be myopic.

Of course the leaders I have just mentioned had moments in which they acted as great statesmen. But in certain historical moments when leaders could have ensured the emergence of a public space and allowed for greater freedom in Israeli society, but perhaps with some loss of personal power, they often chose politicking above statesmanship. Perhaps the most devastating of these choices, upon which I shall soon enlarge, was when Ben Gurion, as Israel's first prime minister, decided that in order to appease the religious parties in Israel he would oppose the drafting of a constitution. He forced this decision through the Knesset (the Israeli parliament) despite the promise given by Israel leaders to the United Nations that Israel would become a constitutional republic. In one parliamentary decision and for some immediate political gains, Ben Gurion and his cowardly, myopic followers were willing to limit for decades the political freedom of the Jewish and Arab citizens of Israel.[5]

Thus the political system set up in Israel under Ben Gurion's leadership reminds one of the weak-sighted Patriarch Isaac mumbling when he was being duped by his son Jacob: "The hands are the hands of Esau, but the voice is the voice of Jacob." The system looks modern, modeled on the English parliament, with a supreme court, a coalition government, and quite

a bit freedom of the press. But, as this book will show, the system greatly
limits the space for political action, and for the realization of a life of spirit.

Martin Buber pointed out that the I–Thou encounter and the dialogical
relationship developed in what he termed the "between," that is, in the space
between persons or between a person and a work of art, or a natural
phenomenon, or God. One may define the realm of the "between" as a space
that comes into being when persons relate dialogically to each other and to
other objects that populate this world. Ontologically this space is different
from the space between two objects in that the "between" may emerge only
when a person relates as a whole being. Thus the ability of human beings to
unite one's entire being in relating is what creates the "between".[6]

A genuine conversation or encounter may occur when one has no wish to
manipulate or to use the individual whom one meets. One meets the Other as
a subject, a partner, with whom one shares the world, not as an object whom
one exploits or utilizes. If such an encounter comes into being Buber holds
that "what happens here cannot be reached by psychological concepts, it is
something ontic."[7] It is important to emphasize this point since a number of
psychologists, including Carl Rogers in a published interview with Buber,[8]
have ignored Buber's admonitions and have attempted to deal with what
occurs in the "between" as psychological phenomena. They seem to have
also ignored Buber's belief that dialogue is the goal of freedom, and the
"between" is the space where this freedom is realized; hence these
psychologists are attempting to eradicate freedom by a two-pronged attack.
First, by using psychological concepts such an approach creates an aura of
determinability. But what characterizes the "between" is that neither its
emergence nor what occurs in this space can be determined beforehand. One
cannot determine the emergence of dialogue, or of love. Second, by reducing
what occurs in the "between" to psychological phenomena, these psychologists are attempting to eliminate the encounter with a partner needed for
dialogue to emerge. One immediate result is that there is no need to attempt
to relate as a whole being or in Buber's terms to relate as a Thou. Buber
rejected such approaches as ontologically invalid, in that they narrow the
common world that one shares with other persons. Only in this common
world can one realize one's freedom and strive to relate dialogically.

The reducing of what occurs in the "between" to the workings of the
individual psyche, coupled with the attempt to attribute determinability to
this realm, effaces personal responsibility. This is a day-to-day danger,
aggravated by the widespread reliance on psychological models and other
models of the behavioral sciences to explain human behavior, and to
encourage certain types of "socially acceptable" behavior. The "between,"
Buber stressed, is the realm where responsibility emerges, through the
response with one's whole being to another person's appeal, or to the

situation in which one finds oneself. This response is not an ego trip, or an outpouring of feelings; it is an act of freedom that often transcends the socially acceptable; and as an act of freedom it cannot be a result of psychological determinations, such as described by Freud or Jung. It is a response in which a person relates wholly to another person and to the world one shares with him or her.[9]

Throughout this book I shall suggest that living in the "between," establishing the relations of wholeness that Buber describes, is crucial if one wishes to develop as a person who acts responsibly. For instance, I believe that the responsibility that emerges in dialogical relations can assist in assuming responsibility in the public realm, albeit in a roundabout manner. One basic reason that persons evade political responsibility is the diminishing of the public space. We have no polis today; and the rule of the bureaucracy, which Arendt denotes as the rule by Nobody, does everything in its power to limit the ability of an individual to influence developments through his or her acts and deeds. A person will find it extremely difficult to act responsibly in, say, struggling against an unjust decree, if there is not a space where he or she can relate dialogically to other persons, and there find repose from such struggles. Many writers, from Kafka to Solzhenitsyn, have poignantly described the loneliness, the feelings of impotence, the degeneration of personal respect, and the flight from responsibility of persons who cannot establish relations in the "between" while being dominated and oppressed by a well-entrenched bureaucracy. Such a plight not only drains a person's courage and fortitude, it often leads him or her to accept thoughtlessness as a way of life, to embrace banality, and to compromise with evil.

Put differently, as Arendt points out, modern humanity cannot return to the wisdom of the Greek citizen who distinguished between the *polis* and the realm of one's private life. In the polis one appeared and was exposed; in one's private life one was hidden from this exposure and could rest from the strenuous demands of participating in political life. As Kafka, Sartre, and other existentialists have shown, today one is constantly exposed to the look of the Other, and this look, in most cases, persistently limits one's freedom; hence, persons need a space which they share with a partner in which they may relate to each other and support each other's freedom. That space is the "between."

This is not to say that Buber's discussion of the "between" can teach us much about living in the realm of politics. This fact has hardly been noticed. Most articles that discuss Buber's political views are merely a rehash of Buber's own writings, and they do not see the political realm as much more than "a demonic force which directs man from the truth and leads him into confusion."[10] As I have shown, when discussing politics Buber limited himself to being guided by a specific relationship—dialogue.[11] He refused to extend the "between" much beyond the realm of the interhuman, although he did attempt to extend it in the direction of what he called a true commune. When he addressed the realm of politics Buber confined himself to the question: How should a person live in the realm of this "demonic force"? The answer was: To attempt to live dialogically, and to be led by one's conscience. But the answer merely reduces what occurs in the political realm to the ontology of *I and Thou*.

Without going further one immediately notes that Buber is limiting the realm of freedom. If human freedom attains its goal in the dialogical "between," what is the significance of political freedom? I don't believe that Buber ever answered this question. When discussing freedom he seemed to overlook a fact that Arendt repeatedly stressed: Central to the grandeur of being human is that persons are endowed with the gift of action, of being able to begin new historical processes; and this gift cannot even be conceived without assuming that political freedom exists, that a person can act within a political organization. Moreover, persons live together in political organizations because such a living together allows them to pursue political action and to express their freedom. In short, "The *raison d'être* of politics is freedom and its field of experience is action."[12]

Buber's lack of attention to and disparaging of the realm of politics was partially a result of his strict distinction between being and seeming, which he held are the two "essential attitudes" a person can adopt.[13] Dialogue and what occurs in the "between" is a manifestation of living according to one's being, while political action, which occurs in the world of appearances, is an expression of the attitude of seeming. Buber sensed that this division cannot be definitive; still, it was often the cutting edge of his emphasizing the significance of the "between." But in politics where deeds and words are what count, and not "essential attitudes," the distinction between being and seeming is often irrelevant. It is of little consequence to determine whether the relations between Anwar Sadat and Menachem Begin during the Camp David meetings were relations of being or of seeming. What is of consequence is the peace treaty that they signed. Even if we assume that while hammering out the treaty Sadat and Begin primarily wished to make an impression— their "essential attitude" was that of seeming—this does not in any manner reduce the importance of their deed. Similarly, even if we assume that when Winston Churchill broadcasted his famous "Dunkirk" speech he was merely striving to make an impression, this does not in any way diminish the historical (or literary) significance of the speech. In short, the distinction between being and seeming have only marginal political implications, hence Buber's emphasis on the "between" has little to teach us about political freedom.

The world lies between people and this in-between ... is today the object of the greatest concern and the most obvious upheaval ... Even where the world is still halfway in order ... the public realm has lost the power of illumination which was originally part of its very nature. More and more people in the countries of the Western world which since the decline of the ancient world has regarded freedom from politics as one of the basic freedoms, make use of this freedom and have retreated from the world and their obligations within it. This withdrawal from the world need not harm an individual; he may even cultivate great talents to the point of genius and so by a detour be useful to the world again. But with each such retreat an almost demonstrable loss to the world takes place; what is lost is the specific and usually irreplaceable in-between which should have formed between this individual and his fellow men.[14]

Much of Arendt's writing is concerned with the trend, described in this citation, whereby persons in the Western World choose to be free *from* politics and thus to abandon one's responsibility for the world. Each person who chooses to retreat from the world and one's obligations within it diminishes the in-between which makes up the public realm and allows others, often inept or corrupt persons, to determine their mutual future. Moreover, as a result of the mass abandoning of the public realm it loses its ability to illuminate persons' lives. Because the great deeds and the resounding words of those persons who attained glory in the public realm—think of Martin Luther King!—can only illuminate and influence the lives of those fellow men and women who join them in creating the in-between. The vicious circle that Arendt describes and rejects can be viewed from two perspectives: Persons use their freedom to abandon the realm of politics, for which freedom is the *raison d'être*. And by such an abandoning of the public realm, administrators reign unhindered, administrators who usually despise persons who wish to act in the public realm and will do everything in their power to minimize the space in which the doer of great deeds or the sayer of important words can appear. This vicious circle slowly destroys the public space.

In Israel, democracy was foisted from above. The political leaders who wrote Israel's declaration of independence and established its political regime decided upon a democracy without conferring with their constituents; scarcely any thought was given to the need for a public space. The limited in-between that emerged as a result of these decisions was accepted by Jews and Arabs, who had almost no experience of political freedom, as a framework for political life. This framework was not examined, thought about, discussed, or determined by these constituents; it was merely accepted. For instance, in January 1949 Israelis elected a "Constituent Assembly," that is, an assembly whose role was to draft a constitution. These representatives met three days as a "Constituent Assembly," and then decided to become a legislative body and to call themselves the First Knesset. The fact that they were not chosen to be a legislative body, and that by changing their role they had betrayed the mission for which they were chosen, bothered almost nobody. Moreover, when in June 1950 this First Knesset, under the forceful pressure of Ben Gurion, decided not to draft a constitution, few people complained. In short, the Jews living then in Israel did not feel that these Knesset members were their paid representatives, who were accountable to them and who should fulfill the role to which they were chosen. They seemed to view the Knesset members in the manner that leaders of the diaspora community were viewed, as important personages to whom the lay person owes allegiance.[15]

Not much has changed in the past four decades. Israel still lacks a constitution. Leaders are still hardly accountable. The outcome is a situation whereby Israelis suffer from many of the vices of democracy without benefiting from most of its virtues, because a necessary condition for the emergence of the virtues of democracy is the existence of the in-between. Or, learning from Plato, a mob-oriented democracy closely resembles a tyranny. What characterizes both regimes is equality before the law, and a lack of the public space in which persons can assume responsibiity for the principles and the manner of their living together in freedom.

Both major parties in Israel, the Likud and the Labor, are mob-oriented. Their leaders and spokesmen are not guided by any principles of responsibility for life in the public realm. They have no vision. Accountability is almost nonexistent. What concerns both parties is power and its benefits, and they have learned that acquiring this power means playing up to the mob. Hence despite their seeming "ideological differences" and their endless bickering about the manner of dividing the fruits of power, they have lived together quite cordially in what they call a "unity government." An immediate outcome of a mob-oriented society, such as is developing in Israel, is that the space for freedom slowly disappears, both Buber's "between" and Arendt's in-between.

Arendt suggested that one reason for the current emergence of the mob as a political factor is the rise of society to prominence in determining human existence. She repeatedly points out that the political realm, to which action is necessary for its existence, disappears when society predominates. Since each society attempts to "normalize" its members, it demands a certain sort of behavior in accordance with certain accepted norms, a behavior that excludes all spontaneous action or outstanding achievement. Few behavioral scientists, or the journalists or political figures that learn from them, have noticed to what an extent their theories are mob-oriented. All of these theories are concerned with examining what equalizes between persons, and at times what equalizes between persons and rats or chimpanzees; they are not interested in what allows for spontaneous action or excellence to emerge. They cannot be. By definition a behavioral science attempts to determine and study what is equal in the behavior of different individuals and not acts of freedom. (Even William James's description of mystical and religious experiences and Abraham Maslow's descriptions of "peak experiences" is an attempt to find what is equal in these experiences.) It is a science of the rise of society and of the attempt to liquidate the political realm, by viewing everything through its lowest common denominator. And that is precisely a mob-oriented view.

As revealed in contemporary literature of societies where a public realm is oppressed—Soviet, Egyptian, South American—the diminishing of the public realm reduces the space where the realm of the "between" may emerge. No less significant is the fact that the political dimension of a person's existence, one's ability to act in the realm of freedom, which one can develop by entering the public realm, disappears. As Arendt pointed out, in the Greek polis a man assumed an additional dimension of existence when he entered the public realm (women were not allowed to enter this realm). He was then not only a person who worked or labored, but also a person who had the courage to discuss principles and to attempt to live in accordance with them. Courage is therefore a political virtue, and only those men and women who are courageous can act in the political realm. Thus, without the in-between, that space where persons can act courageously, an entire dimension of being human does not develop. Persons will therefore find it difficult to relate with the wholeness that concerns Buber, and hence dialogical relationships will be scarce.

In summary, I should like to emphasize once again that a mob-oriented political regime, such as is developing in Israel lately (which is hardly a new development in the histories of democracies), is not only curtailing political freedom, but also limiting personal freedom, including our ability to live a life of dialogue. Buber's mistake was that he did not see the significance of political life and political freedom, including its significance for the emergence of dialogue. Albeit vaguely, he did see the opposite: The importance of a life of dialogue for political freedom. This mistake is significant because linking between the space of dialogue and the space of political existence is necessary if a person wishes to respond to spiritual challenges.

I am suggesting that in order to respond to spiritual challenges a person must live a life of freedom, which means initiating and creating both spaces, the "between" and the in-between. Such must be done in the everyday, in the daily challenges that one encounters. It is no easy task; often one encounters contempt and derision. One can learn about some of these difficulties from the following story.

In the early 1930s, after Hitler came to power many German Jews fled to the land of Israel, among them a landscape architect. No ... One should begin this story with the problem of trees. Israel was once a forested land, but the Turks cut down trees for charcoal to run trains and the indigenous Arabs grazed the deforested land with sheep and goats which relish tree shoots. The land became barren, swampy, infested with malaria. The Jews who returned to Zion planted trees, at first hundreds, later thousands, and fervently nurtured each tree, because only trees could prevent malaria, could redeem the land.

The landscape architect and his family joined a kibbutz. There was little need for landscape architecture in the young kibbutz, nor in all of Israel at that time; he became the kibbutz gardener. One day, after about two years, the kibbutz members were shocked to find that he had cut down two large trees near the dining room and had planted, in their stead, a row of bushes, followed by a column of trees. An uproar ensued, especially since the trees he had cut down had been planted when the kibbutz was established. At the general meeting called to censure him, some members demanded that he be expelled. The architect got up to respond: "I don't appreciate trees? . . . why I planted an avenue of trees . . . I cut down these two trees, because we need some space. Without open space, you . . . your freedom is endangered; these two trees near the dining room were diminishing our space. The problem is that all of you see the garden today. I see it fifteen, twenty years from now, and . . ."

FREEDOM AND THINKING

One of Hannah Arendt's repeated locutions is "the banality of evil," which is evil—at times unprecedented in its monstrosity—that is done by banal thoughtless people. She used this term when she discussed the political significance of lack of thinking while describing Adolf Eichmann at his trial in Jerusalem. What she discerned in Eichmann's responses blatantly countered the tradition concerning evil with which she was acquainted—that evil is something demonic, which a Mephistopheles or a Satan or some other fallen angel brings into the world. What is more, Eichmann's deeds were not a result of envy, resentment, weakness (as with Macbeth and to some extent Hamlet), greed, or any other attitude that leads to and, for the evil doer, often justifies the evil deeds he or she performs (think of Iago). At the Eichmann trial, Arendt recalls,

what I was confronted with was utterly different and still undeniably factual. I was struck by a manifest shallowness in the doer that made it impossible to trace the uncontestable evil of his deeds to any deeper level of roots or motives. The deeds were monstrous, but the doer—at least the very effective one now on trial—was quite ordinary, commonplace, and neither demonic nor monstrous. There was no sign in him of firm ideological convictions or of specific evil motives, and the only notable characteristic one could detect in his past behavior during the trial and throughout the pretrial police examination was something entirely negative: it was not stupidity but thoughtlessness.[16]

Evil has been linked to lack of thought in other twentieth-century writings. Thus, while nineteenth-century existentialists such as Kierkegaard, Nietzsche, and Dostoyevski still linked the performance of evil to envy, or resentment, or pride, or weakness—think of Dostoyevski's Roghozin in *The Idiot* or Raskolnikov in *Crime and Punishment*, or of Kierkegaard's "Diary of the Seducer"—some twentieth-century existentialists, such as Kafka in *The Trial*, *The Castle*, and *Amerika* or Sartre in "No Exit" and "Altona," vividly depict the banality of evil. The accounts of Alexander Solzhenitsyn and other Soviet writers on what occurs in the Gulag Archipelago and outside it in Soviet society, or the writings of Heinrich Boll and Gunter Grass on Nazi Germany and its aftermath, provide a spectrum of literary expressions depicting the linkage between evil and thoughtlessness. Hence, Arendt's importance, beyond pointing to the phenomenon and naming it, is in revealing the relation of the banality of evil to political life in the twentieth century.

In a totalitarian regime and in democratic regimes developing toward fascism, very often those persons who acquire strategies and methods of not thinking will reach political prominence—thoughtlessness is a manner of getting ahead. At his trial, Eichman could not answer questions straightforwardly and coherently, he was unable to remember facts, and he substituted cliches for personal thoughts. Cliches, of course, allow one to pronounce a specific view without having to think it out. Hence, Arendt's conclusion: "The longer one listened to him, the more obvious it became that his inability to speak was connected with an inability to think, namely to think from the standpoint of somebody else."[17] Eichmann himself knew that his speaking ability was limited. He announced: "Officialese [Amtssprache] is my only language."[18] In other words, this deporter of four to five million Jews, in addition to gypsies and other "superfluous human beings," to death camps was unable to communicate except in the language of bureaucracy— and this language, in itself, is built so that one need not think. The bureaucrat needs only to pass down orders and pass up reports. Instead of thinking one solves problems according to rules, and when one has to explain the reason for one's undertaking one relies on cliches. Put differently, in order to communicate meaningfully with another person one must be able to carry on within oneself that inner dialogue which Socrates called thinking, which allows one to think from the standpoint of somebody else. And it is this inner dialogue that totalitarian regimes attempt to eradicate, and in Eichmann's case the Nazis succeeded.

No Israeli political thinker and very few politicians learned from the Eichmann trial how devastating the linkage between banality and evil can be. Nay, perhaps I'm wrong, perhaps they did learn, perhaps they did acknowledge the horrors of this linkage. But if they did it was all academic, because as this book will repeatedly indicate, banality reigns almost unmolested in Israeli political life. I suspect that for most Israelis the Eichmann trial was a manner of reliving the Holocaust—this time without its dangers—and not a lesson on the importance of thinking for a life of freedom. Indicative of this response is the fact that Arendt's book on the trial has never been translated into Hebrew, presumably because her report was critical of the manner the courts and the politicians in Israel dealt with the Eichmann case. Typical of this jingoism and of the lack of thinking that prevails in Israel is the appearance in Hebrew of a book criticizing her report of the trial. In it Hebrew readers can read how a group of academicians denounce

Arendt, but they cannot read her own arguments. Unfortunately, in the decades since the trial lack of thinking has continued to characterize political life in Israel. And few academicians, journalists, authors, or other persons have deplored the fact that this lack of thinking is slowly eroding our political freedom and allowing "the banality of evil" to prevail. Two examples, one general and one specific, will reveal the extent of this erosion.

More than two decades have past since Israel captured the West Bank and the Gaza Strip; with these portions of land more than a million and a quarter Arabs who call themselves Palestinians came under Israeli rule. The manner of ruling these territories has slowly created an apartheid state, with three million six hundred thousand Jewish Israelis having civil and political rights, seven hundred thousand Israeli Arabs having limited civil and political rights, and the Palestinians having few civil rights and even fewer political rights. All discussions, by the two leading political parties, of the manner to deal with this situation are characterized by lack of thinking. The right-wing Likud Party ignores the evolution of an apartheid state and is adamantly against any giving up of conquered land; the Labor Alliance sees the plight of the Palestinians as a problem that has to be solved, say, together with King Hussein. Now, problem solving is not thinking, at least it is not the kind of thinking that contributes to political freedom. The greatness of the political realm, as shown already in Classical Greece, is that in it persons can think not only in order to solve problems, but also to clarify and formulate principles of living together. No such thinking of principles characterizes the manner in which the Labor or the Likud address the apartheid state in which we currently live.

Problem solving requires intelligence, ingenuity, cleverness. It has to do with the matter at hand, with the facts of the case. The problem solver does not assume a more general perspective, say a moral perspective. For him or her these are the facts involved, these are the tasks to be performed, and solving the problem means finding a good way of performing those tasks. Thinking as a problem solver means focusing on what has to be achieved, it has nothing to do with contemplation or with clarifying more general concepts, such as justice, or love, or courage, or knowledge. The problem solver is not concerned with the question of how to live in accordance with these concepts, because these concepts cannot be clarified within the dialectic of means and ends. Nor is he or she concerned with understanding or discussing the principles of the living together of men and women in freedom, which, since the time of the Greeks, is the *raison d'être* of political life. In short, the problem solver attempts to cope with this world by adopting the dialectic of means and ends. Thinking transcends that world and that dialectic. When one thinks as a thinker, one detaches oneself from the world of everyday life, enters the realm of inner dialogue, or of ideas, or of pure concepts, as various philosophers have called this realm, reaches a deeper understanding of human existence and a more perceptive vision of justice, or

of the good, or of the beautiful, or of true faith, and hopes to return to the
everyday world to act in accordance with that vision and understanding.

If Jews in the State of Israel wish to reside in the Middle East, not only as
warriors who can defend their right to exist there, but also on the basis of
acceptance and justice, they must think not only in terms of problem solving,
but also as thinkers. Concerning the West Bank and the Gaza Strip and the
persons who reside there, most politicians persistently evade any thinking
about principles of justice. But when thinking about justice slowly disappears
from the in-between, and every discussion merely becomes an assessment of
means and ends, the level of political discussion is mob-oriented and the way
to tyranny is opened up. The current tyranny that Israeli forces exercise on
the persons living in the captured territories is a case in point. In other
words, I am not only blaming most Israeli citizens, and especially its leaders,
for the apartheid state in which we live. I am not only blaming these leaders
for the lack of foresight which allowed a situation to develop in which Jews
conduct pogroms, kill women and children, and persecute an entire
population. And I am also not only blaming the leaders for converting the
vision of Zionism into a mob-oriented patriotism which has nothing to do
with the Biblical vision of Zion. Here I am blaming them because they refuse
to think—and I suspect that they refuse to think because after one has
thought one must return to the world of appearances and act on one's
thoughts courageously. Yes, I am particularly blaming these leaders and
many of my fellow Israelis because they lack the courage to live their
freedom.

A more specific example has to do with Amos Oz's recent book *In the Land
of Israel*.[19] The book is a series of journalistic interviews that Oz conducted,
primarily with fanatics and mob-oriented persons of every stripe in Israel.
Here and there one finds an interviewee expressing a nostalgic yearning to
the wonderful days of Zionist values. While the book may be a true picture of
some of the views that prevail, what repeatedly emerges is Oz's playing up to
the mob. He is so engrossed in accurately presenting mob-oriented views that
he forgets that he is a person who can take a stance, and not only play the
role of journalist. He refuses to respond to any of the evil views expressed by
his interviewees, he himself refuses to think, and, of course he sanctions the
lack of thinking that underlies the words of all those to whom he listens. This
cowardice and lack of thinking is what allows Oz, whose novels are exercises
in decadence and impotence, to continue to be a spokesman for a large
segment of Israeli society—those persons who themselves fear to think.

What Oz and an entire group of other authors in Israel do not grasp is that
in order to be able to think clearly, one must be willing to take a stance
against evil. But many prominent Israeli authors are quite willing to ignore
or to forgive evil if it is evil done by Jews. In their mob-oriented writings they
have not forcefully come out against the apartheid state developing in Israel,
or against the corruption of Zionism by today's mob-oriented political

leaders, or against persons who promote racism. I shall return to these authors in the chapter on art.

In *In the Land of Israel* Oz reports an interview with a Jew who is a declared Arab hater. This man wants to kill all Arabs residing in the Land of Israel or, at least, expel them forcefully from the land. He presents a Jewish Ku Klux Klan philosophy to support his intentions. Instead of rejecting this philosophy and branding this man as his enemy, Oz listens carefully, recording each word, and ends up drinking whiskey with this Jewish Nazi. In dealing with this embodiment of Arab hatred Oz seems to have accepted the principle that "What is a crime among the multitude is only a vice among the few," which Arendt described as "the very principle by which the slow and insidious decline of nineteenth-century society into the depth of mob and underworld morality took place."[20] Nowhere else in the book, or in other books or statements, has Oz branded this Jewish Nazism as evil.

The tacit endorsement of evil by Oz and other Israeli authors reveals an important point concerning the banality of evil—a point which Arendt's discussions imply, but which she did not present forcefully. It is not only that a person who refuses to think will agree to participate in performing evil deeds, as Eichmann did. The opposite is also the case. By refusing to take a stance against evil a person is limiting his or her ability to think. This idea appears already in Plato's *Gorgias*, and in the first pages of the second book of *The Republic*. In *Gorgias* Plato shows that Socrates's willingness to take a firm stance against evil allows him to think with greater clarity and profundity than his partners to dialogue. And in the second book of *The Republic*, Glaucon and Adeimantus state that they support justice, and then pose the questions that Socrates answers in the remainder of the dialogue. When one refuses to take a moral stance one has difficulties in thinking, because one's vision is clouded by the lack of determination that characterizes one's being. Or, to use Socrates' terminology, in order to conduct an inner dialogue with myself, I must know where I stand or the basis from where my thinking can begin.

Democracy allows thinking. But for a democracy to continue to exist each generation must respond to the challenge of living responsibly in the political realm; such a responsibility includes thinking about the principles of political life and discussing how these principles are to be realized. Thus, although each new generation in the United States can draw inspiration from the writings of the Founding Fathers, such inspiration cannot replace thinking about the principles which they formulated. In short, thinking is essential for political freedom.

In a country, such as Israel today, where there is almost no thinking about or discussion of the principles of justice which must guide our political life, where most democratically chosen representatives do not have to be able to relate to political principles but need only to respond to group interests, democracy is in danger. Arendt repeatedly stressed that the freedom a person has within the political realm must be reenforced and rejuvenated by thinking of the principles of that realm, especially in relation to the new historical circumstances that arise with the emergence of each new generation. Two immediate outcomes arise in a democracy where there is little thinking: First, the bureaucrats begin to reign uncontested, since the cliches which guide their work will never be challenged. Second, the whirlpools of interests that engulf anyone in power totally drown out the possibility of discussing political principles. What is more, in such a democracy, the persons in power are terribly boring. They strive to transform political discussions into insipid platitudes, which serve the mediocrity of their own political interests.

Democracy allows thinking, but thinking will only emerge if persons confront issues and confront each other straightforwardly. Such is not a common practice, especially in the social realm in which confronting is often viewed as impolite, as tactless, as threatening. The confronting of other persons and of issues are linked, and both are crucial if one wishes to struggle for principles in a democracy. If one is willing to confront issues and unwilling to confront other persons, or vice versa, one is seeking ways to avoid confronting in general, because without one mode of confronting the other mode becomes superficial. Above, I could not honestly confront Oz's shallowness without confronting the issue of Israeli apartheid, and I cannot adequately confront the ubiquity of Israeli apartheid without confronting the shallowness of intellectuals such as Amos Oz. Or, as Plato showed in *Gorgias*, *Protagoras*, and the first book of *The Republic*, confronting issues and confronting other persons intermingle in one's attempts to bring thoughts to expression, and especially when one seeks to understand virtue or justice. Or, if we once again glance at Eichmann, he was unwilling to confront issues of conscience; he knew that such a confronting demanded that he confront his Nazi superiors, and that was the one deed Eichmann was determined not to do. (Arendt points out that when Eichmann learned of the mass killings of Jews, his conscience troubled him slightly on this matter for about four weeks.)[21]

When confronting an issue or another person, one's entire being is often involved. (One speaks from the stomach, as we say in Hebrew.) Such an involvement is also a sharing of oneself with other persons on matters of political import. It can lead to the emergence of the political realm which "rises directly out of acting together, the 'sharing of words and deeds.'"[22] On the other hand, the inner dialogue that Plato describes as thinking seems to be a manner of confronting oneself on significant issues. To think one must think against oneself, Sartre often said. In such an inner dialogue one's entire being is involved in this act of thinking. Hence, Socrates, as described in *The Symposium*, could stand "lost in thought" for hours, and not notice the passing of the day.

Thus, if the banality of evil arises when one is unable to think, prior to that one lacks the courage to confront. As Nietzsche repeatedly stressed, when cowardly and mediocre persons sense that they are unable to confront—themselves, other persons, and issues—they will strive to develop approaches and values that will compensate for their cowardice and mediocrity. Eichmann's cliches were such a compensation in addition to being a manner of not confronting reality; the various propounders of "I'm O.K., you're O.K." psychological approaches are advocating another mode of compensation. These psychologists urge cowardly and mediocre persons to "feel good" while evading confrontations. In Israel most politicians, including the current president of Israel and the prime minister, evoke a strong sense of community to compensate for the cowardice of the citizens and of most political leaders. (This trend was reaffirmed in the 1988 election.) These politicians repeatedly tell us that we Jews are an extended family that has to persistently guard its interests against the terrible world beyond the family hearth; hence we should quietly let our politicians lead us, as a herd, to the meadow of their choice.

A point that Arendt repeatedly brings up, in different contexts but always as a source of hope, is that each person that is born is a new beginning. Although this fact is hardly novel, it has political implications that Arendt believes are frequently overlooked. Of course, educational systems do not overlook the fact that these new persons need to be trained so as to join the social and political system in which they were born. What is often overlooked is that each new person, as a beginning, may be able to comprehend with a new mind the reality that confronts him or her, and act in a new unprecedented manner. Arendt writes: "Beginning, before it becomes a historical event, is the supreme capacity of man; politically, it is identical with man's freedom."[23] While processes in nature are generally cyclic—they repeat themselves much as summer follows winter or day follows night —persons, because they have freedom, can initiate processes which are new and which may never be repeated. Thus, living one's political freedom in a democracy means living as a beginner, as a person who initiates new processes and new thinking, by persistently confronting issues and other persons.

As the twentieth century has shown, thinking and living as a beginner are crucial for a life of freedom. Hitler began a new unprecedented process in Western Europe—German totalitarianism—and one reason this process was allowed to continue to its terrifying consequences was that multitudes of persons, both within the Nazi regime and outside it, did not think. Some fled from thinking, others refused to think (Eichmann), still others responded to Hitler's rise to power and establishing of a totalitarian regime as if it were merely another dictatorship or mode of persecution with which one has to live. (Chamberlain, Buber, Gandhi, and many others refused to view this unprecedented development for what it was—with the eyes of beginners.) While it is not possibile to determine the amount of action that may have been initiated if persons did think, there is little doubt that Hitler did everything in his power to block thinking within Germany, and that the lack of thinking of his vicious henchmen allowed them to continue to perform atrocities. Thus, in a sense, the non-Nazi Germans who were questioned about what they knew about the mass murder of the Jews in Europe were telling the truth when they replied that they knew nothing. One only knows about political events when one is willing to think about them. One had to think in order to link between the rounding up of Jews, their deportation, the rumors about death camps, Hitler's speeches about his wish to exterminate the Jews and make Germany *Judenrein*, etc. For a person who did not think, these were merely isolated, unconnected events. Remember, Hitler called this mass extermination The Final Solution. It was merely a problem to be solved, not something to be thought about.

The political system in Israel allows little space for beginners who do not adhere to the line pointed out by the current leadership. One can cite a host of reasons for this situation, prominent among them the fact that in elections one votes for a countrywide party slate of candidates and not for a specific candidate who represents a group of voters. Hence, each voter knows that no person is accountable to him or her personally; at best a voter can turn with his or her ideas, or requests, or criticisms to indifferent clerks of a political party's (Kafkaesque) bureaucracy. On the other hand, the chosen representative knows that the only way to advance in the realm of politics is by adhering strictly to the party line. Needless to say this entire system stifles thinking.

But the indifference and hostility to persons as beginners is hardly confined to the realm of political involvement. As we shall see in subsequent chapters this indifference and hostility to new thought pervades many areas of Israeli society, from the manner in which the problems of security and peaceful existence in the region are grasped to the edicts of the religious establishment, and from the mediocrity of kibbutz existence, to the superficial approach to art. In all these realms the lack of persons who are willing to begin, to cut themselves off from the past and the future in order to see, has created a shallowness of thinking, and a disparaging of all creativity. Israel is slowly becoming a spiritual wasteland.

Such a shallowness and lack of spirituality also emerges in the manner we Israelis relate to Jewish history and to what we can learn from it. Living as a beginner and thinking requires viewing Jewish history not only nostalgically, but as a source from which we can learn, say, how to live justly. Thus, a statement such as the following should guide our daily endeavors:

During the 150 years when Jews truly lived amidst, and not just in the neighborhood of, Western European peoples, they always had to pay with political misery for social glory and with social insult for political success.[24]

A similar degradation is often experienced by Arab citizens of Israel today. It need not be so, and such degradation can be altered by initiating actions and by Jews struggling for true equality for all. Unfortunately very few Jews are even concerned with this problem.

Or consider the manner of commemorating the Holocaust in Israel. Most Jews relate to the atrocities of the Nazis, or the acquiescence of the allies who knew about the annihilation of European Jewery, as if these acts can only teach us not to forget and never to forgive the evil done against the Jewish people. Such an approach adds emotional fuel to the thesis that "The whole world is against us Jews," mentioned above. It also relieves one of assuming responsibility for current developments in the world. In short, the Holocaust and its stories are divorced from one's present-day life and decisions. Thus, Menachem Begin, as prime minister, commemorated the Holocaust each year; in his speech he would describe and discuss the terrible persecution of Jews; a few hours later, in his office, he would forcefully support Jewish persecution of Arabs on the West Bank and in the Gaza Strip. In short, he fled into the past in order not to face the evil he supported in the present.

Begin failed to see the link between the persecution of Jews in Poland and the persecution by Jews in Gaza, not because he wasn't intelligent—he was. And also not because he wasn't perceptive, or sentimental, or lacked the facts. Begin simply refused to think. And he retired from office, when he could no longer not think—when the findings about the Lebanon debacle, which he initiated, screamed in his face and demanded not that he solve problems, but that he think about the principles that had guided his decisions, and had brought undue suffering to all those involved.

The flight into a nostalgic past has one more debilitating aspect to it which many Jews refuse to acknowledge. As Marcel Proust's writings reveal, a remembrance of things past can be accompanied by profound thinking. But in such a remembrance there is no room for dreams, nor is there thought about creating space for freedom to emerge. This fleeing into the workings of one's own mind is a flight from political freedom; but without such freedom, a vision of a better existence will never appear. As I read the Bible, many of the Hebrew prophets sensed this point intuitively. While often nostalgically evoking those periods when relations of wholeness and true faith reigned between God and Israel, they always linked this nostalgia to a demand that their listeners act responsibly in the present: quite often, they also presented a vision of a better future.

CIVIL COURAGE AND EXISTENTIALIST PHILOSOPHY

The Israeli newspaper *Haaretz* of May 3, 1987, described a three-day conference featuring twenty-three (male) Israeli writers and intellectuals who met under the auspices of the newly established Spinoza Center in Jerusalem to discuss "Secular Judaism." After presenting the content of some of the discussions, the article revealed that one session of this conference was closed to the public, so that the professors and authors would have a forum in which they could without fear express what they really believed. The pitiful cowardice of these intellectuals is dwarfed by the fact that organizing such a closed discussion was like spitting in the eye of Baruch Spinoza. It was Spinoza who, as a Jew, was excommunicated, hated, and slandered by his fellow Jews, because he was unwilling to forgo discussing and publishing what he really believed. It was Spinoza who persistently sought for truth and was willing to share what he discovered with all his readers, even if such a sharing would bring him suffering.

Cowardice is the issue. Realizing political freedom and attempting to live responsibly and creatively require civil courage. Such courage is not a virtue currently appreciated in Israeli society—neither in academia, nor in the political realm, nor in the interpersonal realm. (Of course, there are rare instances where courage is appreciated, but they are very exceptional.) Even the supposedly free press of Israel often balks at bringing up issues that might infuriate persons in power. For instance, the press has persistently refused to discuss the question of whether Israel has the atomic bomb, and who would be authorized, and under what conditions, to use such a bomb. But when cowardice prevails, political and personal life become banal and insipid, and there is almost no possibility for spiritual attitudes to emerge.

In contrast to Plato's writings, for instance *Gorgias* and *The Republic*, in the modern age very little political thinking has addressed the question: How does one encourage or educate persons to be courageous, to live responsibly and creatively within the political realm? Political thought, from Thomas Hobbes to Hannah Arendt, perceives "that great LEVIATHAN called a COMMON-WEALTH, or STATE, ... which is but an Artificial Man; though of greater stature and strength than Naturall, for whose protection and defense it was intended"[25] as an object that can be scientifically examined and discussed. From this perspective the thinker attempts to sketch the origin of the state, to determine its legitimacy, to examine its authority, to describe its development. Worthy and enlightening as such a perspective may be, it does not allow one to address the above question—modern political thinking lacks the existential dimension.

This lack is paralleled by the prominence of cowardice in many regimes that are called democracies because they give the people the right to vote. Since quite a few of those democracies were foisted from above, the right to vote does not ensure active participation, as a courageous individual, in the political realm. It often merely forges a link between the mob, the party bureaucracy, and the persons in power. (Mexico is an example of such a linking. One party has been ruling for more than six decades, despite the widespread knowledge of its corruption and of its incompetence in dealing with the country's severe problems.) A person is a member of the mob when he or she participates in the political realm without being willing to assume, as an individual, responsibility for the political outcomes of his or her actions.

The mob is primarily a group in which the residue of all classes are represented. This makes it easy to mistake the mob for the people, which also comprises all strata of society. While the people in all great revolutions fight for true representation, the mob will always shout for the "strong man," the "great leader."[26]

Or, citing one of Nietzche's favorite terms, being a member of the mob means assuming a herd mentality. Thus, the Nazi hordes killed and persecuted Jews, gypsies, and other persons knowing that Hitler assumed responsibility for their actions; to the best of our knowledge such is also true about the atrocities performed by Pol Pot's Khmer Rouge in Cambodia.[27]

The Israeli occupation of the West Bank and the Gaza Strip features no similar atrocities. Still, as has been reported again and again, the human and civil rights and the personal respect of persons in these areas has been disregarded and often trampled upon by Israeli soldiers with a mob attitude. (The above sentence stinks of objectivity—not only has the press reported such trampling, but I and my sons have seen it with our own eyes, as soldiers in the Israel Defense Force. Worse, my sons were forced to participate in such deeds as the demolishing of the houses of suspected terrorists, the forceful dispersing of peaceful demonstrations. They did not participate in beatings and shooting of children and women.)

The emergence of the mob as a political force in Israel is partially an outcome of the occupation. As Socrates pointed out, in order to rule unjustly, a person must learn to not assume personal responsibility for his or her deeds. But the opposite is also true. Israel continues to occupy the West Bank and the Gaza Strip because its politicians refuse to confront and to denounce prevailing mob attitudes. Quite the contrary. The leaders of the Labor Alliance and the right wing Likud Bloc, of the religious parties, and of the racist extremists play up to those who express such attitudes—they openly court the mob. Put more bluntly, from my reading of history I suspect that none of the cowardly intellectuals mentioned above, almost none of the political figures who currently dominate Israeli politics, and probably very few of the citizens of Israel today would have supported Theodore Herzl when, almost a century ago, he brought forth the idea of the return to Zion and the establishing of a Jewish State. For one simple reason: To support Zionism then, one needed civil courage.

Few existentialist philosophers discussed civil courage, or action in the political realm. Yet their writings often emphasize the importance of courage for a worthy human existence, and some of these writings suggest how to educate for courage. This aspect of existentialism was overlooked by Hannah Arendt, despite her emphasis on the importance of courage for political life since the rise of the polis in Greece: "Courage therefore became the political virtue par excellence, and only those men who posessed it could be admitted to a fellowship that was political in content and purpose."[28] Arendt discussed the writings of Kierkegaard, Nietzsche, Heidegger, and Sartre but did not see that many of these works attempt to teach the reader how to live courageously; she viewed them as descriptions of human existence. But Kierkegaard, Nietzsche, Buber, Berdyaev, Marcel, and Sartre—to mention a few—very often appeal to the reader to courageously alter one's mode of existence. In what follows I shall briefly review such appeals, their insights and limitations, in the writings of Buber, Berdyaev, and Nietzsche.

My research into Jewish–Arab dialogue in Israel, and my personal experiences, taught me that a willingness to relate dialogically, and to allow the space that Buber calls the "between" to emerge, demands courage.[29] Above I suggested that this space has little to teach us about action in the political in-between. Still, a person who learns to respond courageously in a personal situation may later be willing or able to respond courageously in the political realm. Consider the Hebrew prophets. What needs to be pointed out immediately is that the Hebrew word *Navi* which has been persistently translated as "prophet" does not mean prophet. *Navi* stems from a word which means to bring; the *Navi* is a bringer of the word of God. In contrast to the priest, for whom "the decisive movement goes out from the human person toward the realm of deity, ... with the *Navi* something descends from the divine sphere upon man: ... word or spirit."[30] Thus the *Navi* is not necessarily a foreteller of the future, he or she is a bringer of the word or of the spirit which descended upon him or her; and many of the sayings and deeds of each *Navi* have little to do with predicting the future. The *Navi* was chosen by God to respond to the situation to which God sent him, by coping—at times wrestling—with God's message (think of Moses at the burning bush, or of Elijah fleeing into the desert!) and bringing it to the people. As Buber pointed out:

God lifts the man [the *Navi*] out of the community, cuts him off from his natural ties; from Abraham to Jeremiah he must go forth out of the land in which he has taken root, away to the land where he has to proclaim the name of God; it is the same story, whether it is a wandering over the earth like Abraham's or a becoming utterly alone in the midst of the people like the prophets. They are drawn out of their natural community; they fight with it, they experience in this community the inner contradiction of human existence.[31]

Scholars have suggested that the reason *Navi* was translated as prophet is that Christian translators wished to read into what they called the Old Testament the foreseeing and the predicting of the coming of Jesus. (Certain chapters of Deutero-Isaiah seemed very relevant to this intention.) In what follows, even when I use the accepted locution, Hebrew prophet, it will mean *Navi*.

Buber noted that the *Navi's* message often emerged in a dialogical encounter, and even when this did not happen the manner of presenting this message was dialogical. When the Hebrew prophet spoke, his or her admonitions, or addresses, or dreams were expressed on a gut level, from person to person. Furthermore, many a *Navi* was entrusted with his or her mission in a personal dialogical encounter with God: think of Moses confronting the burning bush or the young Samuel being called by God at night.[32] It is also evident that the courage aroused and expressed during the dialogical encounter with God had political implications. Moses confronted Pharaoh forcefully; Nathan chastised King David; Elijah admonished Ahab.

Buber believes that the key to the relationship between civil courage and dialogue is wholeness, the ability of a person to act and to live as a whole being. One can only enter into dialogue as a whole being, and when one acts courageously it is as a whole being. In both cases while relating as a whole being here and now, one also transcends the here and now. Thus, wholeness seems to provide an ontological link between courage and dialogue. But the link is problematic. Further clarification is needed.

Consider, once again, the Hebrew prophets. In addition to the wholeness acquired in dialogue, the *Navi* constantly expressed a genuine concern and love for other persons and for God. This love did not always prevent one from acting cruelly, as when Elisha cursed the children from Beth-el who mocked him with "Go up thou baldhead," and two she-bears came out of the forest and killed forty-two children (Second Kings 2, 23–24). But in the daily existence of the *Navi* there is a mission to be undertaken, there are persons in the world to be educated and healed, there is justice to be sought, there is a life of faith to be lived, there is the Decalogue to be obeyed. Each of these undertakings must be done with wholeness, otherwise one will not come near the desired goal. Buber, therefore, was right when he indicated that dialogue can teach us that a wholeness exists which can be expressed in actions enhancing to human existence. But Buber was wrong when he assumed that such wholeness will lead persons to realize their freedom in other realms.[33] Here is one of the points where I, as a student of Buber's philosophy, failed in my work for Jewish–Arab dialogue. As I have shown at length, the dialogue attained between Jews and Arabs rarely encouraged them to, say, struggle for justice in the realm of politics.[34] In short, the wholeness that emerges in dialogue can be the beginning—but only the beginning—of learning to live a more courageous and worthy existence.

Hence, dialogue as a first step in the struggle for justice, for faith, for a life of spirit, a struggle similar to that of the *Navi*, may be a manner of developing civil courage. It is also often true that dialogue can help one learn that one has the courage for such a struggle, and that a struggle which is partially inspired by Buberian dialogue will allow one to see additional dimensions of reality.

But not always! Probably the saddest—and certainly one of the least publicized—episodes in Martin Buber's life testifies to the limitations of dialogue. After Hitler came to power in Germany, Buber, who was already an accepted leader of German Jewry, became an educator; for five years he zealously educated German Jews to embrace Judaism and to immerse themselves in the spirit of its texts in order to withstand Nazi persecution. He did not advocate emigrating from Germany. The end of the story is well known. Most of those Jews who took Buber's advice were murdered by the

Nazis. Buber himself did emigrate from Germany to Israel in 1938, and was thus saved from the results of his teaching. But he never admitted his terrible mistake.

The problem is that dialogue will not teach us how to cope with, or even how to evaluate, evil, and how to deal with those persons who pursue it. Buber's writings show that he always dealt with evil on an abstract level;[35] or as Jochanan Bloch pointed out:

Buber had a lifelong tendency for lack of specifity. A kind of conceptual abstraction prevailed in him, which shied away from a specific commandment, specific contents, and if you like—from the crudeness of life, with its burdens, its materialistic and rigidified element, its cruelty.[36]

Furthermore, Buber never noted that, at times, the ardent belief in dialogue is a manner of not facing up to the emergence of evil in the political realm. For a while I also embraced dialogue so as not to cope with political realities. Slowly I learned that the beating, killing, and exploitation of Arabs by committed fervent Jewish racists—such as have emerged recently in Israel—cannot be dealt with through dialogue; one must brand these Jewish fascists as one's enemies and struggle against them with all the democratic means available, and if they embrace violence as a way of intimidation and a manner of attaining power, one must be willing to struggle against them with violent means. What Buber never recognized was that a fervent committed racist is no partner to dialogue; and the courage emerging in the dialogical encounter has little to teach us about how to counter such evil.

The major concern of Nikolai Berdyaev in his book *Slavery and Freedom*[37] is that each man and woman assume the responsibility of becoming a personality, which means transcending the situation of being an individual. In order to be a personality one must reject the manifold ways in which one is lured to become enslaved; every day, at every moment, one must strive to be free. Already in the names of the chapters of his book Berdyaev describes some of the ways persons become enslaved, and thus forfeit their personality: "The Slavery of Man to Being," "The Slavery of Man to God," "The Social Lure and the Slavery of Man to Society," "The Slavery of Man to Civilization and the Lure of Cultural Values," etc. In relation to courage and freedom he writes:

The freedom of personality is certainly not its right; that is a superficial view. Freedom of personality is a duty, it is a fulfilment of a vocation, the realization of the divine idea of man, an answer to the divine call. Man ought to be free, he dare not be a slave, because he ought to be a man. Such is the will of God. Man likes being a slave and puts forward a claim to slavery as a right, a claim which changes its form from time to time. It is precisely slavery to which man lays claim as a right. Freedom ought not to be a declaration of the rights of man; it ought to be a declaration of man's obligations, of the duty of man to be a personality, to display the strength of character of personality.[38]

Although Berdyaev wrote about man, (he seemed to have had chauvinistic views about women) in what follows the courage to be a person is viewed as an equal duty of men and women. Berdyaev's viewing freedom as an obligation has some parallels with Arendt's description of the polis and of political freedom. Thus in "the life devoted to the matters of the polis, in which excellence produces beautiful deeds"[39] Greek men could live beyond the coercive life of a laborer, the working life of a free craftsman, or the acquisitive life of a merchant—beyond those individuals who were enslaved by everyday concerns. A life "devoted to matters of the polis" meant assuming the obligations, the responsibilities, and the possibilities of freedom, among them the possibility of becoming a person worthy of being remembered, because one had performed excellent deeds or spoken great words.

Without going further, it should be evident that one of the new challenges of Zionism must be the building of a state in which persons will develop their personalities, in Berdyaev's sense of the word—albeit that Berdyaev admitted that he could only vaguely indicate what he meant by personality. The chief rabbi of Hungary in the story in the introduction had personality, in Berdyaev's sense of the word, because he was not enslaved by the religious dogma that he taught and professed; he could see beyond Herzl's sins, he could deeply appreciate his vision. What Berdyaev did not stress (perhaps because of his background which blended Russian aristocracy, Greek Orthodoxy, and Marxism, all of which did not emphasize the significance of the political realm for a life of freedom) is that certain political regimes will encourage persons to assume the obligation of being free, of being a personality, while others will oppress and punish any such inclination. A despotic regime will do its utmost to discourage the development of personality, including killing leaders of any opposition; a totalitarian regime will simply eliminate any person with a slight inclination to fulfill the obligation of developing one's personality. The opposite is also partially true. When enough persons in a nontotalitarian or despotic regime have the courage to strive to be a personality, to declare their obligation to be free, that regime will develop as a political entity which allows, and at times encourages, personality to be realized.

In accordance with Berdyaev, one should read the Bible as a call to live one's freedom and to develop one's personality. The *Navi* demanded that each son and daughter of Israel assume responsibility for fulfilling God's commands; and when the listener assumed such a responsibility he or she fulfilled the obligation to be free. Berdyaev repeatedly emphasized that for such an obligation to be fulfilled one must free oneself from the concept of

God as a Master: "God is freedom; He is the liberator and not the master. God bestows the feeling of freedom and not of subjection. God is Spirit and Spirit knows nothing of the relation of domination and slavery."[40]

In the struggle to be a personality, Berdyaev points out that one of the most dehumanizing forces is socialization. Society wishes to dominate the inward existence of man, it wishes to empty personality of any spiritual content, and to refuse any coherent meaning to the word Spirit. It wishes each person to be as close as possible to average. And in many instances society succeeds. As we shall see, this success within the kibbutz movement has resulted in most kibbutz members being insipid, unspiritual persons, who persistently ignore their obligation to be free. Or to give a personal example, unlike many academicians I use the word Spirit in my classes, including when I am discussing contemporary political problems. Thus in my classes on education for democracy at Ben Gurion University I can say "Mr. Peres, the prime minister, is merely a third-rate bureaucrat who craves power; he has no relationship to a life of Spirit." A few times, after I spoke forcefully, a student approached: "You know, Haim, when I try to use the word Spirit, it doesn't come out of my mouth well, it sounds counterfeit. ... But you, it comes from your stomach." "You know damn well why ..." I reply. "You want to speak about Spirit? ... Stop living a life in which means and ends reign; start struggling against racism and injustice and inequality. ... Fulfill your obligation to be free!"

Berdyaev held that the struggle against the paralyzing forces of society must take place in the inwardness of each person, in what he termed one's "existential center." Like other existentialists he did not suggest that fulfilling the obligation to be free, that developing as a personality, requires entering the public realm. This ignoring of the political realm is most unfortunate. Even for a person to become cognizant of one's own personality, one must appear and interact with others in a realm determined by the obligation to be free—Arendt's political in-between—not the realm of society. (In *Remembrance of Things Past*, Proust has shown poignantly, through his description of Swann, the Verdurins and their "faithful", and others, that appearing in society is very often a continual enslavement which leads to the degeneration of personality; such an appearing has nothing to do with one's existential center, nor with creativity, nor with authentic interaction with other persons, nor with the development of personality.)

Being creative often requires solitude; developing existential relations with another person requires privacy; still, a person must appear in the public realm in order to receive acknowledgment of his or her creativity, or in order that an existential relationship may be affirmed. When two persons for many years nurture a secret love, or when an artist persistently conceals his or her works, they are not fulfilling their obligation to be free. In short, although Berdyaev was politically active—he was jailed and exiled for his speaking out by the Czarist regime, and two decades later, due to similar activities, he was expelled from Russia by the Soviet regime—in his writings he did not explicitly acknowledge that appearing in public is an important component of developing one's personality. He did not mention that in the public realm the courage to be a personality is often tested.

Advocators of personality must engage in a two-pronged attack against "The Social Lure and the Slavery of Man to Society." As personalities, men and women must reject the enslavement to what is acceptable in society. (Today in Israel, in large segments of Jewish society, it is acceptable to despise Arabs and to sanction our exploitation, oppression, beating, and killing of Palestinians. Merely rejecting such a view often demands courage.) The courage developed in assuming the obligation to be free in one's personal life, can often help one struggle in the political realm for matters of Spirit. On the other hand, without struggling in the political realm, the wish to develop as a personality will not be fully realized. Not only because, as totalitarian regimes have shown, once the public realm is eradicated, there are almost no expressions of the human spirit—that argument is true, but it is based on the means–end model, a model which has nothing to do with spiritual existence. Political engagement is central to a life of Spirit primarily because, at least according to Biblical Judaism, such a life is not only a personal undertaking, it is of this world and for this world. As such it must appear in that realm of human existence where excellence is disclosed to everyone—the political realm.

Courage in the political realm is necessary for the spiritual challenges presented in this book. It is not sufficient. To take upon oneself spiritual challenges, a person must not only be courageous in the political realm, he or she must also live as persons of dialogue who struggle against enslavement in their personal life. Although Berdyaev and Buber often ignored the grandeur of the political realm—in which excellence emerges and in which the doers of great deeds and the speakers of great words can appear—it is quite clear that a person who fulfills his or her obligation to be free will not easily succumb to cowardice when he or she enters the public realm. Nicolai Berdyaev and Martin Buber personally exemplified this point. Both of them were not politically active for any lengthy period. But when they did enter the public realm, they often acted courageously.

The linkage between freedom in the interpersonal realm and a life of spirit can be found in quite a few Biblical stories. For instance, if one compares King David and King Saul one finds that both were very courageous in dealing with Israel's enemies. They both were courageous as political leaders of their people. But Saul never became a spiritual leader, while to King David were attributed the Psalms, and according to Jewish tradition the Messiah will be the son of David. Why?

Granted that quite a few scholars have suggested that the editors and the compilers of the Bible were biased: they were against Saul and for David, they attributed the Psalms to David even though it is highly doubtful that he wrote them—still it is interesting how this bias is expressed. One reads that Saul was a very dogmatic person, who was willing to kill Jonathan, his own son, in order to keep a vow, even though Jonathan had single-handedly initiated a victory over the Phillistines (First Samuel, 14, 41–45). David, on the other hand, is described as more of a dialogical person. (Even if scholars may suggest that his dialogical approach was part of his tactics, it is beside the point, since that is scholarly interpretation and not how David is perceived by the lay reader.) Consider, for instance, his resolute loving friendship with Jonathan (First Samuel, 20, 35–42, and Second Samuel, 1, 25–26) or his persistent attempts to convince Saul that he was not his enemy (First Samuel, 26). Hence, despite his many sins, and despite his failings during his dotage, David is remembered as a much more spiritual person than Saul.

Again and again I will emphasize that the linkage between courage in the personal and the political realms is crucial for any attempt to live a more spiritual existence. By spiritual existence I do not mean merely intellectual enhancement, or ascending to a mystical experience, or sailing on the winds of a euphoric feeling. These experiences may be components of a spiritual existence, but in Judaism, since Biblical times, spiritual existence is lived and tested in one's everyday engagements. Making room for dreams in Israel today requires free persons who will undertake everyday engagements in the spirit of peace and justice proclaimed by the Hebrew prophets. (I do not believe that the spirit of the *Navi* is to be realized through a literal adherence to his or her words.) Thus, as will be shown in Part II of this book, both personal and political courage are needed if we Jews wish to establish peaceful relations with our Arab neighbors, if we wish to encourage Jewish (and Arab) women to fulfill their obligation to be free, if we wish to justly distribute our economic resources, to stop exploiting the land, polluting the air, acting ruthlessly toward each other—in short, both kinds of courage are needed if one wishes to undergo what Nietzsche called a metamorphosis.

The three metamorphoses that Nietzsche describes in *Thus Spake Zarathustra* are significant, because a person who undergoes them will become courageous both in one's personal life and as a political being.[41] (The German word that Nietzsche uses is *Verwandlung*, which has been translated as metamorphosis, a change of one's being; it can also be translated as a conversion, a change of one's beliefs.) The link between the *Verwandlungen* and a life of courage has been overlooked by not a few scholars, who bind Nietzsche to a specific philosophical approach. They disregarded Nietzsche's repeated demands that one should ask oneself: What can one learn from these writings about living a more worthy and fulfilling life?[42]

Thus, few scholars noticed that undergoing the second metamorphosis—in Nietzsche's terms, becoming the lion who resides alone in his own wilderness and rejects and challenges all traditional values—requires both personal and political courage. Simply because, when one rejects or challenges traditional values, one changes as a person and one also rejects the political structure which supports these values, and the persons in power who benefit from them. Nietzsche calls the bearer of traditional values a great dragon upon whose golden scales are written "Thou Shalt." The role of the lion is to create a new freedom by rejecting the message on these glittering scales and their inherent values, by forcefully saying "I will."

Let me stop here and turn to a more orderly presentation. First, some personal thoughts about the story of Joseph and his brothers.

A question that many Jewish sages evaded in their commentary of the Bible was: After being sold into slavery by his brothers, why didn't Joseph attempt to escape and to return home? He was sold into slavery, at the age of seventeen, in the Dothan valley, north of Hebron where his father resided. The Ismaelites who bought him traveled south, to Egypt, hence they passed not far from his home. Why, then, didn't Joseph attempt to escape? Especially since he knew that his disappearance would inflict sadness and suffering upon his father?

Some rabbis answer: Joseph knew that the only way to make his dreams of personal grandeur (that were inspired by God) come true—the dream with the sheaves in the field, and the dream with the eleven stars, the sun and the moon (Genesis, 37, 5–10)—was to accept his fate. Others suggest that Joseph was repeating, albeit in a different direction, the wanderings of his father, Jacob, who fled from the wrath of his brother. (The Bible abounds in latter-day repetitions of original Biblical stories.) The problem with these answers is that they are viewing history backward: from the knowledge of the outcome of Joseph's enslavement they assume his attitudes. They do not begin from Joseph's existential situation at the moment of his being sold into slavery by his brothers. My answer, which relys on Nietzsche's metamorphoses, addresses that situation. I would like to believe—and I admit that this is strictly a personal reading[43]—that Joseph suddenly sensed and decided, after being alone some hours in the pit into which his brothers had thrown him—and this decision contributed to his greatness—that in order to grow, to change, to become free, he must learn to bear heavy burdens, including, in his case, the burden of slavery. While suffering from his brothers' betrayal and his newly inflicted degradation, he decided that he had to start anew, while bearing the bane of his past arrogance and vanity.

Undergoing Nietzsche's metamorphoses is a manner of living one's freedom, growing, and becoming creative while bearing a heavy burden. The first metamorphosis is the camel, the spirit who ladens itself with burdens so that it can rejoice in its strength. Nietzsche asks which of a representative list of burdens is most heavy. Here are a few examples from his list.

Is it not this: To debase yourself in order to injure your pride? To let your folly shine out in order to mock your wisdom?

Or is it this: To desert our cause when it is celebrating its victory? To climb high mountains in order to tempt the tempter?

Or is it this: To feed upon the acorns and grass of knowledge, and for the sake of truth to suffer hunger of the soul?

Or is it this: To be sick and to send away comforters, and make friends with the deaf, who never hear what you ask?[44]

Thus, the first step in becoming free and creative is the taking of heavy burdens upon oneself, and the rejoicing in one's strength. When one has become a camel, ladened with such burdens, one can hasten with these burdens into one's wilderness and undergo the second metamorphosis: in the loneliness of one's own desert one can become a lion. Only after living alone with such burdens does one discover in oneself the strength to challenge traditional values. But the challenging of traditional values only allows for freedom to appear, it does not necessarily mean that this freedom will lead to creativity. For creativity to appear, a person must undergo a third metamorphosis, the lion must become a child. Because the "child is innocence and forgetfulness, a new beginning, a sport, a self propelling wheel, a first motion, a sacred Yes."[45] In order to create, one must be able to speak the sacred Yes, that is, to affirm life with one's entire being.

Elsewhere I have suggested that in his life Socrates underwent these three metamorphoses;[46] here the metamorphoses will help me review the development of Zionism.

Establishing the Zionist movement burdened many a Jew with the kind of burdens that Nietzsche described. The biography of Herzl, the charming autobiographical writings of Jabotinsky, and even the boring autobiography of Chaim Weizmann reveal that for the sake of truth these persons suffered hunger of the soul, that Herzl and Jabotinsky were the kind of persons who could be sick and dismiss comforters, or who had to make friends of the deaf, who never heard their requests—in Herzl's case the Turks, in Jabotinsky's case the British. Much the same appears in the Hebrew literature of that perod; being an active Zionist often meant ladening upon oneself Nietzschian burdens. Most of the Jews in the world at that period, and large portions of the Jewish establishment, were deaf to the beliefs and the dreams of the Zionists.

Many of the early Zionists strongly challenged the traditional Jewish values. Herzl challenged the Jews' unwillingness to assume political responsibility for their fate. Jabotinsky challenged the Jewish belief that the power of arms was unimportant in setting up a Jewish homeland, and the worldwide scepticism, including scepticism among Jews, that Jews could successfully bear arms. This challenging of the traditional values allowed Herzl, Jabotinsky, and quite a few other early Zionists to undergo the third metamorphosis and to create new values; Jews began to believe in political initiatives and in the significance of establishing Jewish armed force. Other values attributed to the emerging Zionist movement were communal equality, such as occurred in the kibutz; equality of women, which in truth was very much of a myth,[47] but in lieu of the enslavement of Jewish women for millennia, even bringing up the concept was an act of creativity; a redeeming of the land of Israel, most of which was either mosquito-infested swamp and bog, or wind-stripped desert. In some of the writings of this period one also discerns persons with a childlike innocence, coupled with a constant affirmation of life. (For instance in some of Agnon's stories of Israel.[48])

In short, a few of the more influential early Zionists and some of their followers partially succeeded in undergoing the three metamorphoses. The willingness to undergo such radical changes was an act of courage, and their success and courage often led them to understand that one must constantly go through such metamorphoses if one wishes to be creative. Much of this process stopped with the establishment of the State of Israel. As mentioned in the Introduction, today, within the Zionist movement obsolete values prevail whose realization has become a farce. The kibbutz is today an aristocratic guild whose major—if not only—concern is to raise its standard of living; women in Israel continue to be enslaved by men, and through the enactment of religious laws they are in danger of losing even more of their rights; and the redeemed Promised Land of fifty years ago is slowly but surely becoming polluted, salinated, and in some places contaminated.

Nietzsche's metamorphoses do suggest a direction of development which leads to a courageous creative existence, an existence whereby one expresses one's freedom in the personal and political realms. But there is a catch here. Even to begin undergoing the metamorphoses one needs to be courageous. Here we have reached the final impasse. Education, love, rage, danger—to mention only a few possibilities—can bring a person to be courageous; but in each instance one reaches the imponderable moment when that person takes a leap—or doesn't.

Thus, existentialist philosophy can greatly help in pointing the direction a person who is willing to be courageous should pursue if he or she wishes to live responsibly and creatively in the political realm, if he or she wishes to struggle for spiritual goals. Existentialism, though, cannot help one take the initial leap. That leap, to return to Berdyaev, is the assuming of one's obligation to be free. No philosophy can assist in such a task.

DAILY ENGAGEMENTS

Civil courage, thinking, and creating a space for dialogue and for political freedom are the basis for the spiritual challenges to Zionism described in this book. They are also a criteria for examining various aspects of Israeli society. Thus, when discussing the religious establishment, or the Israeli Defense Force, I shall point to the diminishing of freedom, the obliterating of thinking, and the effacing of civil courage fostered by these institutions. It need not be so: In Plato's *The Republic* the guardians' role is to guard the republic so that thinking can occur in it. Religious leaders such as Moses,

Jesus, and Mohammed educated their followers to undertake the obligations of freedom.

Two issues arise at this juncture. First, in one's daily life the ways of living one's freedom should blend. If one discusses these manners of living freely without demanding of oneself (and pointing out to others) that the "between" and the in-between should emerge in one's daily engagements, one is, at best, living in bad faith. Second, one may ask: What is the relationship of civil courage, or thinking, or political freedom to Judaism? To Zionism? Are not dialogue, civil courage, and thinking beneficial to all persons and societies? I shall discuss the relevance of these manners of living one's freedom to Zionism in the next chapter. Here I shall indicate some ways Israelis evade blending the three ways of realizing one's freedom.

The significance of such a blending is revealed if one examines two misleading questions currently being asked in Israel: Why do the officers and the soldiers in the Israel Defense Force refuse to think, or as we say in Hebrew, why do they have a "small head"? And, why do statistical surveys reveal that anti-Arab racism is spreading among Jewish youth? Not only are these questions misleading; the purpose of the questioner is to evade responsiblity.

The manner of evasion reminds one of the Patriarch Isaac. He knew that his son Esau (who sold his birthright for a pot of lentil soup) was not worthy of continuing and developing the relationship established between Abraham and God. Yet he didn't have the courage to bless Jacob, Esau's twin brother, who was worthy of such a task. The result: Isaac, whose eyesight was weakened, but was not blind, let himself be duped into blessing the worthy son. It wasn't easy. In the darkened tent he had to ask Jacob, "Who are you, my son?" and hear the false answer, "I am Esau, your firstborn." He had to feel the goatskins on Jacob's arms and on the nape of his neck, and say, "The voice is the voice of Jacob and the arms are the arms of Esau." In short, he had to play out the entire melodrama of being duped (Genesis 27).

Posing the question, "Why do the officers and soldiers in the Israel Defense Force refuse to think?" is similar. The politicians and generals who ask are not seeking an honest answer. Asking is a manner of concealing their own unwillingness to assume responsibility. This personal responsibility for lack of thinking cannot be evaded by proposing a general answer (based on Plato): An army that for years oppresses another nation is consistently teaching its soldiers not to think. Because, if soldiers began to think, they would begin to question the morality of the orders they receive. This answer is true, but wrong. It is wrong because it deals with the situation on the plane of objectivity; it thus helps the politicians, the generals, and all Israeli citizens abrogate their personal responsibility for more than two decades of exploitation, oppression, and degradation of Arabs on the West Bank and in the Gaza Strip, and for the "small head" that is one of its results.

Like Isaac, these politicians pose the question knowing that they will get an answer that will allow them to continue to evade courageous deeds. Isaac knew that Jacob's answer to the question "Who are you, my son?" would be a lie. As I read Genesis, between Isaac and Jacob there existed what may be called a consensus to cope with a situation by cowardly means. A similar consensus exists between the politicians and the people of Israel. The politicians and generals will ask with feigned innocence why soldiers don't think, and many journalists, writers, academicians, and other spokesmen will not even respond with the above truth. They will feed their audience half truths: "Good officers leave the army because the pay is low." "For an officer to be promoted, he must join a clique of officers and without much thought follow hints from the leaders of the clique." "The army does not have enough resources to educate its soldiers and its officers; they must be trained to solve military problems." Such half truths do not even touch upon the issue, which is political and existential.

Israeli soldiers and officers do not think because—as will be shown in detail in subsequent chapters, and as I have often experienced personally, including in my ongoing attempts to promote Jewish–Arab dialogue—civil courage and thinking are almost always penalized in the army and in Israel; because the space for dialogue and for political freedom is slowly being eradicated; because persons are finding hosts of ways of living as slaves and denying their obligation to be free. Hence, lack of thinking in the Israeli army is largely a result of the fact that Israelis do not blend the above-mentioned three manners of realizing one's freedom in their daily engagements.

The politicians and generals know all this, much as the people of Israel know it. Together they have agreed to *not* confront or challenge their shallow existence. To appease their anxiety they ask superficial questions knowing that they will receive superficial answers. A consensus of stupidity prevails. (Think for a moment: Wasn't it stupid for Isaac to go through the entire melodrama of being duped, instead of simply getting up from his bed and raising the flap of the tent so he could see, with his weakened eyesight, which son had come to be blessed?) I am saying that many Jews in Israel have learned to be stupid: Nietzsche was right; often, in order to be stupid one must study many hours—so as not to challenge, in their daily lives, the many enslavements that they have gladly assumed.

Evading the queston about racism is much more complex. Lack of thinking can lead to evil, while racism is evil. Most Jews are unwilling to say that racism is a necessary evil that will bring in its wake a new millennium; such a statement recalls *Mein Kampf.* (Meir Kahane and his followers *do say* that anti-Arab racism is a Godly command, and quite a few Jews accept this statement as a legitimate political and religious stance.) Thus the key to stacking the question "Why is anti-Arab racism spreading among Jewish youth?" is by putting the emphasis on the word youth, as if it were merely a problem of the youth. (Although the surveys do reveal that racism among youth is close to fifty percent, much more than among adults, the surveys check responses to questions, not daily behavior.)

Many youth are racist in Israel because anti-Arab racism is what they daily perceive, in thousands of deeds that adult Jews perform, on the bus, in the market, at work, and at home. As Montesquieu pointed out, "It is not the young people that degenerate; they are not spoiled till those of maturer age are sunk into corruption."[49] Unlike most adults, youth often call a spade a spade, and when questioned, admit to being racists. Hence, anti-Arab racism has nothing to do with youth, but with how Jews daily live with Arabs, and especially with the million and a quarter Arabs residing on the West Bank and in the Gaza Strip who have no political rights and few civil rights. By turning the question away from the realities of everyday life, from the political oppression of Arabs, and by focusing on a specific age group the questioner creates the illusion that one merely has an educational problem at hand. The result: Bureaucrats in the Ministry of Education spend months developing educational programs that explain at length that teachers need only clarify how odious racism is, or how important it is to respect each person's beliefs and way of life, and anti-Arab racism will evaporate. Again, stupidity prevails.

The two misleading questions reveal more than a lackadaisical approach to the challenges of Zionism, or an unwillingness to confront some of the existential problems facing Jews in Israel today. The consensus between the political leaders and the people in Israel is based on the tacit agreement that no questions will be addressed on the spiritual level. A question will always be perceived as a problem-to-be-solved. Such a consensus allows all persons to not perform deeds of civil courage, to not think, to not create a space for freedom. The result is not only the stupidity mentioned above, but a loss of the courage needed to make one's life into a story. Persons learn to live a bored, languid existence devoid of the quest for glory. Put otherwise, since most Jews in Israel do not blend the three manners of realizing one's freedom, they have no stories of grandeur to tell.

In one of her *Anecdotes of Destiny* Isak Dinesin describes a dying affluent businessman, Mr. Clay, who suddenly realizes that his life is ending without any memories of glory or grandeur.[50] He did hear, many years ago, a story about an elderly rich man who married a beautiful young woman and was unable to make love to her; the unsuccessful groom drove down to the wharf in his carriage, found a young sailor on leave and asked him to come to his house for that one night, have dinner alone with him, and make love to his wife. Perhaps he would have a son. The delighted sailor agreed. Mr. Clay mentions the story to his male secretary, who replies that the story is told on ever ship, by sailors boasting of their escapades at the last port of call; it has never happened. Mr. Clay decides to have his secretary make the story come true, at least once. His attempt is the haunting and sad anecdote that Dinesin tells—I will not abbreviate it here. It reveals the insipidity and vacuity of a life dedicated to solving problems. Mr. Clay even grasps making the story come true as a problem-to-be-solved.

Only a person who struggles for things that are worthy in themselves—freedom, beauty, justice, wisdom, love, knowledge, glory, dialogue, an authentic relationship with God—has a worthy story to tell. Mr. Clay does not realize that even if, with the help of money, he can make the sailor story happen, it will not be a true story. Not only is the element of surprise partially eliminated. The struggle to express one's individuality and to create a place in this world for things that are worthy in themselves will also be missing.

The consensus between most of the political leaders and the people in Israel resembles the attempt of Mr. Clay and his secretary to make the sailor story happen. Through their speeches and deeds politicans present and pursue a jingoist ideal of an affluent and militarily strong Israeli nation; they suggest that all one need do to realize this ideal is to solve some economic, political, or military problems. Many people agree. An atmosphere of problem solving prevails—quite a few persons sincerely believe that for Israel to become, say, "The Economic Success Story of the Middle East" one need only solve a few problems. They may be right. But such a success will bring in its wake insipidity and vacuity; because, as with Mr. Clay, in the life of many Israelis a struggle for and a spontaneous interaction with those things that are worthy in themselves will have vanished. In short, one cannot make a story come true, one can only strive to courageously attain things that are worthy in themselves; perhaps a story will remain.

In the everyday deed one's mettle is tested. This statement is central to Judaism, and can be traced to Biblical times. During the diaspora the Halakhah was developed, which is a dogmatization of those everyday needs that the Jewish sages believed each Jew must fulfill. For two millennia the Halakhah helped Jews relate to their heritage and to God; but since it did not encourage Jews to be politically active, since it did not encourage them to pursue creative expression in the visual and in other arts, since it often confined Jewish life to a limited adherence to dogma, since it often enslaved Jewish women and certainly did not encourage them to fulfill their obligation to be free, it narrowed the scope of Jewish life, and limited the things that are worthy in themselves to which the Jew could relate. This narrowness emerges when one reads Jewish history and searches for stories that are worth telling. In comparison with the Bible, whose vivid stories depict existential situations in which persons courageously struggle in the world and for the world—the Hebrew prophets are a case in point—the diaspora period is a two-thousand-year wasteland, with here and there a sordid oasis; few, almost no, stories of worldly courage remain from these twenty centuries. The significance of political action and of the struggle for political freedom disappeared from Jewish life and consciousness. Even the Hasidic stories that Martin Buber rewrote and published are, as Buber admitted, anecdotes and legends and not stories comparable to those that abound in the Bible.

Although "every individual life between birth and death can be told as a story with beginning and end,"[51] it is the stories of courageous persons, who struggle for things that are worthy in themselves, which teach us about realizing one's freedom in the world. In the past few hundred years, beginning perhaps with Cervantes, tales of passive, impotent, or grotesque persons, who do not act or speak courageously, have become a major topic of literature. Yet authors often indicated "The Road Not Taken"[52] by their literary heroes which led to their not attaining those things that are worthy in themselves. Shakespeare, Balzac, Dostoyevski, Joyce, Proust, Gide, Kafka, to mention a few, have written fascinating accounts of passive impotent persons who do not act or speak courageously, yet often one senses where they went wrong. (For instance, Proust writes of Swann: "since his mind no longer entertained any lofty ideals, he had ceased to believe in their reality. He had grown also into the habit of taking refuge in trivial considerations, which allowed him to set aside matters of fundamental importance."[53]) Similar accounts can be found in Jewish and Hebrew literature, in the writings of S. Y. Agnon, Y. H. Brenner, Isaac Bashevis Singer, Mendele Mocher Sfarim, and others, but often with hardly a hint as to "The Road Not Taken." Furthermore, while in world literature quite a few writers did describe persons who courageously struggled for things that are worthy in themselves—Brutus in Shakespeare's *Julius Caesar*, Levin in Tolstoy's *Anna Karenina*, Alyosha and Dimitri Karamozov in Dostoyevski's *The Brothers Karamozov*, Robert Jordan in Hemingway's *For Whom The Bells Toll*, and Gavin Steven in Faulkner's *Requiem For A Nun* are good examples—similar heroes hardly ever appear in Hebrew and Jewish literature. This lack of courageous literary heroes merely reflects the fact that neither worldly joy and courage nor political action were appreciated by the Jews of the diaspora. Thus there may be much to describe and analyze when comprehending the two millennia of Jewish life in the diaspora, but stories of Jews courageously acting in this world and for this world will be extremely rare.

Contemporary Israeli novelists are continuing this tradition of impotent literary heroes. They describe at length the psychological and sociological workings that mould their banal heroes—something that Dostoyevski warned not to do—while consistently disregarding the quest for freedom which should animate all literature. They seem not to have understood that for Gide, or Proust, or Kafka, a psychological description always points beyond itself to an ontological situation in which a personal decision was made. In contrast, the heroes described by Israeli novelists swim around in their psychological and sociological opaque reality, like catfish in a muddy marsh, without freedom emerging on the horizon of their being. One can only conclude that for Oz, Kanyuk, Appelfeld, Yehoshua, and a host of other Israeli authors, writing novels is an explanation not an engagement. Hence the result is not a work of art; it is an attempt to flatter the reader, instead of confronting or challenging him or her. Put otherwise, these novels are havens, created by clever chatter and lack of fortitude, which invite the reader to flee from one's own superficiality and cowardice into a forgetting of the possibility of living one's freedom. I shall return to these writers and to how they differ from some excellent Israeli poets.

If in one's daily engagements one does not attempt to realize one's freedom, one lives outside of history. The Jewish people in the diaspora developed a manner of survival by living, most of the time, outside of history. Many Jews in Israel today retain remnants of these manners of survival, one of the most prominent features being the belief that when what they call Jewish values are at stake, one must disregard and disparage the law of the land. This disregard is not civil disobedience, which accepts the laws of the land but rejects a specific law as unjust, such as when Martin Luther King supported the constitution of the United States but organized civil disobedience of laws segregating blacks. Jews are saying that when one is fulfilling what they call Jewish values, all laws can be broken, including the Ten Commandments.

Such fanaticism could perhaps be dismissed if it did not strike a welcome chord in the hearts of many Jews who believe themselves to be supporters of democracy, or of the emergence of the Jewish spirit, or of Jewish–Arab dialogue. These fellow travelers of Jewish fanaticism are, of course, deceiving themselves when they believe that fanaticism can lead to freedom or to spiritual existence. And much too often this deceit stems from an unwillingness, in one's daily life, to be courageous, to take a stance, to create a space for freedom and for dialogue, to think.

Yet someone may say, enough of your criticism! Give us some positive examples of how, in daily engagements, one strives to realize one's freedom.

In two of my recent books I have described at length some of my own attempts, during seven years of educating for Jewish–Arab dialogue, to teach persons and to learn myself how to realize freedom in one's daily engagements.[54] Furthermore, some Israeli Knesset members, such as Shulamit Aloni and Yosi Sarid, are struggling, with some success, for such a realization in Israeli political life. Some Israeli journalists, Kobi Neve for instance, are stressing the significance of daily engagements; and I have met persons outside the public spotlight who, in their daily engagements, strive to realize their freedom. Still, there is a problem in adequately describing how, in daily engagements, one strives to realize one's freedom. Such is usually better expressed in a long story. An anecdote or brief tale illuminates a specific moment; only a story may describe a pattern of daily engagements that indicates how a person realizes his or her freedom. Hence, in whatever manner I shall respond to the above question, and I shall do so partially in Part II of this book, will only be a pointing in a direction which a person who wishes to live his or her freedom may pursue.

There is also a misleading component to the above request. Most intelligent persons know the significance of daily engagements in realizing one's freedom. Presenting positive examples of daily engagements and discussing them might help one clarify, reveal, or determine one's specific existential situation; but many persons know very well how and when a specific daily engagement demands that one act courageously or think, and when and how one is shirking that obligation.

In the fall of 1986, I approached a high-school principal in Beer Sheva and proposed that she integrate into her Jewish school of about 1400 pupils three Israeli-Arab classes (Arabs who are Israeli citizens). I promised to raise the funds for the program. (Jews and Arabs learn in separate high schools in Israel; Jews study in Hebrew, and Arabs in Arabic.) The Arab classes would study in Arabic, but the pupils would have joint activities with Jews, for instance sport; they would meet Jewish youth in casual encounters; and there would be directed activities promoting Jewish–Arab dialogue. The principal decided to present the proposal to her board.

Two weeks later I met with the principal, three vice-principals, and about ten teachers. I explained the need for such a dialogical experiment on the background of Jewish–Arab enmity, and mentioned the pogrom that orthodox Jews in Jerusalem had recently raged against Arabs, after a Jew had been stabbed by two Arabs in Jerusalem. (The police picked up the killers two hours after the stabbing; they were from Nablus, which is about fifty miles north of Jerusalem; but the pogrom went on for three days, with the Israeli press reporting that the police frequently overlooked Jewish violence.) When I finished, two teachers and a vice-principal vehemently opposed my proposal: Arabs are not worthy to be trusted, they are in certain respects subhuman, deserve to be oppressed, and so forth. I kept quiet; I wanted to hear the colleagues of these racists.

I didn't. Not one of the colleagues, including the principal, spoke up for Jewish–Arab dialogue, or for creating trust between Jews and Arabs, or for the belief that we Jews have a land and a destiny to share with the Arab citizens of our country, or for our joint humanity with all Arabs.

The only point I want to make is that every one of the (seemingly) nonracist teachers and administrators who were sitting there, among them a few of my former students, was shirking his or her obligation to be free. And they knew it. Pointing out to such shirkers examples of daily engagements where one can act courageously, think, and struggle for dialogue and political freedom, would be engaging in intellectual masturbation.

NOTES

1. Hannah Arendt, *The Origins of Totalitarianism* (New York: Harcourt Brace Jovanovich, 1951), p. 466.

2. Hannah Arendt, *The Human Condition* (Chicago, Ill.: University of Chicago Press, 1958), p. 198.

3. Here is probably an example of my "existential musings." Unlike Arnold M. Eisen, in *The Chosen People in America: A Study in Religious Ideology* (Bloomington, Ind.: Indiana University Press, 1983), who examined the historical, sociological, and ideological development of the concept of The Chosen People in America, I am not trying to examine the historical or sociological roots of how the concept of The Chosen People is grasped today in Israel. Rather, I am asking myself: What does this concept mean to me in my daily life? If I accept this concept, what should I do today, tomorrow, to live up to its demands? In short, I plead guilty to personally musing about the concept of The Chosen People and of relating it to my daily existence.

4. Arendt, *The Origins of Totalitarianism*, p. 54.

5. Samuel Sager, *The Parliamentary System in Israel* (Syracuse, N.Y.: Syracuse University Press, 1985), esp. chapter 3.

6. Martin Buber's basic work on wholeness and dialogue is, of course, *I and Thou* (New York: Scribners, 1970).

7. Martin Buber, "What Is Man?" in *Between Man and Man* (London: Fontana, 1961), p. 246.

8. See "Appendix," in Martin Buber, *The Knowledge of Man* (New York: Harper, 1965), pp. 166–184.

9. See Martin Buber, "On Education," in Buber, *Between Man and Man*.

10. Robert Weltsch, "Buber's Political Philosophy," in Paul Arthur Schilpp and Maurice Friedman, *The Philosophy of Martin Buber* (La Salle, Ill.: Open Court, 1967), p. 435. An additional article which does not see the limitations of Buber's approach to politics is Jonathan S. Woocher, "Martin Buber's Politics of Dialogue," in *Thought*, Vol. LIII, No. 210, Sept. 1978, pp. 241–257.

11. Gordon, "Existential Guilt and Buber's Social and Political Thought," in Haim Gordon and Jochanan Bloch (editors), *Martin Buber, A Centenary Volume* (New York: Ktav, 1984).

12. Hannah Arendt, "What Is Freedom?" in *Between Past and Future* (New York: Viking, 1961).

13. The distinction is elaborated in Martin Buber, "Elements of the Interhuman," in Buber *The Knowledge of Man*.

14. Hannah Arendt, "On Humanity in Dark Times," in *Men and Dark Times* (Middlesex, England: Penguin, 1969), p. 12.

15. Exact details can be found in Sager, *The Parliamentary System of Israel*.

16. Hannah Arendt, *The Life of the Mind: Part One, Thinking* (New York: Harcourt Brace Jovanovich, 1977) p. 4.

17. Hannah Arendt, *Eichmann in Jerusalem* (Middlesex, England: Penguin, 1976), p. 49.

18. Ibid., p. 48.

19. Amos Oz, *In the Land of Israel* (New York: Harcourt Brace Jovanovich, 1983).

20. Arendt, *The Origins of Totalitarianism*, p. 69.

21. Arendt, *Eichmann in Jerusalem*, especially pp. 93–105.

22. Arendt, *The Human Condition*, p. 198.

23. Arendt, *The Origins of Totalitarianism*, p. 479.

24. Ibid., p. 56.

25. Thomas Hobbes, *Leviathan*, edited by C. E. Macpherson (Middlesex, England: Penguin, 1968), p. 81.

26. Arendt, *The Origins of Totalitarianism*, p. 107.

27. Concerning the leader of a totalitarian movement Arendt writes: "The leader represents the movement in a way totally different from all ordinary party leaders; he claims personal responsibility for every action, deed, or misdeed committed by any member or functionary in his official capacity. This total responsibility is the most important organizational aspect of the so-called Leader principle, according to which every functionary is not only appointed by the leader but is his walking embodiment, and every order is supposed to emanate from this one ever present source." Arendt also points out that this "monopoly of responsibility" is what distinguishes between a totalitarian leader and an ordinary dictator or despot (*The Origins of Totalitarianism*, p. 374).

28. Arendt, *The Human Condition*, p. 36.

29. See Haim Gordon, *Dance, Dialogue, and Despair* (Tuscaloosa, Ala.: University of Alabama Press, 1986) and my articles in Haim Gordon and Leonard Grob, *Education for Peace* (New York: Orbis, 1987).

30. Martin Buber, *The Prophetic Faith* (New York: Harper, 1960), p. 64.

31. Martin Buber, "Biblical Leadership" in *Israel and the World* (New York: Schocken, 1948), pp. 132–133.

32. Buber presents his views on the significance and breadth of the dialogical encounter for the *Navi* in "Biblical Leadership."

33. Buber expresses these views in the section on politics in Martin Buber, *Pointing the Way* (New York: Harper, 1963). A full refutation of Buber's views is beyond the scope of this essay. I have partially dealt with this topic in "Existential Guilt and Buber's Social and Political Thought," in Gordon and Bloch, *Martin Buber, A Centenary Volume.*

34. Gordon, *Dance, Dialogue, and Despair.*

35. Two books in which Buber deals with evil abstractly are; Martin Buber, *Eclipse of God* (New York: Harper, 1952) and Martin Buber, *Good and Evil* (New York: Scribners, 1952). This abstraction is also seen in the fact that Buber, despite his attempts, could never write a good novel or play—since such writing demands that one see evil, concrete evil, as it manifests itself in everyday life—and also in the manner he deals with politics in relation to Jewish–Arab dialogue. See Paul R. Mendes-Flohr, *A Land of Two Peoples, Martin Buber on Jews and Arabs* (Oxford: Oxford University Press, 1983).

36. Jochanan Bloch, "Opening Remarks," in Gordon and Bloch, *Martin Buber, A Centenary Volume*, p. xvi.

37. Nikolai Berdyaev, *Slavery and Freedom* (New York: Scribners, 1944).

38. Ibid., p. 48.

39. Arendt, *The Human Condition*, p. 13.

40. Berdyaev, *Slavery and Freedom*, p. 82.

41. Freidrich Nietzsche, *Thus Spake Zarathustra*, trans. R. J. Hollingdale (Middlesex, England: Penguin, 1961).

42. An example which shows how a scholar murders the live educational message of Nietzsche is David E. Cooper, *Authenticity and Learning: Nietzsche's Educational Philosophy* (London: Routledge and Kegan Paul, 1983). Cooper has overlooked attempts to deal briefly with this educational message in Martin Heidegger, "Who Is Nietzsche's Zarathustra," trans. B. Magnus, *The Review of Metaphysics*, 20, pp. 411–431. Also Haim Gordon, "Nietzsche's Zarathustra as Educator," *Journal of Philosophy of Education*, 14, pp. 181–192.

43. Perhaps I should add that this reading was probably influenced by Thomas Mann's novel *Joseph and His Brothers* (London: Sphere, 1968).

44. Nietzsche, *Thus Spake Zarathustra*, p. 54.

45. Ibid., p. 55.

46. Gordon, "Nietzsche's Zarathustra as Educator."

47. I shall discuss these myths in the chapter on dialogue between men and women.

48. For instance, see Shmuel Yoseph Agnon, *Tmol Shilshom* (in Hebrew) (Tel Aviv: Schocken, 1979). Agnon primarily describes the travails of his impotent hero Yitzchak Kumer, but in the

background of Kumer's adventures one meets persons with the innocence that Nietzsche described.

49. Baron De Montesquieu, *The Spirit of the Laws* (New York: Hafner, 1949), p. 34.

50. Isak Dinesin, "The Immortal Story," in *Anecdotes of Destiny* (New York: Vintage, 1985), pp. 155–231.

51. Arendt, *The Human Condition*, p. 184.

52. "The Road Not Taken" is a poem by Robert Frost. See *The Poetry of Robert Frost* (New York: Holt, Rinehart and Winston, 1964), p. 105.

53. Marcel Proust, *Remembrance of Things Past, Vol. 1* (New York: Random House, 1934), p. 161.

54. Gordon, *Dance, Dialogue, and Despair*. Also my essays in Gordon and Grob, *Education for Peace*.

2

The Reading of the Bible and Zionism

Consider *The Song of Songs*. In Hebrew this collection of love peoms, this celebration of the delights of bodily love, has no parallel. Some scholars suggest that *The Song of Songs* was included in the Bible because the editors of the Bible believed that the earthly love expressed in these poems described the love between God and the People of Israel. This belief—that the earthly love in *The Song of Songs* had nothing to do with love on earth—was accepted by many Jews in the diaspora for two thousand years. It changed with the flourishing of the Zionist movement. When they returned to the land of Israel and revived Hebrew as a spoken language, many Jews began to read *The Song of Songs* as a collection of sensual love poems. Moreover, since the early twentieth century, many verses in this short book have been put to music, as lyrics of popular songs. In short, as the changed attitude to *The Song of Songs* reveals, the Biblical text, like many great texts, transcends the intentions of its editors.

I have already mentioned that I am not a Biblical scholar and that my reading of the Bible is personal and subjective. I believe that the Bible was written not only for scholars to study, or for religious leaders to quote, but also for lay persons like me, who wish, as Berdyaev suggested, to learn from it how to fulfill their obligation to be free. Hence, I can pose the question: How can one read the Bible as a source for realizing one's freedom? In his essay "The Man of Today and the Jewish Bible," Martin Buber suggested that today a person

must read the Jewish Bible as though it were something entirely unfamiliar, as though it had not been set before him ready-made, as though he had not been confronted all his life with sham concepts and sham statements that cited the Bible as their

64

authority. He must face the book with a new attitude as something new. He must yield to it, withholding nothing of his being, and let whatever occur between him and it. He does not know which of its sayings will overwhelm him and mold him, from where the spirit will ferment and enter into him to incorporate itself anew in his body. But he holds himself open. He does not believe anything a priori; he does not disbelieve anything a priori. He reads aloud the words written in the book in front of him; he hears the word he utters and it reaches him. Nothing is prejudged. The current of time flows on and the contemporary character of this man becomes itself a receiving vessel.[1]

Following Buber's suggestion I have for years been reading the Bible spontaneously, nonauthoritarianly, open to its existential message. I have found it to be a source of guidance in my personal struggles for justice, for Jewish–Arab dialogue, for equality between men and women, for true faith. In presenting here some of my personal conclusions I am not advocating that these conclusions are scholarly valid, or exclusive, or necessary. I am not rejecting the possibility that, at times, I may be reading my views into the text. Still, my opening myself to the Bible in the manner suggested by Buber can serve as an example which indicates that in striving to make room for dreams, in striving to fulfill our obligation to be free, we Israelis can—and, I believe, should—read the Bible as a guiding source.

Put differently, the Bible is my personal heritage, much as it is the personal heritage of every Jew and Jewess. It is not, as the religious parties in Israel would like us to believe, a heritage that belongs only to the religious establishment or to those men who spend their life in a yeshiva. It is a heritage that I should not worship, or idolize, but rather learn from in my attempts to live a life of faith and justice, as demanded by the Hebrew prophets.

I have often felt that the core of the Bible is a chronicle of the encounter between the People of Israel, as free persons, and God. Hence, one can read the Bible as an appeal and as a guide to realize one's own freedom. In such a reading one may often struggle to address the spirit of the text, which is not necessarily its literal meaning. (I believe, though, that *The Song of Songs* should be read literally. These love poems clearly indicate that love is expressed in sensual intercourse, in the joy of feeling the presence, the touch, and the caress of a person whom one cherishes.) Thus, although the Pentateuch can be shown to feature many antifeminist laws and attitudes, I do not accept this enslavement and degradation of women as central to Judaism and to the Godly encounter. Unfortunately, many of the rabbis of the religious establishment in Israel not only blindly follow the injunctions enslaving and degrading women in the Bible (which were further developed in the diaspora), they read the Bible as justifying this degradation and also the degradation of Arabs, and of Jews who do not accept the orthodox interpretation of Judaism. They wield the Bible as a tool of enslavement.[2]

Needless to say, I am not alone in stressing the central significance of freedom in the Bible. Berdyaev, as stated above, read the Bible as a demand that he and all other persons fulfill their obligation to be free. And Buber, who saw dialogue as central to the Biblical encounter between Israel and God, assumed the freedom of the people of Israel, since without freedom one cannot enter into dialogue.

For me the central event of the Bible is the liberation of the tribes of Israel from Pharonic bondage, so that they could serve God as free human beings. This struggle for liberation was not undertaken in order to subject the Hebrews and their descendants to a book, or to some rabbis' writings, be they wise or fanatic, fatalistic or enlightening. Any attempt to diminish the centrality of personal freedom in the covenant between Israel and God, even in order to attain a greater adherence to Biblical precepts, is a choosing of the chaff and a throwing away of the kernel.

To benefit from the message of faith and justice central to the Hebrew Bible, reading it in order to understand the text is not enough; especially for the Israeli who reads Hebrew as a living language and can respond to the original force of the writings. One must learn to read these tales, travails, proverbs, appeals, laws, psalms, songs, dreams, and admonitions as embodying a personal challenge: In one's historical circumstances one must take upon oneself the obligation to be free.

Of course, one may argue that my personal reading of the Bible can be challenged by Biblical scholarship. My only response is that any Biblical scholarship which diminishes the Bible's appeal to the freedom of its readers is eroding the basis upon which a life of faith and of justice can be established. As scores of philosophers, theologians, and religious leaders have repeatedly pointed out, faith without freedom is a farce, and justice without freedom does not exist. Hence, any text, such as the Bible, that purports to encourage its readers to live a life of faith and justice must appeal to the freedom of its readers.

Interpretations of a Biblical text may differ. I refuse to accept an interpretation as valid if it does not demand of the Jew, or of any other reader, that one reject all manners of enslavement. What is more, I forcefully disagree with a Biblical text that encourages or concurs with enslavement— for instance, all the laws dealing with legalized slavery. I also vehemently reject all Biblical sources that view women as property, or as impure, or in any way unequal to men. For me, the saying "one man among a thousand have I found; but a woman among all those have I not found" (Ecclesiastes, 8, 28) is unworthy of the Bible; it diminishes the import of the encounter between God and the men and women of Israel as persons who can undertake the obligation to be free.

Let us briefly consider why the enslavement and degradation of women diminishes freedom. One of the spaces where freedom emerges is Buber's "between," which comes into being when persons relate dialogically to each other. But if a woman is considered as mere property of a man, as an object to be owned not as a subject to whom one relates, the possibility of dialogue arising between men and women is diminished, and very often totally eradicated. Not only does the woman suffer because she is related to as an object, she is also not allowed to share the interpersonal freedom that emerges between persons who are subjects. Men are also degraded in the process, because in such a situation a man's love never becomes a giving among equals. It is not only that the woman with whom a man shares his bed, whose naked body the man, in his nakedness, embraces and penetrates, the woman who becomes the mother of a man's children, never becomes a sharer of that man's freedom. It is also that in his most intimate intercourse the man never learns the joy of sharing, which includes the humility of receiving and learning from another sojourner upon earth. Thus an opportunity for love and dialogue is lost; deceit and mendacity thrive.

In the commentaries on Genesis there is much discussion of Jacob's sin, when he stole Esau's blessing. Although there is some discussion on why Rebecca, Jacob's and Esau's mother, decided to deceive her husband, Isaac, thus to ensure that Jacob be blessed, it does not deal with the existential situation in which Rebecca found herself—as an unequal partner to Isaac, as his property. It seems that the (male) commentators wished to overlook the fact that if dialogue and equality had prevailed between Isaac and Rebecca, perhaps none of these sins would have occurred. The commentators and the editors of the Bible seem to have never entertained the thought that Rebecca could share with Isaac, as his equal, the decision as to which of their sons was worthy of being blessed. Thus, Isaac's unwillingness to share his reservations and deliberations concerning the passing on of Abraham's blessing, coupled with his relating to Rebecca as an unequal partner, an object, created an atmosphere of trickery, delusion, and deceit. Persons who live in such an atmosphere forfeit much of their interpersonal freedom.

To read the Bible while espousing freedom one must realise that the message of God, transmitted by the *Navi*, was expressed in a vernacular that would be understood by every person. For instance, the way of life of Israel was patriarchal; hence, the *Navi* spoke in a patriarchal vernacular while demanding of those persons who could be free, the males, to relate to God as free persons. These facts do not mean that patriarchy is essential to fulfilling the message of God. It is not. It is beyond my comprehension to envision a God who demands justice for all and condemns one half of the human race, the females, to being impure and to perpetual enslavement by the males. Nor do I believe that anachronisms like the sacrifice cult, a holy temple, or a priestly caste—to mention a few of the proposals-for-renewal-of-Judaism suggested by some orthodox Jews—are essential for a true faith.[3] What is more, as I shall soon suggest, orthodox Judaism's persistent embracing of patriarchy, and of many other anachronisms, hinders many a Jew's ability to relate to God as a whole person and to fulfill His message.

Since the Bible embodies the demand that the people of Israel serve God as free human beings, I hold that assuming one's obligation to be free means, among other things, reading the text and personally deciding what is the relevance of a specific passage to one's life. In relation to some passages the decisions are almost unanimous—most persons would accept the Decalogue and reject the injunctions to stone a rebellious son, to kill an unfaithful wife and her lover, to sell people into slavery, to conduct a sacrificial cult, or to kill homosexuals. Other passages, such as dietary laws are controversial.

Reading the Bible, and probably any book of revelation, in the manner I am suggesting is exciting and enhancing, because such a book can only retain its vitality if it appeals to persons who will learn from it to live creatively or dialogically, as courageous and whole persons. Of course, allowing each person to decide how to relate to a text of revelation entails no assurances. Khomeini reads the Koran as a tool of enslavement that sanctions and justifies the curtailing of human rights, the oppression of political freedom, a holy war, and murder of nonbelievers. The famous Egyptian author, Naguib Mahfouz, reads the Koran as instructing him to pursue peace and justice, and to educate others to do so. Similarly, in the war-infested period of the Crusades, St. Francis read the Bible and the New Testament as instructing him to love his fellow creatures.

Human freedom brings no assurances—that is why it can be the womb of glory! In the polis, where political freedom was first discovered, Socrates was sentenced to death by a jury of hundreds of his peers. The sentence was also a rejection of freedom of speech in the polis. A few centuries later Brutus killed Julius Caesar to ensure the freedom of the citizens of Rome. He failed. Roman citizens willingly surrendered their freedom and joined Caesar's heirs to defeat Brutus. No, there are no assurances that human freedom will not be trampled upon, or given up willingly. Again and again men and women will worship the golden calf on the slopes of Mount Sinai. Yet, the glory of Socrates's search for wisdom and of Brutus's struggle against tyranny continues to enlighten persons who wish to realize their freedom. Similarly, the glory of the Biblical heroes—from Abraham to Samson and from David to Jonah—is in their struggle to serve God as free human beings, with their fears and dreams, lusts and passions, moments of courage and faults.

Which Biblical commands could one follow? My personal answer is: Only commands that accord with human freedom. The patriarchs and the Hebrew prophets established a relationship with God that forbade worshiping any idol. Unfortunately modern idolatry is a reality; not a few persons enslave themselves by worshiping an idea, or a priestly dogma, or earthly wealth, or a political party, or a charismatic rabbi. I submit that here I am not in agreement with Emil Fackenheim's analysis which sees idolatry in terms of the finite and the infinite: "Only because the finite object is made infinite is the object endowed with its shattering powers, and the idolatrous worship of it, qualitatively distinct from mere superstition."[4] I am closer to the view expressed by Paul Tillich:

Idolatry is the elevation of a preliminary concern to ultimacy. Something essentially conditioned is taken as unconditional, something essentially partial is boosted into universality, something essentially finite is given infinite significance (the best example is the contemporary idolatry of religious nationalism).[5]

The reason I would partially agree with Tillich is that he is presenting the existential dimension of idolatry, showing it as a flight from the obligations of freedom. This is a flight from the possibility of relating to matters of ultimate concern, say, the pursuit of justice, through the elevation of "preliminary concern to ultimacy." Fackenheim, on the other hand, is trying to define idolatry objectively, externally; he is ignoring it as an enslaving mode of being-in-the-world with which each person must wrestle. But the *Navi*, who encountered God, learned that He demanded a relationship with free responsible persons, not with persons who flee relating to matters of ultimate concern. God demanded that the entire manner of a person's being-in-the-world would exclude idolatry, would not elevate to ultimate significance matters that are not ultimate. A case in point is Isaiah's attack on those Israelites who elevate the sacrificial cult to a matter of ultimate concern, while abandoning widows and orphans, while not seeking justice and relieving the oppressed (Isaiah 1). (Of course, the significance of living as a free responsible person while relating to God has been conveyed poetically by Dostoyevski in his description of Jesus' relationship to Catholicism in "The Grand Inquisitor" and in other parts of *The Brothers Karamazov*. Yet the Biblical sources of this theme have often been overlooked.)

It is ironic and sad that I need to argue that relating to the Bible must be based on human freedom. Not only because of the centrality of freedom to the Biblical message, but also because the problem of Jews living in freedom acquired great import in the twentieth century. The success of the Nazis in destroying millions of Jews was partially a result of the lack of political action and political experience that has characterized Jewish existence during two millennia of living in the diaspora. On the other hand, with the establishment of the State of Israel, Jews are experiencing, in terms of personal and political freedom, the most exciting and promising century of Jewish history since the Macabean era—one must go back at least two thousand years, eighty to a hundred generations, to encounter a similar experience of Jewish freedom. Yet many—if not most—of today's Jews, including politicians, writers, poets, ignore the blessings of human freedom and the Bible as a possible source of such blessings.

In Israel today the Bible is often read to justify idolatry and superficiality. So-called religious Jews continue to regurgitate the Halakha, and its Biblical sources, as if learning these texts were central to a relationship with God, were of ultimate concern in this world. Quite a few of these Jews grasp themselves as holy, and above worldly justice, since they spend their life analyzing and digesting what they consider to be holy texts. As the Israeli press repeatedly reveals, without qualms they often sanction corruption, deceit, exploitation, and, in general, a trampling upon the freedom and the property of their fellow Jews as long as these deeds are done to further the learning of the Halakha or to support the religious parties.

Other Jews relate to the Bible as a source for justifying feelings that dominate their existence. For instance, Menachem Begin repeatedly played on the remembrance of Jewish suffering to arouse Jewish sentiment. He interspersed his speeches and writings with Biblical epigrams. Speaking in the Knesset after his government initiated the Lebanese war, Begin announced that thanks to this war Jewish suffering would lessen and the land would have "rest [for] forty years" (Judges 3, 11). But the war backfired. Instead of bringing peace and alleviating Jewish suffering it brought greater suffering to all involved. Begin resigned, at least partially because of this backfiring of his plans and deeds. Still, since it is much easier to be sentimental than to be free, many Jews choose to follow persons like Begin who use the Bible to justify one's feelings.

What does it mean to read the Decalogue as a free responsible person? I believe that it means attempting to realize each command in its broadest possible interpretation. An orthodox rabbi who believes that he is fulfilling the second commandment when he refuses to hang a reprint of Van Gogh in his house, because it is a graven image, yet who daily elevates money, or status, or power, or learning the Talmud to ultimate concern is not only living in bad faith. He is a fool. His way of life clearly contradicts the Decalogue, and he need only think to discover this contradiction. Similarly, Israeli religious leaders who support a ruthless vice-laden politician like Ariel Sharon, because he will help them force other Jews to keep certain religious injunctions, are not only immoral and living in bad faith. They are also fools—and yet, perhaps they aren't. Perhaps, like Dostoyevski's Grand Inquisitor, they have begun to serve the Adversary and not the true God, because they refuse to trust their fellow Jews with freedom.

One can also narrowly interpret the commandment *Thou shalt not steal*. As such, it is merely an injunction against burglars, or white-collar criminals. I believe in a broader interpretation, according to which one views oneself as a sojourner upon earth who is entrusted with this planet and its bounty, which one must share with forthcoming generations. In this case, depleting the resources of the earth, polluting its rivers and seas, contaminating its air and land, is stealing from other persons with whom one shares this earth, and from the generations who will be entrusted with the fate of the planet in centuries to come. A no less broad interpretation demands that one not exploit one's fellow sojourner by unfairly dividing the bounty that has been reaped or wrested from the earth.

Thou shalt not kill also has broad interpretations. It has been reiterated *ad nauseum* that there is no direct object to this commandment. Thou shalt not kill, *period.*[6] What has not been noted are the political implications of this commandment. A political community that creates circumstances—such as those prevailing on the West Bank and in the Gaza strip—in which Jews repeatedly kill Arabs, is no less responsible for the death of those Arabs than the soldier doing the shooting. In Israel the responsibility of the political community is reemphasized by the fact that many of the soldiers who perform the oppression are in the reserves; they are citizens most of the year, and are called up for a few weeks of active duty during which they are sent to enforce the oppression in Gaza and the West Bank, to beat up the rebelling women and children. These soldiers cannot argue that they are merely obeying commands. In politics, as Hannah Arendt stressed, obedience is support.

Once Golda Meir was asked if she would ever forgive the Arabs for killing so many Jews. Golda replied: "I will be able to forgive the Arabs for killing Jews. But I will not be able to forgive them for making Jews into killers." The answer is beautiful. But Golda evaded mentioning her own responsibility for making Jews into killers. No wonder that with such self-delusion active support of *Thou shalt not kill* is rare in Israel today. Many Jews don't mind being killers, or friends and supporters of killers. There are three political parties in the Knesset—among them two religious parties—which openly support a group of Jews who decided to become a death squad and were caught after a series of Arab killings. What Golda refused to acknowledge was that in the past two decades, which include her tenure as prime minister, Israeli oppression of Arabs, which was a political decision, has helped make Jews into killers.

Comparing the relationship between Israel and the Promised Land in the Bible to relationships to the earth in other religions, Buber pointed out: "In Israel the earth is not merely, as in all other primitive peoples or peoples that preserve their primeval energy, a living being, but it is also a partner in a moral God willed and God guaranteed association."[7] The Bible repeatedly stresses that true faith in God and following His moral precepts are the conditions under which Abraham's descendants will be entitled to reside in the Promised Land. It is a portent that few of the early Zionists discussed these conditions. Views prevailed that the conditions were fulfilled by Ben Gurion's demand that Jews work the land, or by Jabotinsky's directing the Jews to capture and to own the land. These views do not accord with my reading of the Bible. Ben Gurion's and Jabotinsky's policies were, in certain circumstances, necessary; they were never sufficient. The Hebrew Prophets repeatedly appealed to their listeners to pursue a spiritual existence while residing on the land. And the land itself had to be related to as a partner to the covenant with God. Or, as Buber puts it, "The Promise [of the land] means that within history an absolute relationship between a people and a land has been taken into the covenant between God and the people."[8]

How does one relate to the land as a partner? Especially today, when only four percent of Israel's population work the land, producing enough for the country to be almost self-sufficient agriculturally and to export fruits, cotton, and other crops? One aspect of such a relationship, mentioned in the Introduction, is living on the land as a sojourner, not viewing the land as an asset to capitalize on, or as property to exploit. The sojourner knows that one is merely passing through the land in one's earthly life, much as the shepherd passes with his or her herd through a lush pasture, and that one must leave the land fertile for those who will follow in one's wake. But such is not enough—much as redeeming the land from mosquito-infested swamps and festering bogs, as the early Zionist pioneers did, was not enough. If the land is a partner, it is a partner to one's everyday way of life.

Architecture is an instance. Look first at the bland uninspiring highrises that prevail in Israeli cities and towns, making them mediocre and ugly. Consider also the boring and alienating facades of almost all buildings in Israel. Walk a bit in the alleys of the recently rebuilt Jewish quarter in the Old City of Jerusalem, which resembles the Jewish Ghetto in Rome more than a section of Jerusalem in which Jewish freedom should be lived. And to crown this pattern of alienation from the land, stroll through the newly constructed Hebrew University on Mount Scopus. Built as a hybrid between a medieval fortress and a fascist monument, this architectural monstrosity houses Israel's oldest university. Students studying within this ugly fortress cannot relate to the land of Israel, they cannot even comprehend the arresting vistas of Jerusalem; they are closed in, incarcerated in a stone and brick ivory tower.

Relating to the land as a partner to one's endeavors is expressed in the way one lives, in the houses one builds, in the cities one establishes, in the roads one constructs, in how one works the land and relates to the plants and animals that it sustains. As Israeli architecture reveals, such an attitude hardly prevails in Israel. If one judged by architecture alone, Israel has almost become a fascist country, since one encounters fascist architecture wherever one turns.

What does the Bible mean by pursuing a spiritual existence? And, does the Biblical quest for spirituality have anything to do with pursuing a spiritual existence today?

There seems to have always been a necessary and sufficient condition that must be fulfilled for spirituality to emerge. Pursuing a direction in which one endeavors to perfect oneself, while striving to give of oneself to the world and to its inhabitants, is the necessary condition. The Biblical example of persons who fulfill this condition is the *Navi*. The sufficient condition is that one attain wholeness—albeit only rarely—while pursuing that direction. Love, dialogue, creativity, and the attaining of excellence in any field in which one relates as a whole being, be it sports (as the Greeks viewed it), science, arts, or crafts, can lead to the emergence of spirituality.

The necessary condition is something a person can strive to fulfill. Not so with the sufficient condition. Moments of wholeness are moments of grace in which suddenly everything seems to come together; hence, they never can be planned, or sought after, or pursued. One cannot plan to fall in love on Monday at 2:00 p.m., or to encounter the Thou in genuine dialogue tomorrow morning, or to be creative before lunch. Hence attempting to live a spiritual existence is a daily striving to perfect oneself and to give of that perfected self; it is also an opening of oneself to moments of wholeness, if and when they may occur, while recognizing that nothing can be assured.

Thus, the Jew who wishes to learn how to live a life of spirit from the *Navi*, who lived upon the Promised Land as a sojourner, should relate to the *Navi*'s entire way of life, not only to his or her admonitions or visions. Analyzing, interpreting, or scholarly discussing the *Navi*'s message while ignoring his or her way of life will often block the path to a life of spirit. A central characteristic of that way of life is that spirituality can only emerge if, in the process of perfecting oneself, one has struggled courageously in this world for things that are worthy in themselves.

My experience has taught me that this "existential" message of the *Navi* can only be appreciated and absorbed by persons who are themselves assuming their obligation to be free. A central aspect of the Bible, as I read it, is that the *Navi* needs listeners, who are willing to live in freedom, much as the people need the *Navi*. In such a reading, Moses's greatest challenge was educating and encouraging the Hebrew tribes to live as a free people. Thus, Moses could break the tablets of law at the foot of Mount Sinai, but he could not continue in his mission without admonishing the Israelites, without demanding that they renew their faith in God and kill those who danced around the Golden Calf; put briefly, he had to appeal, once again, to the freedom of each person in Israel and to demand a life of faith from that free person (Exodus 32–33). Of course, Buber was right when he stressed that the greatness of the *Navi* stems from his or her addressing a specific situation, and presenting a vision or a demand pertinent to that situation.[9] But he overlooked the fact that these visions and demands could only be listened to and absorbed by persons who wish to live their freedom.

Relating to the Bible as conveying a message of freedom is often hindered by the ghetto mentality espoused by many Jews. The vast majority of Jews who emigrated to Israel came from countries in which the ghetto, either as imposed by the regime or as chosen by the Jews themselves, was a way of life—Iraq, Morocco, Yemen, Poland, Roumania, Russia. Hundreds of thousands of Jews who came from these and from many other countries had never experienced political freedom. Neither have the Jews of the two latest waves of emigrants, from Ethiopia and from the Soviet Union. Consequently, a large majority of Israeli citizens, including the Arabs, relate to Israeli political life as if it had nothing to do with the principles of justice. They believe that interests and survival are what are at stake in politics, and they read the Bible as legitimizing their cluttering the political realm with petty requests and demands for personal mediation—as if Israel were a huge ghetto.

Why does the Bible lend itself to such a reading? The main reason is that, although it gives a direction for life, as does every book of revelation, the Bible focuses on daily deeds, *Mitzvoth*, as important to following that direction. Here is where for many centuries the cart changed places with the horse. Jews in the diaspora could not live the life directed by the Bible, since such a life required some measure of political freedom and a space in which they, as Jews, could live that freedom. They lacked such a space and did not have the courage, or the will, or perhaps the capability to struggle to establish it. To hold onto their tradition and beliefs and to justify their lack of vision and courage, they fetishized the *Mitzvoth*. In the ghettos, where survival and taking care of one's interests were paramount, fulfilling the *Mitzvoth* became the essence of Judaism.

Such may, perhaps, have been necessary in certain periods in the diaspora; I do not want to judge here. But today, when the Jews have returned to Zion and have set up a political entity, our primary goal should be the pursuit of justice and of true faith, not the study of the Talmud or the fulfilling of fetishized *Mitzvoth*. Let me stress one last time that the only way I can read the Bible is as a book that appeals to the freedom of its readers; in such a reading pursuing a direction of life which leads to justice and true faith is central to the Biblical message, not certain *Mitzvoth* which some priest, or rabbi, or Biblical editor determined.

Persons espousing the ghetto mentality read the history of the last two thousand years as a mirror image of their own existence. They assume that the dedication to learning, to the Halakhah, and to an otherworldly God was the only way to ensure Jewish survival. I wonder. Could it not be the case that, if a Zionist movement had arisen, say, fifteen hundred or nine hundred years ago the Jews could have survived, differently of course, yet with a space for political freedom? Some scholars may respond: It didn't arise since the conditions were unfavorable. This response can only evoke a smile of contempt. Doesn't this scholar grasp that he or she, together with all the orthodox Jews, are reading history backward, from the results to supposed causes? Don't they perceive that once one makes history inevitable one eradicates human freedom? And finally do they really not see that such an interpretation of history contradicts the central message of the Bible?

I am arguing that one could just as reasonably say, and this saying would accord with the emphasis of the Bible on freedom, that no Zionist movement arose because the Jews lacked the courage and the will for it to arise. I am also arguing that making history into a process with predictable outcomes, like a chemical process, is stupid, since it could always have been different. The history of the twentieth century would definitely have changed if Hitler had been assassinated in one of the attempts on his life. But I am mainly reiterating that reading the Bible in accordance with its spirit demands the courage to live as a free person in one's political and personal life. Such cannot be done with a ghetto mentality.

Wait! Aren't you shortchanging two thousand years of Jewish life in the diaspora? By disparaging the ghetto mentality so vehemently, aren't you spitting into the well that sustained Jewish existence for millennia? And remember this period also had its greatness: The Talmud, Sadyah Gaon, the Golden age of Spanish Jewry, Maimonedes, Rashi, the Kabbalah and Jewish mysticism, Hasidism, to mention a few of the highlights. How can you, how dare you flippantly discard twenty centuries of Jewish existence and great spiritual achievement?

I am not shortchanging the highlights of Jewish life in the diaspora; I am advocating that in order to see what needs to be done today in Israel, in Zionism, we must cut ourselves off from our past, in the manner described in the Introduction. Only if we go forth, only if we undertake the new challenges that living a life of freedom in Israel entails can we hope to relate as free persons to the highlights and to the squalor of the diaspora. Because, great as the spiritual heritage of the diaspora may be, it has very little to teach us about how to live in freedom, how to undertake political action; it also has little to teach us about how to live a life of dialogue. The ghetto mentality, the fear and obeisance that characterized Jewish life for these two millennia, were not the ground upon which Buber's "between" and Arendt's in-between could emerge. Only the Bible, and perhaps the Books of the Maccabees and other sections of the Apocrypha, can teach us about political action, about dialogue. Or put differently, only a mentality cut off from the ghetto mentality can read these books and learn from them how to live a life of freedom and of dialogue.

Consider, once again, the Hebrew prophets. For me their glory stems from their acting as free persons in this world, in short, in their acting in stark contradiction to many precepts of the Jewish ghetto. From Moses to Jonah to Ezekial they all understood, even if many of them did not articulate it, that their message had political implications; and when one enters the public realm, one is no longer concerned with petty interests and personal survival. Unlike the ghetto Jew the *Navi* intuitively knew that

it requires courage to leave the protective security of our four walls and enter the public realm, not because of particular dangers which may lie in wait for us, but because we have arrived in a realm where the concern for life has lost its validity. Courage liberates men from their worry about life for the freedom of the world. Courage is indispensible because in politics not life but the world is at stake.[10]

Hence, a central message of this book is that we Israelis can only learn to live as free persons with the spiritual achievements of diaspora Jewry if we cut ourselves off from the way of life of diaspora Jews and live our freedom. Like the *Neviim* we must learn to live with courage, like them we must assume responsibilities in our life so that our deeds will reveal that not life but the world is at stake.

Look a bit closer at how Jews in the diaspora ignored the message of freedom emanating from the *Navi*. Emphasizing the *Navi*'s religious message was what concerned them for centuries. Since the nineteenth century quite a bit has been written about the moral implications of this message; rarely has it been mentioned that the *Navi* spoke and acted in the public realm. For instance, Moses' demanding of Pharaoh that he free the Hebrew slaves while struggling with the Hebrews to accept this freedom and its obligations is the epitome of the prophetic mission. Yet Jews repeatedly examined, elaborated upon, and analyzed this mission only as a religious event. They ignored its political dimension. Such is also true of their relation to the lives and the missions of the other *Neviim*. Of course, as already mentioned, nothing resembling the polis existed in Israel; still, what concerned the *Navi* was not interests and survival but the fate of the world. This concern had nothing to do with an eternal hereafter; it related to this specific portion of the world in which he or she lived, acted, and spoke. Redemption for the *Navi* is in this world.

The Hebrew prophet was called to his or her mission to demand that every man and woman in Israel endeavor to live in accordance with God's message. That was the test of Israel's chosenness. As already stressed, Israel was not chosen because it was genetically superior, as many Jewish chauvinists suggest. Israel was chosen because Abraham, Isaac, and Jacob and their progeny chose to attempt to live in accordance with God's commands. This attempt showed that striving to attain a life of the spirit is a human possibility and that the fate of the world would be altered if all persons and nations endeavored to realize that possibility. But as I have repeatedly stressed, one can only attempt to realize a spiritual life if one is free, if one can interact in the "between" and the in-between.

The disregard of the political realm by readers of the Bible is perhaps most striking in relation to God's love for Israel, which is a recurring theme in the *Navi*'s appeals and admonitions. The religious implications of this love are incorporated into the Jew's daily prayer. Unfortunately, in daily life the ethical implications of God's love are rarely mentioned, and the political implications have been completely ignored. One reason for this unbalanced reading is superficiality, which in many instances is linked to cowardice, to a wish to remain within one's four walls. Another reason is the fanaticism and fatalism that for centuries has been an accompanying component of Jewish thought and life. Of course, the Bible highlights Israel's religious involvement with a loving God, emphasizing again and again how Israel will be punished, or was punished, for betraying God and worshiping the gods of the land. This emphasis may have been posited by the editors of the Bible, who often were more concerned with priestly dogma than with religious existence. Still, the Bible repeatedly reveals that love cannot be confined to the religious realm. God's love for Israel demands developing ethical relations in this world and assuming political responsibility for the fate of the world. Why?

Love is an act of giving of oneself. A full and authentic accepting of God's or of another person's love can only be done by a giving of oneself to this love. But as the entire saga of Abraham shows—which began with his cutting himself off from his past and reached its climax with his willingness to sacrifice Isaac and to cut himself off from his future, and which included his bargaining with God for the saving of the wicked of Sodom and Gomorrah—such a giving must be realized in the everyday world, with its problems, exigencies, and deficiencies. To borrow a metaphor from Mozart's opera *The Magic Flute*, one can only follow the magic flute of love if one is willing to attempt to slay dragons while struggling against one's own and other persons' unethical words and deeds. In other words, although love arises in the "between," for it to endure it must continually lead to acts of freedom and for freedom in the in-between. And finally to be much more specific, I am saying that those Jews—and there are many—who announce that their love of God leads them to deliberately trample upon the freedom of fellow human beings are blatant liars. One cannot love the God of Israel while resolutely degrading, oppressing, and exploiting one's fellow sojourners upon earth.

I have been showing what I learned from reading the Bible in accordance with Buber's suggestions. But I acknowledge that these suggestions are problematic. Is only the Bible to be read in this manner? How is one to read Shakespeare, or Plato, or Livy, or Dostoyevski? In his essay Buber indicates that the Bible teaches a person how to live with three aspects of human existence: Creation, revelation, redemption. (Buber acknowledges that he gleaned these aspects from Franz Rosenzweig's *The Star of Redemption*.) But anyone who is willing to become a "receiving vessel" to the works of great writers, from Shakespeare through Goethe and Proust to Faulkner, will learn much on how to live with creation, revelation, and redemption. In short, Buber does not indicate how reading the Bible may be different from reading other great books; the manner of opening oneself to a text which he suggests is merely a first step for reading any great writer.

The difference between a text of revelation such as the Bible, the New Testament, or the Koran, and a work by a great writer is that the text of revelation poses a very clear direction which it demands that its readers pursue. It is deliberately educational, not merely educational through its ability to enlighten certain aspects of human existence. Hence, unlike the reading of great literature, the only way to read a text of revelation faithfully is to be willing to cope with its demands and appeals, in short, to attempt to follow the direction indicated. (One of the very few recent books resembling books of revelation, more in tone, poetic expression, and intent than in profundity and scope, is Nietzsche's *Thus Spake Zarathustra*.[11])

I hold, therefore, that reading the Bible as a free person must lead to deeds. Here is where a danger lurks. Generations of Jewish history reveal that the Bible can easily be read as an enslaving text, which tells persons exactly which deeds to do and which deeds not to do, thus eradicating human freedom and its own central message. To benefit from its message of freedom one must learn to read the Bible as a free person. In short, one must be willing to defy and disregard certain Biblical commands and beliefs while learning from the text. The Bible itself describes persons who defied God's commands, and instances where God's own decisions disregard accepted beliefs about Him. As against *Thou shalt not steal* one reads about Jacob stealing the blessing from Esau, Rachel stealing her father's teraphim, and David stealing Saul's arms. As against the repeated description of God as a God of mercy, one reads of Jacob wrestling an entire night with an angel on his way back to the Promised Land, and of Job, who suffered because God yielded to Satan.

But let me give a more positive, and personal, example. For the past eight years I have been working for Jewish–Arab dialogue in Israel. Put briefly, I have been trying to teach Jews and Arabs to relate to each other dialogically, in the spirit of the writings of Martin Buber. In the process, I have done many things which disregarded Biblical beliefs and defied Biblical commands. (For instance, I held many activities on Sabbaths, when the Decalogue prescribes that one should not work. In addition, I related to women as equal to men, and demanded that my students also do so.) Furthermore, I did not always follow Buber's philosophy when faced with difficulties and exigencies; I was not only not a saint, I was often vicious and oppressive. Still, I believe that I was closer to the spirit of the Bible than those Jews who fulfill *Mitzvoth* but sit back and let hatred between Jews and Arabs run rampage in Israel, or who devote their entire existence to interpreting abstruse Talmudic texts. Not only because I can cite Abraham, or Elijah, or Nathan, or Jonah as Biblical persons who struggled to relate dialogically in difficult situations, and not only because I believe, as Buber holds, that dialogue is ontologically central to the Godly message. I was closer to the spirit of the Bible because I was engaging my freedom to create a space of freedom for others. And even when I failed miserably, which at times happened, it was a failure in a struggle for freedom and integrity.[12]

To summarize, I would like to return to a question formulated in the previous section: What is the relationship of civil courage, or thinking, or political freedom to Judaism? To Zionism? Are not dialogue, civil courage, and thinking beneficial to all persons and societies? Of course, dialogue, civil courage, and thinking are beneficial to all persons and societies. But in

showing the significance of these ways of life one must speak from within a
situation and one must address a specific situation. The eloquence and
lasting relevance of the *Navi's* message was at least partially a result of his or
her speaking from within a situation and addressing a specific situation.
(Such can, of course, also be said of the judge, or the psalmist, and of other
Biblical writers and figures. The *Navi* is merely an example.) Learning from
the *Navi*, I have been attempting to speak from within the Jewish heritage
while addressing specific problems in Israel. Thus, if I had discussed the
significance of dialogue for spiritual existence today in Israel without
addressing the problem of Jewish–Arab dialogue it would have been a farce,
a cop out.

There is a beautiful story by S. Y. Agnon, which I can only abbreviate
here, but which encourages me to continue to read the Bible in the manner I
briefly described.

Among the Children of Israel gathered at Mount Sinai there was an old
man who had everything he needed: cows and sheep, donkeys and camels,
children and grandchildren. The only thing that he lacked was some peace.
On his bed at night he turned from side to side but found no rest. When
Moses prepared to ascend Mount Sinai the second time the old man
approached.

"Moses," he said. "I have always followed your injunctions. When you
told us to leave Egypt before our bread had baked, I carried the unleavened
bread in a sack on my back; when you told us to jump into the raging waters
of the Red Sea and a path would open, I controlled my fear and leaped into
the sea. Even when we wandered in the desert for three days without water, I
sucked my thumb to alleviate my thirst but I didn't complain. When you
went up to God and tarried for forty days, I did not join those who danced
around the Golden Calf. Now, you're ascending to God for the second time,
could you ask Him to grant me a request?"

"What is the request?" Moses asked.

"I have cows and sheep, donkeys and camels, children and grandchildren.
The only thing I am lacking is some peaceful rest. Please, Moses, ask God to
grant me some rest."

Moses agreed.

Moses ascended Mount Sinai. After receiving the Ten Commandments he
recalled the old man. "Almighty God," he said. "There is a man in my camp
who has done everything that you requested. Could you please grant him
some rest."

"I cannot do that," answered the Almighty.

"How can that be?" asked Moses. "You youself indicated that your power
is unlimited."

God replied: "Everything that I created, I created in six days. Rest I did
not create."

And I would add: Only persons who struggle to realize their freedom, who create and do not merely follow orders, will attain the inner peace that allows them to rest.

NOTES

1. Martin Buber, "The Man of Today and The Jewish Bible," in *On the Bible* (New York: Schocken, 1968), p. 5.

2. Anyone who has been to a Jewish religious court in Israel, especially in a case that deals with marriage and divorce, will witness striking evidence of this degradation of women in the name of a "pure" Judaism. For instance, in divorce cases women can often be branded prostitutes, while men almost always come out clean. Recently, in a religious court ruling a man was allowed to take a second wife because his wife was sterile. No woman would be allowed to take a second husband if her husband were to be found sterile. Additional instances of degradation are described in the chapter on faith.

3. For a philosophical justification and presentation of such views see, for instance, Michael Wyschogrod, *The Body of Faith* (New York: Seabury, 1983).

4. Emil Fackenheim, *Encounters Between Judaism and Modern Philosophy* (New York: Basic Books, 1973), p. 186.

5. Paul Tillich, *Systematic Theology, Volume 1* (Chicago, Ill.: University of Chicago Press, 1951), p. 12. Although the definition presented by Tillich is acceptable, I do not accept the basis of this definition. Thus I disagree when Tillich compartmentalizes theology: "Theology should not leave the situation of ultimate concern and try to play a role within the arena of preliminary concerns. Theology cannot and should not give judgements about the aesthetic value of an artistic creation, about the scientific value of a physical theory or a historical conjecture, about the solution of political or international conflicts" (p. 11). This book is a partial refutation of Tillich's approach, which seems to see only salvation and faith as ultimate concern. I am also ultimately concerned with the pursuit of justice, peace, and equality. My faith must be realized in the everyday of this world.

6. Needless to say, I reject the Biblical injunction to kill all the Amalekites. Personally, I do not believe that this command issued from God, but was added later by the priestly caste, or perhaps by the editors and compilers of the Bible.

7. Martin Buber, *On Zion* (New York: Schocken, 1973), p. 14.

8. Ibid., p. 18.

9. Martin Buber has made this point many times, as have others. One essay where he presents it forcefully is "Plato and Isaiah," in Martin Buber, *Israel and the World, Essays in Time of Crisis* (New York: Schocken, 1948), pp. 103–112.

10. Hannah Arendt, "What Is Freedom," in *Between Past and Future* (New York: Viking, 1961), p. 156.

11. Nietzsche, Friedrich, *Thus Spake Zarathrusta* (Middlesex, England: Penguin, 1961).

12. I have described my work for Jewish–Arab dialogue, and my failures, in *Dance, Dialogue, and Despair* (Tuscaloosa, Ala.: University of Alabama Press, 1986) and in my essays in Haim Gordon and Leonard Grob, *Education for Peace* (New York: Orbis, 1984). Failures in such struggles should not deter us. Buber repeatedly pointed out that the role of the *Navi* often led him to fail. Jeremiah is a prominent example of such failure from whom one can learn. For Buber's description of Isaiah's failure see "Plato and Isaiah".

PART II

CHALLENGES

3

Introduction

The proffering of a vision, if it is to be a viable vision, entails presenting daily challenges that accord with this vision. The challenges that I shall present are few in number, but they give some indication of the direction that the vision of political freedom and dialogue that I have been advocating could follow. In suggesting these challenges, I will continue to describe the deterioration of freedom and the lack of dialogue in Israeli society, a situation that I believe we can alter.

The fulfilling of the specific challenges may mean reliving the story of Rabbi Eisek of Krakow.[1] For three consecutive nights Eisek dreamed of a treasure buried under the bridge in Prague. Since the devout rabbi was very poor, he decided to travel to Prague. Perhaps the dream was true. After a week of wandering he reached Prague and found the bridge that had appeared in his dreams. It was guarded by an officer and a squad of soldiers. Rabbi Eisek strolled back and forth on the bridge for some hours, looking for a hint of the treasure. At last he aroused the officer's suspicion, who asked why he was loitering on the bridge. When Isaac told him, the officer laughed. "Stupid Jew. If I were to believe everything I dreamed," he said, "Why today I would be on my way to Krakow. Because last night I dreamed that under the hearth of a Rabbi Eisek there, a treasure is buried." Rabbi Eisek thanked the officer, returned to his home and promptly dug up the treasure.

Responding to the challenges resembles this story in the belief that it is in one's being, under one's hearth, that one can find the strength to create the space for freedom to emerge. A new spiritual direction for the People of Israel is not a treasure guarded by some remote officer; it is here, waiting to be dug up from our past, and to be undertaken today. Tarrying until some outside development evokes one's response is irresponsible. Such irresponsibility and the damage that results from it will emerge vividly in the following chapters.

The five challenges that I shall discuss may not blend into an entire vision, but they are necessary components of any vision of freedom and dialogue. If more Israelis would struggle for justice, peace, faith, dialogue, and creative expression, our entire situation would be different. If more Israelis would even think about and discuss what is wrong in these areas, instead of accepting the current situation as it is, perhaps new directions would emerge. Even though the combined challenges do not cover all areas in Israeli life which need to be addressed, the approach developed in dealing with these areas can help a person attempt to bring about change in other realms.

Often I will be linking a challenge to a segment of Israeli society—the kibbutz, the Israel Defense Force, the militant orthodox Jews. Not because only in that segment is the challenge relevant; mainly because that part of society is where I can most vividly describe the need to cut ourselves off from the past and the future, to be willing to see new possibilities, and to dream.

It should be clear at the outset that my critique of the kibbutz, or of the Israeli military, or of militant orthodox Jewry, is not an in-depth scholarly study of these societies and institutions, although I shall be citing some such studies. My description is a report of the existential situation in which these societies and institutions find themselves and an indicating of how this sad situation reflects the lack of spirituality in Israel. Put differently, dreaming and vision can only partially be based on scholarly findings. Persons— especially academically oriented persons—tend to forget that accepting the challenge to live spiritually, to courageously go forth and pursue things that are worthy in themselves, begins where scholarly research ends.

NOTE

1. I have abbreviated the story of Rabbi Eisek told by Buber in Martin Buber, *Tales of the Hasidim: Later Masters* (New York: Schocken, 1948), pp. 245–246.

4

Justice and the Demise of the Kibbutz Myth

Recently Yehudah Harel, a kibbutz member from Kibbutz Mrom Hagolan, established a Workshop for Strategic Planning whose primary goal is to outline, in a series of workshops held with kibbutz functionaries, means and methods that will allow the kibbutz movement to survive. Harel believes that the kibbutz movement resembles a truck driving full speed toward a wall, and only a supreme effort will bring it to deviate from its path; surviving an imminent crash is the kibbutz movement's most crucial challenge. Disregard the pathos in Harel's presentation, and skip over his methods which are taken from group dynamics and business administration textbooks. The fact that kibbutz members flock to his workshops, and that one must reserve a place six months ahead, suggests that although Harel's initiatives may be merely a fad, they point to a problem. Many kibbutz members sense that their way of life is amiss. To borrow a phrase from Sartre, the kibbutz seems to have outlived itself.

What is sad about this situation, and Yehudah Harel's workshops epitomize it, is that most kibbutz members believe that certain technical changes will suffice "to save the kibbutz." (Most group dynamics like much psychotherapy has, after all, become a technique, which has almost nothing to do with a person's soul.) Furthermore, those who wish to save the kibbutz do not see that making the kibbutz way of life into a goal is idolatry or dogmatism or both; and without a goal that transcends the way of life, the kibbutz will continue to deteriorate.

Why has the kibbutz movement—once Israel's "proud contribution" to socialism and to communal living—begun to outlive itself? Persons will point to economic developments, or to the fact that the era of pioneering that gave birth to the kibbutz has passed, or to other areas of the world where the socialist dream has foundered or failed. These are excuses, not explanations. The kibbutz is deteriorating because *it has no spiritual goals, no goals that are worthy in themselves;* it is a failure because it has become part of the means-end problem-solving (capitalistic) dialectic. Kibbutz members cannot envision new spiritual goals because the space for freedom has been eradicated in the kibbutz; in their life there is no room for dreams. The prominent kibbutz members with whom I have consulted know this; I suspect that they also know that a lack of spiritual goals has much deeper sources than the excuses they often cite. But they refuse to acknowledge these sources. In short, there is a skeleton in their closet.

The kibbutzim were originally established as socialist communes, where each person supposedly gave to the commune according to his or her abilities and received from the commune according to his or her needs. Such a way of life was the basis of what they termed justice, and it was a primary goal of the kibbutz movement. From the 1920s to the 1960s the kibbutz movement boasted that it was a bastion of social justice within a ruthless capitalistic society. But there was a hollowness to this boasting, because it relied on the Marxist assumptions concerning social justice that the kibbutz members presented. In those years and even today when speaking to a kibbutz member, if one tried to envision justice beyond the communal (Marxist) paradigm to which he or she adhered, one encountered dogmatic responses. Kibbutz members had no wish to examine the existential and political principles underlying their communal life. Their superficiality resembles that of the orthodox Marxist whom Sartre unmasked.

In *Search for a Method* Sartre explains his adherence to Marx's writings while rejecting contemporary Marxism. Marxist thinkers, according to Sartre, have been striving to fit everything into their Procrustean interpretation of Marx. In the process they not only disregard reality, they have lost the ability to read. Like these Marxists, kibbutz members read, but they understand absolutely nothing. "To understand is to change, to go beyond oneself."[1] And such a going beyond oneself is exactly what kibbutz members refuse to do. "This is because *they insist on standing in their own light.* They reject the hostile sentence [that they are reading] (out of fear or hate or laziness) at the very moment that they want to open themselves to it"[2] (my italics). The roots of this arrogance among Marxists and kibbutz members was in their fervent belief that they had discovered the just way of life, or the final truth, or both. Today, in the atmosphere of imminent crisis that characterizes the kibbutz, the outer wrapping of this arrogance has often been discarded. But the belief that what is amiss in kibbutz life can be remedied by some technical or functional changes is a continuing to stand in one's own light.

The skeleton in the kibbutz closet is not only the fear or the laziness to think and to encounter reality that Sartre described. The skeleton emerges when one realizes that under the camouflage of "social justice" the kibbutz way of life has eradicated the two spaces essential for human freedom to emerge, the "between" and the in-between. Hence any technical changes will resemble Gorbachev's *Glasnost*, which has initiated some openness and criticism in Soviet life, but will never allow the space for political freedom and for dialogue to emerge in the Soviet Union. Of course, I am presenting a dynamic situation as frozen; kibbutz life could perhaps change; members *could* strive to reestablish the spaces of human freedom and to realize spiritual goals. A kibbutz friend indicated recently that she senses a longing for spiritual existence among her comrades. Still, my presentation reveals where those who are longing for a life with spiritual goals should begin.

But why does kibbutz life eradicate the "between" and the in-between? And how does such an eradicating diminish justice? To answer both questions one must consider another aspect of Hannah Arendt's thought.

Daily life on a kibbutz is based on the belief that the most important human activities are labor and work. Kibbutz members judge each other by their competence as laborers and workers. But as Hannah Arendt has shown, since ancient times "To labour meant to be enslaved by necessity";[3] labor is not an activity that will lead to the emergence of freedom. When one labors one is performing the necessary activities for life to continue functioning— one washes the dishes, cleans the windows, weeds a garden, sweeps the floor. Labor is repetitive, and has no enduring result. "It is indeed the mark of all laboring that it leaves nothing behind, that the result of its effort is almost as quickly consumed as the effort is spent."[4] In contrast, the product of one's work is a durable object: one builds a house, weaves a rug, constructs a table, paves a road. These products create the human artifice in which we live and upon which we rely. But except in rare cases, work also has little to do with creating a space for freedom. Hence, although labor and work are crucial for human existence, living a life of freedom is based upon other activities. It is speech and action that can create the in-between, and except in the special case of an artist who succeeds in relating to a portion of the unhuman world as a subject, it is through speaking and acting that a person establishes the "between."

(In the first two decades of the twentieth century, one of the early Zionist thinkers, A. D. Gordon, developed a mystical approach to labor which viewed it as a pathway to freedom, and which for some years enthused Zionist youth in Europe and pioneers in the Land of Israel. Despite his influence between the two World Wars, I doubt that A. D. Gordon's thoughts can serve as a basis for spiritual development in Israel today, primarily because they largely ignore the political realm as crucial to human freedom. Since the 1940s these views have been considered an anchronism, at least in their practical implications, within both the kibbutz movement and the Israeli labor movement.[5])

In *The Republic* and in other writings Plato repeatedly emphasized that justice can only emerge in a polis, in that political space in which persons, through words and deeds, express their freedom. In a way of life that gravely limits such freedom, there is almost no possibility of persons bringing up the question of justice, discussing it, and attempting to pursue it. To borrow a phrase from Sartre, it is an impossibility of those persons' possibilities—they cannot envision themselves pursuing justice. Such has occurred in communist regimes, in fascist regimes, and in states ruled by religious fanatics, such as Iran. But there are many other subtle ways of limiting a person's freedom, which have been developed in more open, democratic societies. In the kibbutz, these manners have been linked to the emphasis on labor and work, and to the look of the other.

Once again courage is crucial. The pursuit of justice often demands acting courageously; in Plato's terms one must be a guardian or a warrior. Hence, the kibbutz, which highlights labor and work as those activities by which a person is evaluated, is suggesting to its comrades that one can attain personal fulfillment without acting courageously. I doubt it. But even entertaining such a notion entails that the "fulfilled kibbutz member" has sold his or her freedom for a pot of lentil soup. As already indicated, a person in the kibbutz is not judged by personal ideas, or by personal struggles for justice, or by personal acts of courage, in short by the worthy story a person makes of his or her life. A person is judged by those activities that can hardly become stories, such as one's diligence in and devotion to one's work, or by the economic success of one's branch of agriculture or industry. Kibbutz members evaluate a "comrade" by *what* he or she is, not by *who* he or she is. Not only are the necessary conditions for the emergence of the political realm and for the pursuit of justice thus eradicated, freedom as a transcending of oneself disappears.

To help in this process of mutual reification the kibbutz member relies on the relentless alienating power of the Other's look. As Sartre pointed out, the look of the Other can eradicate one's freedom by giving one a nature. "Strictly speaking it is not that I perceive myself losing my freedom in order to become a *thing*, but my nature is—over there, outside my lived freedom—as a given attribute of this being which I am for the Other." The kibbutz member finds his or her nature in the eyes of a comrade, he or she grasps him/herself primarily as an object-for-others, not as a subjective freedom. This situation creates an impotency to act as a free individual. With Sartre, the kibbutz member could say that during his or her entire life "I grasp the Other's look at the very center of my act as the solidification and alienation of my own possibilities."[6]

The kibbutz member cannot flee the look of the Other. This is because the center of his or her existence is the social realm. As already mentioned, Arendt pointed out that in antiquity there were three realms in which persons existed, the private, the social, and the political. In the private realm inequality and slavery existed, and with it violence and the degradation of women; but a person who returned to the privacy of his home from participating in the political realm was sheltered there from the look of his peers (only males were allowed to enter the political realm). He could rest from having to appear to the Other, and from having to act and to speak in a manner that would be constantly judged by his fellow participants in the in-between. Sartre, of course, believes that the look of the Other pervades all three realms, and such does often occur. Yet Arendt would hold that the main reason for the ability of the Other's look to prevail in our life is the rise of the social realm. In any event, everyone knows that in one's private realm there is, at least, more possibility for respite from the look of the Other. Furthermore, friendship, which can occur only beyond the alienating judging look of the Other, requires a privacy, a space one can call one's own, which Sartre's philosophy does not admit.

Thus it is no surprise that many kibbutz members admit that friendship is very rare on the kibbutz; members have no place to rest from the look of the Other, since there is no private realm that is recognized as being excluded from the judging look of other persons. Language upholds this situation. The kibbutz member calls the entire kibbutz "home," while the apartment in which one resides is called room or apartment. Hence there is no clearly defined spatial area in the kibbutz which a member can call a private home, and shut its door upon the look of his or her "comrades."

If one is unable to free oneself from the look of the Other, one has no place to gather one's powers so as to act courageously. But cowardly people do not join together to create a public space. Furthermore, the emergence of this in-between relies on the fact that persons are different, that they adhere to different principles, and that they are willing to struggle to convince each other to act in a specific manner. But the critical look of the comrade in the kibbutz wants to eradicate these differences. In the kibbutz personal differences and differences on matters of principle are discouraged and disparaged. The role of the general meeting, or of the committees, is to solve problems, not to encourage thinking or to examine and to discuss matters of principle.

Put differently, the kibbutz is a society without philosophers, because it already "has a philosophy" which is embodied in the kibbutz way of life and which supposedly answers all questions. It is a society without a political realm, because anyone with civil courage will soon be ostracized as "uncomradely." Deviating from the accepted kibbutz norm is rarely—if ever—appreciated. The critical look of kibbutz members upon each other is the look of the lowest common denominator, of the fickleness of popular democracy, of envy and gossip. The vices of the social realm reign unmolested.

Here, perhaps, is the place to mention the story of Ran Cohen from Kibbutz Gan Shmuel, who was recently elected to the Knesset as member of a party not sanctioned by his kibbutz movement. In the Knesset he is very active in struggles for civil rights and political freedom. But as he revealed recently in an interview, in his kibbutz and in the movement he continues to be criticized, and often rejected, for not adhering to the "party line," for breaking with the flock.

One distinction between the social realm and the political realm is that persons flee from their loneliness into the social realm, while they enter the political realm from solitude, as persons willing to act courageously. A person in solitude is truly alone, but he or she is not lonely; more often than not he or she is thinking, meditating, or contemplating. Furthermore, as Merleau-Ponty puts it "We are truly alone only on the condition that we do not know we are; it is this very ignorance which is our solitude."[7] In the kibbutz, a member who cherishes solitude is viewed askance, and often severely criticized. Persons exist primarily in the social realm, they are motivated by their own cowardice and the cowardice of their fellow establishers of this realm; their mutual loneliness leads to a unanimity or likemindedness that seemingly supports them. But in order to continue to exist, this unanimity and likemindedness must eradicate the "between" and the in-between; because these realms of freedom threaten the consensus that arises in the social realm and which, to its participants, seems to be the glue that binds them together.

Thus, spiritual challenges do not emerge on the horizon of the kibbutz member's vision. He or she is daily reminded, by the look of fellow members, to adhere to a likemindedness that stifles originality, to a unanimity that rejects thinking, to a living in the social realm that breeds cowardice, and to a comradeship that undermines dialogue. As a result, kibbutz members live a life that contains no stories, only anecdotes; and the individual member is often lonely and bitter, unfulfilled and unfree. The pursuit of justice is no longer his or her concern.

Most kibbutz members and many Israelis evade the pursuit of justice by taking the world seriously, which as Sartre points out is a manner of fleeing the anguish of being free. The serious world that they establish is not only characterized by lack of humor; it is primarily characterized by an inability to play. "What is play indeed if not an activity of which man is the first origin, for which man himself sets the rules, and which has no consequences except according to the rules posited?"[8] Sartre linked living in a serious world to materialism and to Marxism, which view persons as objects in a world ruled by objective historical processes upon which an individual has little influence; he did not notice that the devouring of the political and of the private realms by the social realm implies eliminating two crucial areas where one can live one's freedom, set the rules, and play. If one lives only in the social realm one views everything, including oneself, as part of a whole, as a process; never as one who can set the rules. One is therefore constantly concerned with the consequences of one's acts and with one's acts as consequences. Life is a fatalistic journey. "The serious man is 'of this world' and has no resource in himself."[9]

As indicated above, the greatness of the public space and of the "between" is that upon entering these spaces and living in them, one acts as a beginner, who begins a process whose consequences are unknown. The pursuit of justice can only occur in such a space; it demands beginning every morning anew to struggle against the greed, the exploitation, the mendacity, the banality of evil that one encounters. It may require countering accepted rules and demanding the acceptance of new rules. It often demands initiating processes whose outcomes may boomerang against the initiator. It calls for courage and love of this world, and a willingness to live with the anguish of freedom. But in the kibbutz the space where such a struggle may emerge has disappeared; one no longer lives the anguish of freedom, one exists in a serious world where one has outlived oneself.

Perhaps the best example of this lack of play in kibbutz life is the general meeting, which supposedly is the embodiment of democracy. Instead of kibbutz members setting the rules, and understanding that there are no consequences except according to the rules that they have posited, they transform the kibbutz into a Medusa-like being which sucks up the freedom of its members and which, carried by the waves of history, posits values and rules. They firmly believe that one attains meaning in life by immersing oneself in the sticky protoplasm of this younger sibling of Hobbes' *Leviathan*. In the meeting comrades speak thus: "Such is according to kibbutz principles," "that would be for the best of the kibbutz," "The kibbutz demands that you . . .," "I suggest that the kibbutz respond in the following manner . . .," and so forth. As these phrases reveal, they dismiss human reality and endow the kibbutz with a soul and a will whose dictates they must follow. In short, the general meeting is an assembly in which comrades, through the language they use, assist each other in the process of hiding from oneself the consciousness of one's freedom.

Another example of seriousness is the above-mentioned belief of kibbutz members that labor and work will bring about the establishment of a new and just society. They are wrong on two counts. As already indicated, the most that labor and work can bring about is the establishment of a human artifice; justice arises when persons take responsibility in the political realm. Such an assuming of responsiblity is denied kibbutz members by the society they have established. In addition, labor and work are not realms where a person can play; in many languages play and work are antonyms, at least in common vernacular. More often than not kibbutz members embrace the common interpretation of play, while making labor and work into the basis of all values. In short, by embracing seriousness they not only live in bad faith, they slink away from acts of freedom into a superciliousness, which holds that only in their communes is a worthy life attainable.[10]

It would be fortunate if the situation of the kibbutz was not that of Israel at large. But at least in relation to the pursuit of justice the kibbutz is, in many respects, a microcosm that reveals what ails the macrocosm.

I previously intimated that the pursuit of justice can only be undertaken by persons who have assumed what Berdyaev called the obligation to be free. Most contemporary political regimes strive to "free" persons *from* this obligation by restricting the emergence of the in-between. Their methods range from totalitarianism and terrorism to economical incentives for those who "mind their own business." In Israel the public space is persistently destroyed by the major political parties, who despite their so-called differences, have together embraced and developed some of the alienating and reifying processes developed in the kibbutz movement. Party members soon learn that party interests are what counts, not principles of justice; that loyalty to a leader is more important than merit; that speaking and acting in the public realm must always accord with these interests and this loyalty. The pursuit of justice has been traded off for the procuring of narrow party interests. Furthermore, in the public realm the quest for personality has disappeared; political leaders are surrounded by lackeys and are often themselves toadys who rose to power; boredom, quibbling, and pettiness prevail.

More than two decades ago, Uri Avneri wrote: "To paraphrase Mirabeau's famous dictum about the army in Prussia; Elsewhere the state has parties; in Israel, the parties have a state."[11] Today Avneri's description is still true, with devastating results for the pursuit of justice. No, let me start differently.

Anyone who discusses the political situation in Israel with a person who is concerned and knowledgeable, even if that person is a party member, will almost always encounter an ingrained cynicism that frequently borders on despair. (One need not be an astute psychologist to discern that a sycophant is a coward, and frequently a disguised cynic.) This cynicism is a defense and a way out. It defends a person against seeing the meaning of the countless injustices that have become part and parcel of Israeli political life; it is a way out because Israelis have learned to doubt the truth of any fact, statement, or commitment stated by politicians. They know that these politicians have been hypocrites for so long that they no longer distinguish in their own soul between truth and falsehood; hence the only way to view them is with an uncommitted derisive humor. Or with repugnance. Or with despair. But no, repugnance or despair may lead one to attempt to do something about the situation. And that is what the cynic fears. So, better to drown one's fear, repugnance, and despair in the sour mead of cynicism.

In allowing cynicism to flourish the concensus between the politicians and many Israelis is most powerful. The politicians let the cynicism prevail as long as it does not threaten their power—they know that cynicism can be ignored, and the cynic will do nothing—and the population is satisfied that it can view its leaders derisively. Thus, they believe, they are ensuring their freedom of speech. But it is a hollow freedom of speech. Because the Israelis only rarely suggest an alternative direction for development and mainly limit themselves to responding to the acts and words of politicians whom they despise. In short, the cynic uses his or her freedom of speech to become *free* from the responsibility of acting in the public realm. In the meantime, to borrow a phrase from Sam Ervin, justice weeps.

Recently, a committee headed by a retired supreme court judge, Justice Landau, published a report on the prosecuting procedures of the Israeli

Security Service against suspected terrorists, most of them Arabs. According to this report, for sixteen years Security Service agents have been torturing suspects in order to get them to confess to crimes of which they were accused. When suspects who had confessed complained in court that the confession had been extracted under duress, and described some of the torturing procedures, the agents categorically denied the complaints. They lied to the judges blatantly, knowing that torturing suspects and lying in court was the accepted policy of the Israeli Security Service. The Jewish judges always accepted the version of the Security Service.

The committee's recommendations were that in future the Security Service should only use light manners of torture, and that they should refrain from lying in court. In short, torturing is permitted, lying in court is to be condemned. The committee also recommended that none of the Security Service agents who had tortured suspects or committed perjury be prosecuted, that the ministers in charge of the Security Service not be held responsible, and that the condemned be allowed to appeal their sentence. In the press, and the Knesset, there were some strong responses. One commentator asked at what voltage does running an electric current through a suspect's genitals stop being "a light manner of torture." Shulamit Aloni, a Knesset member asked: "Where during these sixteen years were the judges? Did it never occur to them that the Security Service agents consistently committed perjury?" Others asked: "Who is to promise that Security agents will not lie now as to the severity of the torture?" But the government adopted the report and its recommendations. It thanked the judges.

I suspect that the judges who participated in this juridical farce aren't ashamed. They flee shame into seriousness. As in the kibbutz they are more concerned with likemindedness than with original thinking, with unanimity than with justice; they dare not challenge accepted norms, they are slaves of the social realm. In their defense, they will probably speak of the security needs of Israel, of the State being surrounded and threatened, in short, that conditions in the Arab world and in Israel made them reach their decisions. I disagree. Learning from both Plato and the Hebrew prophets I hold that our strongest line of defense is a just way of life. Only when justice prevails will Jews be willing to defend the Jewish State wholeheartedly. I will return to this point in my discussion of the Israel Defense Force.

What is more I am ashamed; ashamed when I think of hundreds of beaten, tortured suspects and of sentences handed out on the basis of a confession extracted by torture, ashamed that Mr. Landau was a supreme court judge, ashamed of the superficiality and banality that emerged as characterizing the judicial system, ashamed that the government could approve such a report, and that torturing and injustice will continue. I can only console myself that from shame some change may arise, from cynicism none.

Once shame disappears from a political realm, justice and freedom no longer concern most persons who participate in that realm. Many examples presented in this book reveal that shame hardly plays a role in Israeli politics. Scandals arise and are discussed in the press, but the minister in charge never resigns. He or she is not even ashamed that they occurred in his or her area of responsibility. The politicians throw some stupid excuse at the public, who swallow it, or respond with cynicism, and wait for the next scandal. Thus with the Lebanon war fiasco, with the Pollard espionage case, with the selling of arms to Iran, and with many less publicized scandals. The politicians in charge lie with chutzpah to the public, and never take responsibility for their words or deeds.

How has shame which, at least since Sophocles's *Ajax*, played a crucial role in public life disappeared from the Israeli political scene? One answer is the structure of the political parties. Representatives to the Knesset are not elected individually, as a representative of a constituency, but as a name on a countrywide party slate. Consequently, loyalty to a leader and adherence to party interests is what ensures one's place in the party slate, and in the party hierarchy. As a result the structure of most political parties somewhat resembles the totalitarian movements that Hannah Arendt described. Perhaps it is not a linguistic incident that many parties in Israel today are also called movements—the labor and the Herut movements are two cases in point which together represent about two-thirds of voting Israelis.

Shame disappears when loyalty without thought prevails, or as Arendt wrote "Total loyalty is possible only when fidelity is emptied of all concrete content, from which changes of mind naturally arise."[12] This thoughtless loyalty also shields the leader from the look of other persons which can be the source of shame. Borrowing a metaphor from Arendt, each leader embeds him- or herself in the center of onion-like layers of loyal followers. At the layer immediately surrounding the leader are persons whose loyalty will not be affected by any development; for them the leader cannot make mistakes. At the next layer are persons whose loyalty is strong, but who may be open for mild criticism of the leader. They are never allowed to enter the inner layer, but they guard that layer and the leader from the next layer of party adherents who are more open to criticizing the leader. The second layer also represents an external reality for the innermost layer. This scheme continues until it reaches regular members of the party and finally fellow travelers. Each layer of adherents shields internal layers from criticism and gives persons at those layers the feeling that it represents external reality. Like all models, this is not the entire truth, yet it partially describes how shame and thought can disappear from the innermost circles of major parties. One should add that even when a party is divided among two or three leaders who are competing for power, each leader strives to become encompassed with layers of followers.

A leader surrounded by such layers of loyalty slowly loses contact with constituents and with thoughts of other persons. The leader's only concern is ensuring his or her power. (Richard Nixon during the Watergate scandal exemplified this approach. Even today, Nixon declares that he feels no shame—despite the fact that his crimes have been broadly publicized.) Structure, though, is only a partial explanation. The disappearance of shame has also to do with the disappearance of integrity and of innocence, because if one refuses to be ashamed of one's failings one ends up losing one's innocence, and with it one's personal integrity.

In the public realm shame is important because it reveals to the individual that one's repugnant act has been seen by an Other, with whom one shares this world. This Other can make one into an object of derision. But he or she can also act differently. As a fellow sojourner in the world, the Other can also help one to correct oneself, can help one to begin anew. Dostoyevski's Raskolnikov is unashamed of the murder he committed. In his mind he relives his repugnant act, superciliously justifying it, accepting it, rationalizing it, reifying it as an object that has a nature. Throughout the book he seeks innocence while rejecting his guilt and refusing to live with his shame—an impossible project. Only in the epilogue, and with the help of Sonya who was the first person to whom he revealed his crime, is he finally overcome by shame (and by his guilt). Innocence returns; he can think of beginning anew.

When they are caught in a scandal, the large majority of Israeli politicians resemble Raskolnikov. They refuse to live with the shame. (Let their be no mistake. I am pointing to the president of Israel, to the prime ministers, to the foreign and defense ministers; the refusal to live with shame commences at the peak of the political pyramid, or, if you wish, at the center of the political onion, and permeates all other layers.) From a political point of view there are three immediate results. Intelligent Israeli citizens relate cynically to these politicians, knowing that all their rationalizations and justifications are cover-ups and lies. The leaders lose their personal integrity, even if they retain their power. To retain some semblance of dignity, and to hold onto their power, leaders appeal more and more to the mob; they seek support from those who admire anyone in power, and who despise all discussions of principles. Consequently, to borrow a phrase from Ludwig Wittgenstein, for many Israeli citizens and politicians, the riddle of justice doesn't exist.

Innocence and integrity are necessary because any honest pursuit of justice must transcend the means-end problem-solving dialectic which prevails, and must think about principles of life together without preconceived notions or prejudices, and especially without the promise of personal gain that might result from adopting certain principles. One might think that the kibbutz could create an existential situation in which innocence and integrity prevail and the pursuit of justice comes naturally. Quite the opposite has happened, largely, I believe, because of the tyranny of the social realm. In the kibbutz shame is hardly ever forgotten. Hence, the kibbutz member will do everything so as not to be put to public shame. One of the best ways to ensure that even if one falters one will not be shamed, is by persistently expressing loyalty to the kibbutz. But such loyalty stifles all discussion, and thought, and vision. One cannot honestly discuss justice if one's initial premise is that whatever the outcome, one will remain loyal to the kibbutz or to the platform of one's political party. In short, since very few kibbutz members and leading party members are willing to risk being put to shame, they do not pursue justice.

Someone may point out that there are kibbutz members or party members who struggle for Arab rights, or against oppression of women by the orthodox religious establishment, or against the unjust way the economic pie is divided. Of course there are. But their struggle strengthens the point I have been making. These persons are struggling outside the kibbutz, or the party, on behalf of kibbutz or party ideology. The entire kibbutz supports their endeavors. They are not pursuing justice within the kibbutz. They resemble the many Israeli politicians and citizens who have embraced the cause of freedom for Soviet Jews, but who do little for freedom of Jews and Arabs in Israel. Incidentally, the parties who canvass most vigorously for freedom of Soviet Jews are those who fervently participate in the oppression of Arabs in Israel. In their own eyes they are pursuing justice, but it is a pursuit that does not demand that they themselves strive to live justly.

Today in Israel the pursuit of justice must begin with a struggle for the emergence of the public space, and of Buber's "between." It is a crucial struggle—although Israel is called a democracy, in many areas it is moving toward fascism, toward tyranny, toward an apartheid state. A number of examples of this process have already been presented: the emergence of the mob as a political force and the treaty between it and the pseudo-intellectuals of the right; the anti-Arab racism; the fanaticism of the religious establishment; the worshiping of the Israeli Defense Force; the emphasis on unreserved loyalty by the political parties, which awards toadys and punishes free discussion and thinking; the rising power of the bureaucracy, and so on. Of course, many Jews would argue that these developments need not necessarily lead to fascism, that Israeli democracy is merely suffering from structural, or economic, or political deficiencies, such as a governing system with few checks and balances, or a need to spend much of its resources on security, or a need to hold on to the West Bank and the Gaza Strip until Israel's security is ensured. These points are, at best, partially valid; they are mainly excuses whose underlying assumption is that certain technical changes will suffice to put Israel "back on the right track." Worse, by ignoring the fact that Jewish life in Israel lacks spiritual goals, that it is a life with no room for dreams, those who offer such excuses refuse to see the fascist tendencies that are daily emerging.

Mussolini once defined fascism as a regime in which the entire nation marches together as an army. Anyone who has participated in an army march will immediately discern that during the march there is no space for freedom. The "between" and the in-between have disappeared. The unanimity of those marching together restricts freedom on at least two levels: the personality of each individual, which is necessary for the space of freedom to emerge, loses its significance; in addition, the person who is marching is surrounded by fellow marchers, who rigidly restrict one's space and the realm where one's personality can develop. This unanimity, which allows one to evade responsibility and freedom, is what attracts weak, incompetent persons, and especially members of the mob, to fascist movements. Hence, the political parties in Israel which stress loyalty, discourage discussion, and demand that all party members march to the same tune behind a specific leader have adopted—whether they know it or not—fascist methods.

The pursuit of justice is not a challenge to which one can suggest clear, well-defined actions. It is much easier to point out where justice is being trampled. But one can indicate why a struggle to establish the "between" and the in-between is crucial for justice. Consider one of Isaiah's visions:

And it shall come to pass in the end of days,
That the mountain of the Lord's house shall be established as the top of the
    mountains,
And shall be exalted above the hills;
And all nations shall flow unto it.
And many peoples shall go and say:
"Come ye, and let us go up to the mountain of the lord,
To the house of the God of Jacob;
And He will teach us of His ways,
And we will walk in His paths."
For out of Zion shall go forth the law,
And the word of the Lord from Jerusalem.
And He shall judge between the nations,
And shall decide for many peoples;
And they shall beat their swords into ploughshares,
And their spears into pruning hooks;
Nation shall not lift up sword against nation,
Neither shall they learn war anymore. [Isaiah 2, 2–4]

Faith in God is, of course, central to Isaiah's vision; how one can today link faith to vision will be discussed in the next chapter. Although Isaiah seems to indicate that faith must precede justice, one could also hold that a necessary component of true faith is the pursuit of justice—one cannot have true faith in the God of Abraham while exploiting and oppressing other persons. What appeals to me in this vision is that Isaiah speaks with innocence and integrity and assumes that his listeners can also live innocently and with integrity, and thus make room for dreams. As I read the text, he does not want to create a mass movement that will march together like an army; he wants the nations to flow to the Lord's mountain, as peoples who in innocence wish to learn from God how to live. He does not want all nations to merge with Israel, but each individual nation, with its integrity, will come to hear the judgement of the Lord (which is not a dogma created by some priests or rabbis). This innocence is the basis of the inter-national trust that will develop and prompt persons to beat their swords into ploughshares.

Similarly, today any person who wishes to present a vision and to pursue justice must at least partially retain his or her innocence and integrity. Even before entering the public space, one can learn to live innocently and with integrity by engaging in dialogue, by striving to relate with one's whole being to other persons, to nature, and to spiritual beings. Put differently, in Buber's "between," in the space where dialogue emerges, a person can again and again attain the wholeness needed to struggle for justice. This should not suggest that dialogue is merely a means to attain wholeness. Relating dialogically is a way of life; a person who endeavors to live such a life learns to relate with wholeness, with integrity, with courage; hence he or she may often relate to the world and its inhabitants with the personal involvement and concern needed to pursue justice.

A life of dialogue is also a life of trust in the world and in one's fellow human beings. One cannot engage in dialogue if a deep mistrust pervades one's being. Neither can one seek justice or a vision. Only a person who trusts the world can share with other persons his or her visions, feelings, thoughts, and dreams. Even nightmares.

A recent personal incident exemplifies this last point. It began with my saying at one of my lectures in a course, "Education for a Life of Democracy," that I would be happy if Mr. Ariel Sharon, the minister of trade and industry, and initiator of the Lebanese war, would be stricken with a fatal heart attack. "He is a nightmare for freedom in Israel," I explained. "Sharon is so power hungry and corrupt that if he only could, he would overthrow the democracy in Israel and seize power." I also described the banality of other ministers in the government, and indicated how this banality leads to evil deeds. A student described my views to a reporter and one newspaper dedicated half a page to how I utilize my academic freedom. A prime-time interview on nationwide television followed. There have been three responses to this story, until now. A person in Sharon's party asked the chief of Israeli police to investigate if during my television appearance I had not been inciting to murder. I have not yet heard from the police. Another member of his party brought it up in the Knesset, and asked the minister of education to inquire whether my views represented those of my university. The university administration denied any responsibility for my publicized views. And finally, I received supporting letters and calls, and, of course, many threatening calls and much hate mail. One fact that surprised me in the supporting mail and calls was that many persons had nightmares similar to my own, since Sharon's many acts of deceit and abuse of power have been described at length in print, but they did not trust the world enough to express them.[13]

While helping to develop trust, living a life of dialogue also teaches a person who to mistrust. Here I am going beyond Buber. Dialogue may be a way of life, but it is not a panacea, as Buber often seemed to believe. From my personal endeavors to live a life of dialogue I have learned that many persons reject dialogue.[14] Not only do fanatics, fatalists, members of the mob, super-loyal party and kibbutz members, ruthless businessmen, power-hungry politicians, toadys, and hosts of other persons who do not strive to develop their personalities consistently evade dialogue, many of these people endeavor to eradicate its basis by establishing a world where mistrust is the prevailing way of life. I do not want to be misunderstood. A person striving to live a life of dialogue should allow for the possibility that these spiritual children of Thomas Hobbes may change their way of being-in-the-world. But, learning from the *Navi*, he or she should not hesitate to view these persons as enemies of dialogue, of freedom, and of spiritual existence. Furthermore, if their mistrust leads to racism or to other manners of oppression one should not hesitate to view them as personal enemies, whose disappearance from the political realm is necessary for a life of freedom. In short, one should mistrust them as destroyers of the "between," while knowing that if change in them occurs one will always be open to trusting them.

As mentioned earlier, although living a life of dialogue is important for living justly, justice must be pursued in the political realm. Hence the challenge of justice requires the establishing of a public space and the encouraging of persons to enter that space. This is no simple task. In relating to political issues, many Israelis have already adopted the habits of the mob. These habits suit most of the politicians who prefer to play up to mob instincts and perceptions, thus evading issues of principle. This vicious circle can only be broken by education, in its broadest sense, by the emergence of persons who are willing to pursue justice, by painstaking work for justice and freedom at the grass roots level. There is no panacea; there is only a lifelong struggle. Put differently, here is the point where my argument ends, and only dreams and stories can speak. Why?

Look again at Isaiah's vision of peace. For persons and nations to attempt to live that vision, arguments can, at best, provide some enlightenment; but only persons who are willing to dream with Isaiah, and follow up the dream with daily deeds and words through which they struggle for peace and justice, can bring about even a partial fulfilling of that vision. Stories of these persons reek of blood, sweat, and tears, with only here and there an insight into the meaning of their struggle for justice, or a moment of satisfaction when one has briefly triumphed over injustice. Yet, without such stories a people has no claim to glory.

So let me present a few dreams.

Hitherto I have ignored economics, but any dream of justice must have an economic basis. Israel is a cross between capitalism and socialism, with few of the virtues of either political system and with the vices of both. The Israeli must face both the economic ruthlessness of capitalists and a gigantic well-entrenched and sycophantic bureaucracy established during forty years of flirting with socialism. Economic inequality abounds; large segments of the population live on the border of, or in, poverty while at the other end of the spectrum top socialist managers and well-established capitalists enjoy enormous expense accounts that allow them to live affluently and to acquire excessive holdings and wealth.

Consider four examples of the growth of inequality and of its links to government policy. The kibbutz movement—that so-called bastion of equality, of socialism, and of economic justice—has for two decades focused on raising its standard of living through industrialization. Thanks to much government economic support it pretty much succeeded and most kibbutz members enjoy a standard of living well beyond the average. Often in the kibbutz fields or industries hired labor is employed—at times even cheap Arab labor from the occupied territories—which according to the kibbutz socialist *Weltanschauung* is exploitation of fellow workers. The religious parties, who are needed to set up any coalition government, sell their votes in the Knesset for exorbitant sums which go to support yeshivas, schools, and many other institutions run by their constituents. About half of these religious parties are anti-Zionist, but they have no qualms in fleecing the Zionist State. The Histadrut, the Labor movement, blocks any law suggesting general health insurance since one of its power bases is Kupat Holim, a health insurance empire that owns and runs most of the hospitals and clinics in Israel. And finally, most of the major parties in Israel are not so much political groups as they are clearinghouses for jobs, contracts, loans, financial support, or put succinctly, official plunder.

The many examples mentioned in this book of official fleecing and plunder are merely the tip of an iceberg. For most Israelis, accepting economic injustice has become a way of life, a habit. Connections count much more than competence, personal achievement is devalued, honesty is frequently deemed worthless. Everyone accepts the fact that the way the economic pie is divided is mainly a result of power struggles and bickering between party officials. Add to all this that few—if any—persons are thinking about ways of coping with these injustices and of how to attain greater economic equality. Economists and social workers, laborers and artists, party functionaries and housewives, professors and rabbis—all agree that the way the economy is run is a travesty of justice; few endeavor to do anything about it.

Two numbers describe the extent of the inequality. The press recently disclosed that Israeli top bank executives earn the highest salary of all bank executives in the world, including a bank such as Citicorp or the top Japanese banks. (The bank with the highest salaries, Bank Leumi, was set up by Herzl, and formally still belongs to the Jewish people.) On the other hand one hundred forty-three thousand elderly families live off social security alone, which is less than $200 a month. Remember, this economic plundering by persons in power developed under the banner of socialism. It merely reached new heights when Menachem Begin and his right-wing cohorts came to power.

There is no question that Israelis must begin to feel shame at the gross economic injustice that prevails and to dream of greater economic equality. Proposing methods of realizing this dream requires a competence in economics which I lack; but I can outline some general points that should not be ignored. First, some of the thinking about economic equality must be meta-economical or philosophical, in other words it must question assumptions. Thus although such thinking must take into account the significance of economic incentives, it must not view human existence solely in terms of economics. Second, as a guiding principle one must accept the fact that greater economic equality is necessary for freedom to emerge. It is a necessity if one wishes to encourage more persons to struggle for things worthy in themselves; without a minimum of funds and of free time few persons will be able to relate to spiritual goals. Third, only freedom can check exploitation. If persons do not live their freedom, and do not have ways of combating another person's greed, exploitation will grow. Fourth, economic equality is merely a means; the goal is striving for a spiritual existence. What Marx did not note is that even after the economic pie is divided equally there are many ways a person can pursue a mediocre, stupid existence. Hence, in striving for economic equality one must always keep in mind that the ultimate goals are freedom, justice, and creating the conditions that will encourage persons to seek a more spiritual existence.

The lack of thinking and of dreaming about economic justice in Israel does not reflect the situation in the West, at least in academic circles. Sartre and Merleau-Ponty in France, Adorno, Horkheimer, and Habermas in Germany, Marcuse and Rawls in the United States—to mention a few contemporary thinkers—all presented original thinking in this field. In seeking to bring about change one could start with a seemingly simple principle, such as Rawls' second principle of justice:

All social values—liberty and opportunity, income and wealth, and the bases of self-respect—are to be distributed equally unless an unequal distribution of any, or all, of these values is to everyone's advantage.[15]

This principle puts the burden of justifying an unequal economic distribution, such as exists in Israel, on those persons who benefit from it. Often merely demanding an explanation of a certain inequality, while refering to Rawls's principle, can be a beginning of the pursuit of justice. Thus, the kibbutzim must show that their receiving national land and water at highly subsidized prices, including land and water for industrial uses, is to everyone's advantage. The religious parties must—no, I don't know how their rapaciousness can in any way be to everyone's advantage, unless one believes that they are paving the way to paradise for all Jews, something they themselves do not believe. The Histadrut must prove that general health insurance is to everyone's disadvantage, as against the current program which gives the Histadrut power and funds. And the bank executives must prove that their outrageous salaries are beneficial to all Israelis. Am I dreaming? Yes, I'm daring to dream.

Equality of opportunities is another dream. Those suffering most from inequality are women and Arabs. Equality of opportunity implies the possibility for each person to realize one's potentials by living one's freedom constructively; hence it requires the emergence of the public space. Because, as mentioned above, without a public space there is no place for excellence to appear, to develop. And without excellence appearing and being appreciated—and excellence cannot be appreciated if one does not value courage and truth—there is no possibility of setting standards and of seeking justice. Here is one of the greatest dangers of the unwritten treaty between the pseudo-intellectual and the lackey, between the political toady and the mob, which is so prominent in Israeli politics. Together they not only destroy the public space, they also destroy all standards of excellence and justice.

Living one's freedom while pursuing excellence means being able to initiate. When the public space is gravely limited, as has occurred in the Knesset, in the political parties, in academia, and in the kibbutzim, persons in these environments mainly respond to what happens, they do not initiate. Many Israelis have learned that initiating is a risk not worth taking, unless one has the support of the political establishment—and I would gravely doubt that such support can lead to a pursuit of excellence. Even when they are enraged, most Israelis merely respond. Thus, when a Tel Aviv university professor discovered by chance, while doing research on the stock market annual reports, the enormous salaries of bank executives, almost everyone in Israel was enraged. (The salaries were subsequently cut down, although they still remain very high.) But despite the anger, I do not remember anyone initiating a discussion on the principles of economic equality or on how such salaries thwart equality of opportunity.

Accountability of political leaders is an aspect of the pursuit of excellence, and of equality of opportunity. Since in Israel the public space hardly exists, most leaders do not pursue excellence and do not grasp themselves accountable. But let me stop here.

Before summarizing, I do want to suggest a few practical steps that could help to enlarge the public space. Regional elections would make Knesset members more accountable to their constituency. Having the executive power chosen by the electorate would also help; as would reducing the bloated government bureaucracy, enlarging freedom of the press, which would include having television and radio stations that were not run by the government, and reducing the number of court cases judged behind closed doors. But remember, my suggestions will be worthless if Israelis do not strive to live as free persons, if they evade political action, if they flee their obligation to be free.

More than a hundred years ago Nietzsche wrote:

All political parties today have in common a demagogic character and the intention of influencing the masses; because of this intention, all of them are obliged to transform their principles into great frescos of stupidity, and paint them that way on the wall. Nothing more can be changed about this—indeed it is superfluous even to lift a finger against it; for what Voltaire says applies here: "Once the populace begins to reason, all is lost."[16]

Although Nietzsche is indicating a direction pursued by many political parties, I doubt if his generalization is true and that in all political parties today principles are transformed into great frescoes of stupidity. I also reject the fatalism of his second sentence and his ardent belief in the citation from Voltaire. But Nietzsche does point to a problem that accompanies the struggle for political freedom: the continual courting of the mob by political parties. His words are a warning well worth heeding.

Nietzsche's insight does describe many aspects of the political situation in Israel today; at times one senses that, wherever one turns, principles have been transformed into frescoes of stupidity. Hence any attempt to make room for dreams, including the dream of justice, must begin by tearing down these frescoes and demanding that the discussion be dedicated to principles. Put otherwise, one of the greatest hindrances to the pursuit of justice today is the disappearance of principles from public discussion. Like kibbutz members most Israelis believe that some mere technical changes will lead them back to the correct path. That they are wrong gives little consolation.

One way to reaffirm the significance of pursuing justice is to follow the path indicated by the structure of the first seven books of Plato's *Republic*. First, one must viciously reject those who believe that greed and the pursuit of power is the essence of political existence. Next one must suggest principles of living together that will allow one to pursue justice; and finally one must convey to all participants in the republic that this pursuit is in itself a pursuit of excellence and of the good. This chapter has attempted to indicate, albeit vaguely, such a direction.

NOTES

1. Jean Paul Sartre, *Search for a Method*, trans. Hazel E. Barnes (New York: Vintage, 1968), p. 18.

2. Ibid., pp. 38–39 (footnote).

3. Hannah Arendt, *The Human Condition* (Chicago, Ill.: University of Chicago Press, 1958), p. 83.

4. Ibid., p. 87.

5. For instance, see A. D. Gordon, *Selected Essays*, trans. Frances Burnce (New York: League for Labor Palestine, 1938).

6. Jean Paul Sartre, *Being and Nothingness*, trans. Hazel E. Barnes (New York: Washington Square Press, 1956), p. 352.

7. Maurice Merleau-Ponty, *Signs*, trans. Richard C. McCleary (Evanston, Ill.: Northwestern University Press, 1964), p. 174.

8. Sartre, *Being and Nothingness*, p. 741.

9. Ibid.

10. One may ask as to the sources for my critique of the kibbutz. In addition to having personally grown up on a kibbutz and lived on a kibbutz as a member for thirteen years, my wife also grew up and lived on a kibbutz for the first thirty-five years of her life. In addition, I submitted this critique to two prominent kibbutz members from different kibbutzim and they agreed that it is valid. Perhaps I should add that my Ph.D. thesis also dealt with the kibbutz, and then I went through all relevant literature, which shows that spirituality is rare if not extinct in kibbutz life. Here my critique is built more on my personal experience than an examination of literature, for the simple reason that to the best of my knowledge there are no scholarly writings on problems of spirituality or political freedom or dialogue in the kibbutz.

11. Uri Avnery, "The Establishment," in Gary V. Smith, *Zionism, The Dream and the Reality* (New York: Barnes and Noble, 1974), p. 164.

12. Hannah Arendt, *The Origins of Totalitarianism* (New York: Harcourt Brace Jovanovich, 1951), p. 324.

13. Sharon was of course much attacked in the press. For books that describe his deceit and abuse of power see Ze'ev Schiff and Ehud Ya'ari, *Israel's Lebanon War* (New York; Simon and Schuster, 1984); Shimon Shiffer, *Snow Ball: The Story Behind the Lebanon War* (published in Hebrew under the title *Cadur Hasheleg*; Tel Aviv: Yediot Aharonot Books, 1984). A book that deals specifically with Sharon is Uzi Benziman, *Sharon: An Israeli Caesar* (published in Hebrew under the title: *Lo Otzer B'adom*; Tel Aviv: Adam Publishers, 1985).

14. Haim Gordon, *Dance, Dialogue, and Despair* (Tuscaloosa, Ala.: University of Alabama Press, 1986) and my essays in Haim Gordon and Leonard Grob, *Education for Peace* (New York: Orbis, 1987).

15. John Rawls, *A Theory of Justice* (Cambridge, Mass.: Harvard University Press, 1971), p. 62.

16. Friedrich Nietzsche, *Human, All Too Human*, trans. Marion Faber, with Stephen Lehmann (Lincoln, Nebr.: University of Nebraska Press, 1986), p. 210.

5

Faith Versus a Religious Obstruction of Belief

Ask a person in Israel to name the two major events in Jewish history during the twentieth century and the answer will most probably be the Holocaust and the establishment of the State of Israel. What is surprising, therefore, is that both events play almost no part in what most orthodox Jews define as the Jewish religion. Many an orthodox Jew will fast, sit on the floor, read the Biblical book of Lamentations, and conduct special prayers on the ninth day of Ab, which commemorates the destruction of both holy temples in Jerusalem, the first by the Babylonians under Nebuchadnezzar around twenty-five hundred years ago, and the second about five hundred years later by the Romans. But he (in this chapter I shall often use the male pronoun because orthodox Judaism is strictly patriarchal) will do nothing out of the ordinary on the day set aside in Israel to commemorate the six million Jewish victims of the Holocaust. He will celebrate the Passover Seder fervently, and discuss with his sons the significance of the Hebrews emerging from slavery to freedom, but he will not link this freedom to the political freedom that Jews can realize today in Israel. Unfortunately, these narrow-minded approaches cannot be dismissed as merely myopic and stupid. Underlying the myopia is an attempt, through living a religious life based on a blending of fatalism and fanaticism, a life dedicated to the embracing of a dogma, to block the development of any Jewish spirituality that does not accord with their precepts.

If one reads the Bible, not in order to justify the tenets of orthodox Judaism developed in the diaspora, but innocently, with no preconceived notions, one cannot but see that the God of Israel is a God that relates to history. It is in the flux of daily events, with their relation to the near and far past, that the people of Israel are called upon to establish their relationship with God. As I read the Bible, it does not encourage ascetics who flee from human interaction into the desert to eat locusts and roots and to seek divine revelation. Elijah, who fled from confronting the sins of King Ahab and his fellow Israelites into the Sinai, unto God's holy mountain, was commanded by God to return to his fellow Israelites and to relate to them and to the events unfolding before his eyes. A large majority of the orthodox Jews living in Israel today, and especially those hundred fifty thousand orthodox Jews who militantly endeavor to impose the diaspora dogma on their fellow Jews, refuse to learn from Elijah's experience. They live in Israel as if they were blindfolded, declining to see the history developing before their eyes. Most of these militant orthodox Jews do not relate to God in the flux of historical events—and if they do relate to historical events it is fanatically or fatalistically, as the disaster of the drowning which I shall soon cite exemplifies—hence the God they worship has no relationship to the life of the Jews who are striving to establish a political entity in the Promised Land.

Here is one of many painful examples. Many Jews in Israel despise war. Still, there is no doubt in our minds that after the Holocaust we must take the rhetoric of those people who define themselves as enemies of Israel seriously. After patently ignoring Hitler's declarations that he would make the world *Judenrein*, we Israelis dare not ignore similar threats about the Middle East by Assad, or Khomeini, or Kadaffi. Most Jews in Israel believe that we must sustain the military power needed to defend ourselves against those who vow to annihilate us. Hence, there is a consensus among Jews in Israel that we need a strong army, and most Jews, among them many religious Jews, fulfill their compulsory service in the army and in the reserves willingly. Except many of the militant orthodox Jews. With the establishment of the State of Israel the anti-Zionist orthodox religious parties agreed to join Ben Gurion's coalition under the condition that a law be passed by which men studying in a Yeshiva would be released from service in the army. The law was passed and today between thirty and forty thousand male orthodox Jews of army and reserve age—about five percent of this age group—have never served in the army and do not serve in the reserves. There is little point in arguing with more than thirty thousand legal draftdodgers about the immorality of their letting other Jews, among them religious Jews like themselves, expose themselves to Arab bullets and bombs so that they can regurgitate the Talmud. But I do want to argue that this organized draftdodging is an evasion of the responsibilities of relating to God, as described in the Bible.

A vivid example of such a responsibility appears in the book of Jonah. Called upon by God to "go to Nineveh, that great city, and proclaim against it; for their wickedness is come up before me" (Jonah 1, 2), Jonah flees "from the presence of the Lord" (Jonah 1, 3) by boarding a ship headed to Tarshish. The remainder of the first half of Jonah's story is well known: A fierce storm arises, Jonah bids the sailors to throw him into the deep so as to save the ship, and when they do so the storm abates. Jonah is swallowed by a

large fish; in the stomach of the fish he prays to God, and is thrown up onto
the beach and told to once again undertake his mission. Here begins the
second half of the story, which contains a major message that militant
orthodox Jews do not heed.

So Jonah arose, and went unto Nineveh, according to the word of the Lord. Now
Nineveh was an exceeding great city of three days' journey. And Jonah began to enter
into the city a day's journey, and he proclaimed, and said: "Yet forty days and
Nineveh shall be overthrown." And the people of Nineveh believed God; and they
proclaimed a fast, and put on sackcloth, from the greatest of them even to the least of
them. [Jonah 3, 4–6]

God decides to forgive the people of Nineveh, who have all turned to Him
and repented their sins. Jonah sulks and complains against God's
compassion and mercy. He has fulfilled the mission, only to have his words
not come true. God responds by having the gourd that arose in one day to
shadow Jonah from the sun and vehement east wind, killed the next day by a
worm. He then reprimands Jonah, who had pity for the gourd, but not for the
six hundred thousand people of Nineveh and their many animals.

Stop a minute and ask. What is Jonah's greatness? Why is he truly a *Navi*?
Seemingly, the four-chapter book which describes his mission mainly
recounts his sins: First he fled his mission, then he questioned God's mercy.
Aside from these two events and from his prayer to God from the stomach of
the fish, we know very little about him, neither his ancestry, except his being
the son of Amitai, from the town of Gath Hahefer, which historians place in
the tribe of Zevulun, nor his missions, except that he advised the second
Yerovam. And all this additional information is known from one Biblical
verse (Second Kings 14, 25). He emerges momentarily on the Biblical stage,
like a shadow or a ghost, only to disappear again.

Jonah's greatness is that while he struggled with bringing God's message
to the people of Nineveh, he rebelled against God. Of course he sinned—who
doesn't? But a major message of the book, as I read it, is that it is better to
rebel as a free person against God's words and deeds than to accept God's
intervening in history as a slave following the commands of one's master. Not
only because by such a rebelling one can learn from God, but mainly because
whoever never rebels will never express his or her freedom. And a person
who never expresses his or her freedom will never be able to bring God's
message into the everyday exigencies that make up history; he or she will
never be able to worship the God of Israel through acting as a free person in
the world, or, in short, as God demanded to be worshiped.

In fleeing God's mission, Jonah is not alone among the Hebrew prophets.
Moses asked God to send someone in his stead; Elijah, as mentioned, fled
into the desert. Jonah is alone, though, in rejecting God's mercy so
straightforwardly and forcefully. The message, therefore, is clear. A rebel
who questions God, while struggling to bring His message to other persons in

the world, is worthy of being a *Navi*; those who flee history and involvement in the world, never.

Now reconsider the orthodox draftdodgers. By their deeds they are evicting God from the history of the world. The God they worship is served by rejecting responsibility for the day-to-day lives and well being of their fellow Jews and, instead, dedicating themselves to prolonged studying of abstruse Talmudic texts. This God of Talmudic scholars is not the God of Israel described in the Bible, who encourages human freedom and responsibility, and who accepts rebellion against His mercy.

Someone may respond that Moses, Isaiah, Jonah, and other *Neviim* were never told to go join an army, but rather to preach the word of the Lord. Hence the orthodox Jew is emulating the *Navi* when he wishes to learn this preaching and to not join the army. This (diaspora) interpretation is an ignoring of key Biblical texts, because Abraham, Moses, Joshuah, and Deborah all participated in battles. What is more, Moses, who by many is considered the greatest *Navi*, killed an Egyptian with his own hands. But what is more misleading in this response is that it does not see that the *Navi* responded to the exigencies of the situation that confronted him or her. When Deborah called Barak and told him to raise an army to battle Sisera, and he responded: "If thou wilt go with me, then I will go; but if thou wilt not go with me I will not go," Deborah answered immediately "I will surely go with thee" (Judges 4, 8–9). In short, Deborah responded to the immediate need of the situation, which included stopping to judge under the palm tree and going to join an army.

Thus, the deliberate ignoring of the political and existential situation in which the Jewish people in Israel find themselves, as militarily threatened by a number of despotic and fanatical Arab regimes, is one of the greatest sins of the militant orthodox Jews in Israel today. Justifying this sin by telling us, who do serve in the army, that we do not understand the message of Moses, or Isaiah, or Jonah, either by quoting passages of the Talmud that stress the importance of learning, or by making the *Navi* into a preacher who is not involved in the making of history, is a distorting of the moral issues confronting us and of Biblical history. It is also adding insult to injury.

On a number of occasions I have stressed that involvement in this world as a free person is crucial in relating to the God of Israel described in the Bible. Such involvement requires, of course, creating the space needed for freedom to emerge, the "between" and the in-between. But it also require an attitude conspicuously lacking in the way many militant orthodox Jews in Israel today grasp Jewish liturgy, prayer, dogma, and religious life: joy in this world. Except perhaps within the remnants of the Hasidic movement, which is still following some of the precepts of the Baal Shem Tov and his immediate followers,[1] most orthodox Jews embrace the belief that life in this world need not be joyous, since it is merely a corridor which leads to the parlor of afterlife.[2] I shall soon show that fatalism and fanaticism—which I defined elsewhere as "Siamese twins, born of the same wish: to allow one *not* to assume personal responsibility for one's life, especially for one's passions"[3]—never dally far behind such a belief. But first one should note that there is a basic contradiction inherent in a faith in God which views this world with disdain. Just think. Tens of thousands of Israeli Jews read the Bible literally, believe that the world is God's creation as described in Genesis, that Israel is His chosen land, yet they deliberately ignore, despise, disparage, and flee the everyday manifestations of this divine creation.

Leaving aside the historical reasons for this contradiction one should recall that there is little joy in a life lived without dialogue, without a striving for an an appreciation of excellence, and without a struggle for things worthy in themselves. Furthermore, joy in this world is crucial for faith in the God of Abraham. Dostoyevski clarified the link between joy and faith in his descriptions of Dimitri, Alyosha, and Father Zosima in *The Brothers Karamozov*.[4] Joy can only emerge when a free person relates with his or her whole being to other persons or to what occurs in this world. A person whose soul is divided may at times be happy, but he or she will never experience the welling up of joy that accompanies giving oneself fully as a free person. Such a giving of oneself fully, one learns from the Biblical chronicle of Abraham, is the basis of establishing a relationship with God. Jewish tradition believes that we all are forgiven for our sins thanks to Abraham's righteousness. But few militant orthodox Jews, who believe this tradition fervently and often fanatically, go one step further and see that this righteousness was a result of Abraham's courage, freedom, and willingness to involve himself as a whole being in the world and for the world. Thus the lack of joy in this world which emerges in the daily religious life of the militant orthodox Jew, indicates that beyond being a source of enslavement, Jewish orthodoxy is sick.

Look at the clothes the militant orthodox Jews wear. A black suit with a black or fur hat, black pointed shoes. They always wear these tight uniforms proudly, in muggy weather as in a vehement khamsin, like volunteer soldiers on parade. Many of these blackhats, as they are called in Israel, live in Jerusalem, God's holy city, yet they never expose their body to its mild sun in spring or to its first soft rain in fall. Each blackhat alienates his body from the world, concealing it under thick layers of clothing so as not to sense the natural delights of Jerusalem and of Israel. But as we all know, and as Nietzsche repeatedly reminded us,[5] there is no joy without bodily joy; we can only conclude that these persons are addicted to taking themselves seriously. In short, they are sick with their own seriousness.

Consider a recent disaster which is definitely not out of the ordinary. A student group from the Gur Yeshiva with its rabbi-teachers went on a summer trip to the Gallilee and Golan Heights. One evening they reached a pool in the Jordan river, and since they were alone, the boys asked permission to enter the pool with their black suits and shoes to enjoy the water. They knew nothing about the pool and did not know how to swim. As it turned out this was a dangerous pool for nonswimmers, with deep sucking muck as a bottom; within moments of their plunging into the water fifteen of the yeshiva boys were drowning. Their heavy clothes filled with water pulled them under, as did the muck. The rabbis in charge, who also did not know how to swim, stood on the shore and screamed or recited Psalms. Luckily five or six secular Jews arrived at that moment for a picnic, and quickly jumped into the water to save the yeshiva boys. Eleven were saved, some only after respiratory first aid. Four drowned.

One of those saved by respiratory aid arose when he felt better, and approached a policman who had arrived after the incident to file a report, and who wore a skull cap. "Thanks for saving my life," He said.

"I didn't save your life, go thank those men over there. They saved you," the policeman answered.

"We don't speak to those kind of people.They don't wear skullcaps. They're Goyim," responded the yeshiva boy.[6]

Perhaps I should add that neither at the funeral, nor in their response in the media, did the heads of Gur Yeshiva ever thank the secular Jews who saved eleven of their students. Nor did they personally accept blame for encouraging their students to live a life so alienated from the land of Israel, that entering into a pool can result in disaster.

Nietzsche, in his somewhat polemical exaggerated manner, described the existential decision that leads to a way of life such as that adopted by the black hats:

The Jews are the most remarkable nation of world history because, faced with the question of being or not being, they preferred, with a perfect uncanny conviction, being at *any price*: the price they had to pay was the radical *falsification* of all nature, all naturalness, all reality, the entire inner world as well as the outer. They defined themselves *counter* to all those conditions under which a nation was previously able to live, was *permitted* to live; they made of themselves an antithesis to *natural* conditions—they inverted religion, religious worship, morality, history, psychology, one after the other in an irreparable way into the *contradiction of their natural values.*[7]

It is not my concern here to discuss Nietzsche's theory concerning Jewish history. The drowning disaster of the students of Gur-Yeshiva proves that the attitudes and the values that Nietzsche describes are dominant among many blackhats in Israel. One need only imagine plunging into a pool while dressed with a full suit and coat, with one's shoes on, tied (no, one need not imagine: there were photographs of the drowned yeshiva boys, lying there all dressed up), because of one's fervent belief in some dogma, to see how much of an "antithesis to natural conditions" these blackhats have become, how much they falsify nature, how little they are willing to bodily experience the joys of the world. Faith in the God of Israel who created and intervened in this natural world must vehemently reject their "contradiction of all natural values."

Hold it! Why are you continuously attacking the militant orthodox Jews, the blackhats? Why do you point to them as distorting the Jewish faith? Is it not the secular and semireligious Jews, who through their lukewarm adherence, render Jewish religiosity a farce?

I am attacking the militant orthodox Jews for three reasons. First, their holier than thou attitude; second, their political immorality; third, and most important, because through their striving to make us all slaves of a diaspora dogma, they are obstructing the way to God. I am continuously attacking them because they are not a peripheral phenomenon. Rather, due to their political involvement they often set the standard for other religious Jews and for other religious parties. In the past decade these radical militants have repeatedly determined for almost all religious Jews what Jewish religiosity is all about. For instance, radical militant Jews keep finding ways of excluding women from political and religious institutions. Lately, through a few court battles this principle has been challenged. But the religious Jews keep seeking for ways of working around court decisions so as to continue oppressing women.[8] Thus Jewish religiosity has become, at best, a daily nuisance to every nonorthodox Jew in Israel and, more often, a fanatic adversary of personal and political freedom. The lukewarm Jew may not be seeking a life of faith, but he or she does not threaten the freedom of fellow Jews. And the only way to appeal to the nonorthodox Jews to relate to God is by appealing to them as free human beings, not as slaves who have escaped their master's fold. Each reason merits further explanation.

Any reader of the Bible will soon discern that one cannot determine God's whims and ways. Despite a strict patriarchy God often chooses a younger son as His elected one; King David is an example. (And remember, King David had a great grandmother who was not an Israelite—Ruth, the Moabite.) Furthermore, the *Neviim* repeatedly determined that a whole-hearted faith which leads to a pursuit of justice is more important than adherence to many of the dictates of the Torah; thus moral deeds in this world are more pleasing to God than a giving of sacrifices. These basic tenets of Judaism are ignored by many orthodox Jews in Israel. They are seldom concerned with the pursuit of justice. They act as if they know God's deepest thoughts and decisions. Some blackhats speak as if God has become a puppet who sits on their knee and, with the help of their ventriloquist ability, recites the dogma of orthodox Jewry.

Here is an example. After a recent school bus accident, in which twenty-three primary school children were killed, the minister of the interior, Mr. Peretz, a fervent blackhat and a leader of one of the orthodox political parties, notified the entire country that these Jewish children had died because in their school the Mezuzoth had not been affixed properly. He was never censured for this announcement by any member of the religious establishment, and he never retracted his statement. Ignore for a moment that this statement by Mr. Peretz, which was supported by his orthodox cohorts, is insensitive, obnoxious, and vile. Only a fervent fanatic who is sure he knows God's will and who cannot at all relate to the sorrow of his fellow Jews—parents, relatives, and friends of the dead children—could make such a public statement. More significant in our context, though, is that such a holier-than-thou attitude, which is daily expressed by many blackhats, begins by diminishing and depreciating human freedom, and ends by eliminating God's freedom.

The militant orthodox Jews are politically immoral in their continual attempts to use democratic means to limit the personal and political freedom of their fellow Jewish and Arab citizens. Yishayahu Lebovitz, himself an orthodox Jew, has explained at length that this immorality stems from the unwillingness of orthodox Jewry to move beyond Halakhic dogma and to undertake decisions as to how a modern state should be run.[9] Of course, this unwillingness is partially a result of diaspora life which made little room for the "between" and the in-between, or for dreams of earthly freedom and responsibility. But it is also a result of the orthodox Jews' lascivious lust for power over their fellow Jews. Only freedom can limit this lust for power. The religious establishment knows this, hence under their stated concern to preserve and to spread the diaspora heritage, they do all they can within Israeli democracy to limit the space for freedom. As mentioned, they pressured Ben Gurion in 1950 not to agree to the drafting and accepting of a constitution and have since then vehemently opposed a bill of rights.[10] Through the rabbinic courts, which alone in Israel are allowed to deal with marriage and divorce of Jews, they enforce Halakhic principles which view women as property of men. They have repeatedly opposed women being chosen to political office, and vehemently opposed Golda Meir being appointed prime minister.

Here is another example. The Israeli newspapers of August 12, 1988, report the establishment of a terrorist group called Keshet, from among the militant orthodox Jews in an orthodox neighborhood called Bnai Brak, who have been terrorizing the stores in their neighborhood that sell secular newspapers, like the major newspapers of Israel: *Hadoshot, Yediot Ahronot, Maariv.* This group recently blew up a few of the kiosks in their neighborhood that refused to discontinue selling these newspapers. What I found significant was that no major rabbi in Israel, no leader of a religious party, came out with a statement supporting freedom of the press or censuring this violence of religious Jews against their fellow Jews.

Beyond matters of principle, Jewish orthodox parties, some of which are anti-Zionist, have developed what may be ironically called "a pork barrel" response to their being courted to form any coalition government. Among their so-called achievements are a "generous" government support program for yeshivas; a bloated bureaucracy to approve kashrut in hotels, restaurants, food factories, supermarkets, fast food stores, and so forth which provides well-paid jobs to members of the religious parties; a similar bloated bureaucracy for the rabbinic court system; and an independent religious school system which is government-funded. The press has repeatedly revealed that in the process of disbursing these funds many instances of impropriety arose, ranging from administrative defects to corruption and bribery. But those religious leaders who perform such greedy and criminal acts always seem to save face, even if they end up in jail; their adherents continue to believe that God is on their side.

The militant orthodox Jews' demand that all Jews in Israel adhere faithfully to a diaspora dogma is linked to the sickness of taking oneself seriously (which is similar to the kibbutz member's taking oneself seriously, described above). The Bible repeatedly emphasizes that faith in God, which is of this world and in this world, is a present given to Abraham and passed on to his progeny, a present the Jew must accept with joy. A person will be worthy of this present only if he or she attempts to joyfully and courageously realize the worldly demands of this faith. Expressed in political terms, the Jewish faith accepts responsibility for the fate of the world, by acting *in the world*. This means not only defending Israel against its avowed enemies by the use of military force, when needed; it also means pursing justice in this world, here and now. If such attitudes were not central to the Biblical experience Abraham would never have pleaded with God so as to save the people of Sodom and Gomorrah, Moses would not have decided to battle Amalek, Isaiah would never have expressed the vision cited above in the chapter on justice, Jonah would never have been charged with a Godly mission. Of course, there is an element of fear in relating to God, but one must always remember that even when one serves the Lord with fear, one should "rejoice with trembling" (Psalms 2, 11).

Now Jonah's second sin becomes clearer. Instead of rejoicing that the people of Nineveh turned to God, he complained that his prophecy would prove to be untrue because of God's mercy. The message of God that he presented was more important to him than the turning of the people of Nineveh; his words were more important than the historical developments that he encountered. Jonah is the epitome of a person who is sick with taking himself seriously, in short, he is a dogmatic and callous egotist.

This second sin is daily performed by the militant orthodox Jews. Even though they fervently read the book of Jonah while fasting on Yom Kippur, since it is part of the Yom Kippur afternoon prayer, they learn nothing from their reading. Because, like the kibbutz members mentioned above, *they insist on standing in their own light*. Hence these blackhats do not see that God accepted Jonah's rebellion while rejecting his taking of himself seriously, his extreme egotism, his being dogmatic. Worse, they try to force all other Jews to adhere to the seriousness and the dogma that they embrace. In the process, they not only anger these Jews, they also block the path to a faith based on freedom.

I submit that not all orthodox Jews are as extreme as those I have been attacking, but in the polyphony of orthodox voices heard in Israel those whom I have been attacking are often the loudest, and much too often the most influential. For instance, a large group of orthodox religious Jews, who for almost three decades opposed the fanaticism of the blackhats and related respectfully to the secular Jews, are called the "knitted kipot," since they wear secular clothes and don a knitted kipa. The men of the knitted kipot do serve in the army. But in the past decade the knitted kipot have become radicalized and in almost all political decisions most of them have sided with the blackhats. In short, the blackhats set the standard and their militant Judaism is the dominant voice of orthodox Jewry that one hears in political and religious discussions. Since the death of Abraham Isaac Kook in 1935, who was chief rabbi of Israel, there has not been a spokesman for orthodox Jewry who was willing to relate positively to secular Jews in a Jewish State (or in Rabbi Kook's time in the British mandate) if these Jews pursue justice and renew the relation of Jews to the land of their forefathers. I believe that the reason for his breadth of vision is that he personally put love of existence above adherence to dogma. Consider one of Rabbi Kook's poems:

The Whispers of Existence

All existence whispers to me a secret:
I have life, take it, take it—
If you have a heart and in the heart blood
Which the poison of despair has not soiled.

But if your heart is dulled
And my beauty does not charm you—existence whispers—
Leave me, leave
I am forbidden to you.

If every gentle whistle,
Every living beauty,
Stir you not to the glory of holy song,
But to the stream of an alien fire,
Then leave me, leave, I am forbidden to you

And a generation will yet arise
Who will sing to beauty and to life
Who will draw unending tenderness
From the dew of heaven.

From the Carmel and the Sharon,
A live people will lend its ear
To the plentiful secrets of existence
And from the tenderness of song and life's beauty
A holy light will abound.
And all existence will whisper,
My beloved, I am permitted to you.[11]

Yes, one of my major criticisms of the blackhats is that they stubbornly refuse to listen to the whispers of existence.

A person who hearkens to the whispers of existence will not view this world merely as a corridor to the afterworld, he or she will not elevate a dogma above personal integrity and freedom. To wholeheartedly "sing to beauty and to life" one must give of oneself to the world, one must open oneself to the "between." Contrarily, seeing this world as a corridor breeds fanaticism and fatalism; the embracer of such a way of life relates to what one does in this world merely as a means to a euphoric afterlife; hence, there are no things on earth worthy in themselves, and worthy of being struggled for here and now. I have shown elsewhere that in viewing one's life as a corridor the fanatic projects him- or herself as an inert object in God's domain. He or she becomes a rock in God's edifice of reality, or a pebble in God's slingshot.[12] The fanatic flees freedom, communion with God, joy in the world, and accountability for his or her deeds into the rigidity of a stone, a rigidity in which there is no room for dreams.

Consider an event that occurred during the Israeli war of independence. In the last month and a half of the seige of Jerusalem by Arab forces, when no food could reach the city, specifically between April 23 and June 11, 1948, the army in Jerusalem had at its disposal a small amount of kosher meat and a large warehouse full of canned pork, left behind by the British army. When this situation became known to the chief rabbi of Jerusalem, he issued a demand to the headquarters of the Israeli army in Jerusalem that the pork be immediately fed to the nonobserving Jews in the army, and that the kosher meat should be given only to Jews who are "truly religious" (those who observe the precepts prescribed by the orthodox religious establishment). Following this demand headquarters started a process of distinguishing between religious and nonobserving Jews, and of setting up kosher and nonkosher kitchens. This process aroused bitter resentment in the entire army, including among the "truly religious" soldiers, and also in parts of the religious and the secular Jewish population of Jerusalem. They demanded that the entire army eat kosher, as long as there was kosher meat, and then all soldiers eat nonkosher. In response to this criticism, spokesmen in the office of the chief rabbi of Israel expressed some reservations as to the demand of the chief rabbi of Jerusalem, but they never contradicted it or indicated what should be done.[13]

Remember, the demand to discriminate between Jews concerned the chief rabbi of Jerusalem while the city was besieged, with little water to drink or food to eat, and with bombs falling daily. No wonder that such a person, who ignores the screams of existence, let alone its whispers, will never be able to dream of a more worthy life of faith. No, if one wishes to dream, one must go beyond these myopic fanatics.

One of the basic tenets of Judaism is that faith in God is expressed in one's relations with other persons. Six of the Ten Commandments deal with relations between persons. With each New Year the Jew is given ten days to ask forgiveness of fellow inhabitants upon earth for misdeeds against them;

only after asking such forgiveness can the Jew pray wholeheartedly on Yom Kippur, the one day in which one asks forgiveness of God. But these and other examples deal primarily with what one should not do in relations with other persons—the last five commandments of the Decalogue open with the words "Thou shalt not." And in order to dream one must suggest positive directions, which stem from a life of freedom. Hence the significance of Buberian dialogue for a life of faith. Dialogue is a positive possibility for each person, and a life of dialogue can lead to a life of spirit. In addition, Buber's emphasis on dialogue as central to a life of faith and to one's relation to God not only redeems faith from the narrow confines of dogma, it also helps one make room for dreams.

I submit that Buber often writes poetically, unclearly, and at times mystically. In pointing out the linkage between the dialogical encounter and God, whom he terms the eternal You (Thou), one discerns these trends:

In every sphere, through everything that becomes present to us, we gaze toward the train of the eternal You; in each we perceive a breath of it; in every You we address the eternal You, in every sphere according to its manner.[14]

Extended the lines of relationships intersect in the eternal You. Every single You is a glimpse of that. Through every single You the basic word addresses the eternal You. ... The innate You is actualized each time without being perfected. It attains perfection solely in the immediate relationship to the You that in accordance with its nature cannot become an It.[15]

Although scholars have argued as to the exact interpretation of these and other passages in I and Thou[16] the direction to which Buber is pointing is not too obscure. He is advocating that in a dialogical encounter with another person, or with nature, or with a spiritual being, such as a work of art—one's being fully present in such an encounter, is also a presence to God. Thus, one learns about being present to God and having faith in Him through one's dialogical encounters.

In a series of books and articles Buber showed that in the Bible the dialogical encounter is central to establishing a relationship to God.[17] More important in our context is that dialogue opens a possibility of establishing a life of faith which is based on simple, yet wonderful and meaningful, encounters in this world. If one accepts Buber's guidance wholeheartedly, then, not the study of abstruse texts, not the fulfilling of six hundred thirteen daily mitzvoth, neither fatalism nor fanaticism, will lead to an establishing of a true faith in God based on human freedom. Only dialogue can lead to such a faith.

Hence a life of faith based on freedom must go beyond listening to the whispers of existence. It only *begins* with a personal response to the final whisper: "My beloved, I am permitted to you." Here is where Kook's lyric poem ends, perhaps because relating lovingly to existence requires courageously living in the world and making a story of one's life, such as only epic poetry can describe. Such a life of faith may resemble the lives of *Neviim* and their listeners; it will have little to do with the lives of most of the diaspora sages whom today's orthodox Jews attempt to emulate. Such a life of faith will strive to relate to God through one's encounters with the dusty red of a desert sunset, with the innocent glance of a trusting child, with music, with the fragrance of a budding flower. Relating to God will be expressed in one's joy in being alive and being able to smell, and to hate, and to love, and to weep, and to struggle for justice and beauty and truth and knowledge, and to create, and to speak, and to do. Such is a faith of God in this world and a faith in God of this world.

Before an additional dream, a nightmare. Consider Joseph Conrad in *Heart of Darkness*:

I've seen the devil of violence, and the devil of greed, and the devil of hot desire; but by all stars! these were strong, lusty, red eyed devils, that swayed and drove men—men, I tell you. But as I stood on the hillside, I foresaw that in the blinding sunshine of that land I would become acquainted with a flabby, pretending, weak-eyed devil of a rapacious and pitiless folly.[18]

That is my nightmare. That, as in Iran today, where neither greed, nor desire, nor even violence are what make Khomeini tick, but rather a fanatic belief in Allah intermingled with a rapacious and pitiless folly, such attitudes will spread to all peoples of the Middle East. Certainly, some Jewish religious leaders in Israel do not lag very far behind Khomeini (Rabbi Meir Kahane, but not only him). The problem is, as Conrad brilliantly explained, that among the nonfanatics such a leader inspires "neither love nor fear, nor even respect. He inspired uneasiness. That was it. Uneasiness."[19] Many secular and observant Jews experience such an uneasiness when confronted by the fanatic blackhats in Israel's religious establishment. For these secular and observant Jews, who live primarily in a means–end dialectic, who have problems with establishing a personal relationship to transcendence, the uneasiness stems from the suspicion that perhaps, after all, there is fact in the folly presented by the fanatics. Otherwise, why would they pursue it so fervently?

The religious establishment thrives on this uneasiness. It is one of its major sources of power and of influence. It has no need that, say, in the example cited above, the observant Jewish soldier wholeheartedly accept that he is entitled to eat kosher meat while his secular buddies eat pork. All that is needed is that both the religious and the secular Jew feel uneasy about rebelling against such a decree. The fanatic rabbis do not need that religious women wholeheartedly accept their degraded existence and their enslavement to males according to the tenets of Halakhah. All they need is that these women feel uneasy about rebelling against this tradition.

Judaism, like other religions, rejects "the devil of violence, the devil of greed, the devil of hot desire." But often in Biblical times—much as those who danced around the golden calf were detested and killed—*Neviim* instructed their listeners to detest the "devil of a rapacious and pitiless folly." Today he has representatives, who quote scriptures as their guidance, in the Israeli Knesset and government.

Hence my nightmare.

From the Bible one repeatedly learns that a life of faith means acting in the in-between. The *Navi*, from Abraham and Moses, through Samuel and Nathan, to Jeremiah and Jonah, was active in the political realm. It is from these knights of faith, to borrow a phrase from Kierkegaard, that the Jew today must learn how to live a life of faith. Consider Nathan. He came to King David to admonish him with the story of the poor man's ewe lamb after David had slept with Bath Sheva and ordered the death of her husband, Uriah the Hittite (Second Samuel 11–12). Nathan was acting within the political realm, he was admonishing a gross injustice committed in this world. He was defending the rights of a person who had been killed to cover up the lusts of King David. And don't forget, Uriah was a Hittite, not an Israelite. (He was literally a Goy.) I dream of Jews whose faith in God will lead them to follow the path of Nathan, Jews who will admonish those who, through violence, satisfy their greed and desires, while exploiting, oppressing, and inflicting suffering and death upon other persons. Put otherwise, I dream of a revival of worldliness in Judaism, based on a reading of the Bible as a divine text that demands that we assume our obligation to be free, and inspired by many Jews whose faith in God will instruct them to struggle for justice and against the fatalism, the fanaticism, and the rapacious folly that characterizes many, if not most blackhats, and the Israeli religious establishment.

Here and there one may encounter such religious Jews; Yeshaiyahu Lebovitz, whom I mentioned and cited above, embraces the Halakhah while struggling for justice. Some Jews with knitted kipot, disillusioned with the radicalization of all religious political parties, have recently set up a political party that will endeavor to be less radical, and pursue justice while adhering to religious dogma. Their spiritual leader is Rabbi Amital. Martin Buber spoke out at times for a rejuvenation of Judaism in the spirit of his writings, but he and his writings have been almost totally ignored by the orthodox religious establishment. A number of members of this establishment despise Buber and refuse to relate to his writings because he did not live according to the tenets of orthodox Jewry. Still, some orthodox Jews and quite a few secular Jews hearkened to his calls. But the limited response to the demands of these redeemers of the Jewish faith reveals that myopia and fanaticism are deeply entrenched in orthodox Jewry, or, put otherwise, the religious establishment has no wish to allow Jews to assume their obligation to be free.

For my dream to come true all this must change. Many religious Jews, and especially the blackhats, must, like Abraham, trust in their faith in God while cutting themselves off from much of their recent religious history, from fanaticism, from blind adherence to dogma, from myopic support of some rabbis' lust for power. This moment in history through which we are living, with the establishment of Israel as a political state, is also a wonderful moment—which the militant orthodox Jews have until now missed—for such a cutting off. Among these fatalists, fanatics, and embracers of dogma, some are lazy, some refuse to think, some are cowards. All of them do not trust enough in their faith in God to begin anew.

NOTES

1. Martin Buber has written extensively about Hasidism, including their joyous way of life. See, for instance, Martin Buber, *Hasidism and Modern Man* (New York: Harper, 1958); *The Origin and Meaning of Hasidism* (New York: Harper, 1960); *The Legend of the Baal Shem* (New York: Schocken, 1969).

2. S. Y. Agnon, himself an orthodox Jew, has described life among orthodox Jews in some of his stories. I do not recall him describing an orthodox Jew who had joy in worldly life. See especially his well-known story "Tehila" (in Hebrew this story appears in *AD HENA*; Tel Aviv: Schocken, 1951).

3. Haim Gordon, "Beyond Fatalism: Education for Peace Within Judaism," in Haim Gordon and Leonard Grob, *Education for Peace* (New York: Orbis, 1987), p. 45.

4. While Zosima discusses and describes the link between joy and faith on his deathbed, Dimitri and Alyosha experience this link in their lives through their wholehearted actions in the world. Thus Dostoyevski presents both the philosophy and instances of its realization.

5. See for instance the first essay in Friedrich Nietzsche, *On the Geneology of Morals* (New York: Vintage, 1967). Also "The Despisers of the Body," in Nietzsche, *Thus Spake Zarathustra* (Middlesex, England: Penguin), pp. 61–63.

6. The drowning occurred on July 31, 1988, and was reported in all Israeli newspapers. See, especially *Maariv*, August 2, 1988. Every year Yeshiva students drown under similar conditions; before the disaster of July 31 there were this year, according to my recollection, three other drownings of yeshiva boys who entered the water fully dressed, not knowing how to swim.

7. Friedrich Nietzsche, *The Anti-Christ* (Middlesex, England: Penguin, 1968), p. 134.

8. Here is a recent example, one of many. A new rabbi had to be chosen as chief rabbi for the city of Tel Aviv. The nominee (a blackhat, of course), after consulting with the chief rabbis of Israel, agreed to run for office only if all women members of the city council were not allowed to participate in the voting. The mayor, Mr. Lahat, agreed to his condition, and convinced the mostly male city council to go along with him. Mr. Lahat and his co-chauvenists were vehemently attacked in the press. To no avail. Only after the women members of the council filed a suit in the supreme court, demanding their full rights to participate in any matter brought before the council, since they were democratically chosen members of the council, only after they won this suit, was their participation in the voting ensured.

9. Yishayahu Lebovitz, *Yahadut Am Yehudi Vemedinat Yisrael* (in Hebrew) (Tel Aviv: Schocken, 1979).

10. Samuel Sager, *The Parliamentary System of Israel* (Syracuse University Press, 1985), especially Chapter 3, "In Quest of a Constitution."

11. I translated this poem by Abraham Isaac Kook. Rabbi Kook did not publish his poems. This and other poems appeared in the journal *Sinai*, edited by A. M. Haberman, in 1945, about ten years after Rabbi Kook's death.

12. Gordon, "Beyond Fatalism," p. 46.

13. Lebovitz, *Yahadut Am Yehudi*, p. 211.

14. Martin Buber, *I and Thou* (New York: Scribners, 1970), p. 57.

15. Ibid., p. 123.

16. See, for instance: Jochanan Bloch, *Die Aporie des Du: Probleme der Dialogik Martin Bubers* (Heidelberg: Lambert Schneider, 1977). Also, Jochanan Bloch "The Justification and the Futility of Dialogical Thinking" and Yehoshua Amir, "The Finite Thou and the Eternal Thou in the Work of Buber," both in Haim Gordon and Jochanan Bloch, *Martin Buber, A Centenary Volume* (New York: Ktav, 1984).

17. See, for instance the following books by Martin Buber: *Moses: The Revelation and the Covenant* (New York: Harper, 1958); *The Prophetic Faith* (New York: Harper, 1960); *Good and Evil* (New York: Scribners, 1952); *Two Types of Faith* (New York: Harper, 1951).

18. Joseph Conrad, *Heart of Darkness* (New York: New American Library, 1980), p. 81.

19. Ibid., pp. 86–87.

6

Peace Versus the Idolizing of the Israel Defense Force

The return of the Jewish people to the land of Zion has not been a peaceful return. Welcomed by a wasteland, one half desert and the other half mosquito-infested, the pioneers who came at the turn of the century had to struggle with malaria, dysentery, and other ailments and also with the active hatred of the scattered Arab inhabitants, who were supported by Arabs in neighboring countries.[1] Thanks to the efforts of many Jews the wasteland has receded; the hostility of most of our Arab neighbors has not. Jews in Israel live with some Arab neighbors who tolerate our presence in the Middle East and with a majority of Arabs who declare that they wish to evict or to annihilate us. Jews who returned to the land of Zion soon learned that they must defend themselves against such hostilities. Since Arab rhetoric has been followed by wars and acts of violence, for most Jews suspecting our Arab enemies has become a habit, and for many Jews despising Arabs has become a norm. Dreams of peace have all but disappeared. Living in Israel for many Jews means, primarily, being strong enough to face one's enemies. Unfortunately, the Arab way of life can hardly encourage Israelis to change their perceptions or beliefs.

Anyone who has spent some time with Arabs, or who has read contemporary Arab literature,[2] or followed contemporary Arab politics, will discover that many of T. E. Lawrence's keen observations, written more than half a century ago, still hold.

They [the Arabs] were a people of primary colours, or rather of black and white, who saw the world always in contour. They were a dogmatic people, despising doubt, our modern crown of thorns. ... They knew only truth and untruth, belief and unbelief, without our hesitating retinue of shades.

121

These people were black and white, not only in vision, but by inmost furnishing: black and white not merely in clarity, but in apposition. Their thoughts were at ease only in extremes. They inhabited superlatives by choice. Sometimes inconsistencies seemed to possess them at once in joint sway; but they never compromised: they pursued the logic of several incompatible opinions to absurd ends, without perceiving the incongruity. . . .

They were a limited narrow-minded people, whose inert intellects lay fallow in incurious resignation. Their imaginations were vivid, but not creative.[3]

All this from Lawrence of Arabia, who stated that he had raised a "wave" of Arab rebellion which "rolled before the breath of an idea, till it reached its crest, and toppled over and fell at Damascus."[4] Lawrence learned that the Arabs with whom he lived and fought knew how to fight for freedom, but they did not know how to live with political freedom once they had helped rout their Turkish rulers. Neither were they dialogical persons. Hence, the first buds of democracy, of political freedom, and even of dialogue appeared in the Middle East with the establishment of the Jewish State. Forty years after this event the Arab peoples have yet to reveal an inclination to democracy or to political freedom; they have yet to establish a democratic state.

In many Arab countries, and in the personal lives of multitudes of Arabs, adherence to dogma and a tendency to fanatically embrace extremes reign unmolested. Arab males still zealously oppress women. It seems that most Arabs are still a people of creeds who, to quote Lawrence again, "could be swung on an idea as on a cord; for the unpledged allegiance of their minds made them obedient servants."[5] As Arabic literature repeatedly reveals, they are ruthless in pursuit of wealth and its pleasures, and in many Arab states those who succeed do so at the expense of millions of their fellow countrymen who rot in poverty, ignorance, and squalor. In many Arab countries corruption is an accepted norm. In interpersonal relations Arabs seek adherence more than friendship, identification with their sad plight and not dialogue. They eagerly blame enemies for their own inability to get their act together, especially when these enemies are not Allah's servants. Black and white are still the primary colors of their mind and vision.

This does not mean that among Arabs one cannot find faithful friends, or supporters of democracy, or workers for dialogue and peace. One can, as I have repeatedly discovered in the years I have been working for Jewish–Arab dialogue. Still, I believe, on the basis of my limited experience, that these persons are rare exceptions, and that Lawrence's description is still true. Both recent history and Arabic literature add support to my belief.

Thus Israelis live on an island of limited political freedom surrounded by Arab regimes that are theocratic, or dictatorial, or both, and in which ruthlessness, bigotry, fanaticism, and violence are common. The longest war of the twentieth century raged between two Moslem nations, Iran and Iraq. At any given period in the past decade at least two wars were underway between Arab nations or groups. The two decades of internal strife in

Lebanon, where treaties are brokered and broken daily, where civilians are killed cynically, epitomizes the fratricide that characterizes Arab "brotherhood." In the early stages of the return to Zion Jews learned that guarding their freedom against the erupting orgy of violence and mutual annihilation which has characterized Arab existence for decades is a major commitment that all Jews in Israel must daily undertake. Before the establishment of Israel Jews responded to the need to guard themselves by establishing a volunteer people's army, which enlisted men and women, the *Haganah* (which literally means defense), and which later became the Israel Defense Force.

The initial role of the *Haganah* was defense of Jewish existence in Israel, then Palestine, against Arab marauders. For this role a volunteer people's army sufficed. With the establishment of the State of Israel and with the repeatedly expressed wish to annihilate the Jewish State becoming the official policy of Arab states, the need for a professional army that could repulse Arab attacks became a dire necessity. As the years passed, Arab enmity continued unabated, and Arab nations received sophisticated weaponry from the Soviet Union. Israel responded by enlarging its professional army, by acquiring arms from France and from the United States, and by developing an arms industry. The Israel Defense Force and the arms industry grew like a eucalyptus tree in a fertile swamp.[6] This military–industrial complex soon became a major employer of Israelis and an enterprise dominating much of the economy. Parallel to these developments the army, which began as a means of guarding Jewish freedom, became a source of pride and of values and, for many, an idol that Israelis could worship and Jews in the diaspora could admire.

There was good reason for pride. Jews in the diaspora, and even in Israel around the turn of the century, had little experience with firearms and with self-defense. Creating a Jewish army that could hold its own and later defeat the joined armed forces of Arab nations meant changing many aspects of the Jewish ghetto mentality. Perhaps the most important of these changes was the belief that Jews should no longer rely on external authorities, as Jews in the diaspora were prone to do, to defend Jewish lives and interests. Another change was the belief that Jews could attain glory in this world by heroism in battle, by fighting for Jewish existence in Israel. This heroism was often linked to the pioneering epic, to settling in a border settlement which together with other settlements guarded Israel's frontier. (For many years in the ghetto, glory was attained by being well versed in the Talmud, or by amassing worldly wealth.) Thus, through the years the Israel Defense Force not only guarded Jewish freedom, it also helped the Jew understand that one is capable of a life of freedom and of attaining glory when one successfully defends oneself against one's enemies.

As long as defense of Jewish lives and freedom was the goal of the Israel Defense Force, imperialistic tendencies were not prominent in the minds of most Jews. But with the acquisition of sophisticated weapons by parties in the Middle East conflict in the late 1960s, border settlements, for instance, were no longer the first line of security, they were no longer outposts that could justify their existence by holding that they guarded Israel's integrity and freedom. They needed to be guarded by advanced weaponry and became a military burden—much as today the Jewish settlements on the West Bank and the Gaza Strip are a military burden and need to be guarded by the Israel Defense Force. Jewish settlers' pride in their being able to guard their freedom was threatened, and when pride is threatened some people always seek salvation in contempt for those whom they can rule. Furthermore, with the burgeoning of the military–industrial complex, with our repeated military victories, with the taking over of great portions of Arab land in 1967, pride in one's being able to guard one's freedom often became arrogance, and arrogance often became superciliousness and hauteur.

To put it bluntly, today the power we have justly amassed to guard our freedom has encouraged many Jews to embrace imperialistic views and to pursue unjust ends. Even if these Jewish imperialists were merely intending to spread the idea of freedom, they are wrong. Freedom can hardly ever be exported through domination, it very rarely follows in the wake of violence. The means of violence are justified only in order to guard political and personal freedom, not to pursue it. These insights are hardly new—they go back to Plato, to Burke—yet they are ignored or discarded by many Jews in Israel.

That is only the first half of the problem. No less important is the fact that when the means of violence are used to limit the freedom of others, they begin to dictate the way of life of those who espouse freedom, and to undermine their political principles. Almost two centuries ago Edmund Burke warned, "the House of Commons ... is indeed great; and long may it be able to preserve its greatness; ... and it will do so, as long as it can keep the breakers of law in India from becoming the makers of law in England."[7] In Israel today, the Jewish breakers of law in Gaza and the West Bank are very often the makers of law in Jerusalem.

Who are these breakers and makers of law? I previously mentioned the Security Service who, after it was revealed that for them torturing Arabs and lying in court had become an accepted norm, received from Justice Landau permission for "mild torture" of Arab suspects. With the support of the Israeli government, Justice Landau's conclusions have been accepted as law of the land, and an Arab suspect is no longer innocent until proved guilty. He or she is in the hands of the Security, who have legal permission to torture suspects. They only need to explain in court that this degradation of another human being, this inflicted physical pain, was done mildly. Furthermore, recent cases reveal that the Security has begun to use "mild torture" in dealing with Jewish suspects.

Another such area is economics. It is acceptable that minimum wage laws in Israel do not hold for Arabs from the West Bank and the Gaza Strip who work in Israel. The exploiters of these Arabs are linked to both major parties in Israel and would not allow any law to pass which would give those Arabs equal wages. Also, in the past twenty-one years, while Israel has ruled the occupied territories, Arabs in these territories have not been allowed to develop indigenous industries. A colonial approach prevailed whereby these Arabs could only be menial workers of Israelis, or small farmers who export cheap crops to Israel. Some white-collar or blue-collar Palestinian workers exist, but they are a small minority. Note that white-collar workers for the Israeli government, such as teachers, receive much lower wages than in Israel (around two-thirds of the Israeli wage scale, at most). Hence, even if a few Palestinians did become affluent in the past two decades, it was as a result of their being merchants, not a result of economic development.

With the Palestinian uprising, the *Intifada*, these trends acquired velocity. Now under the "iron fist policy" initiated by Israel to curb the uprising, almost any law broken in dealing with Arabs who participate in the uprising is soon sanctioned in Jerusalem. Thus Israel has become a country with concentration camps in which today 2,500 Arabs are detained for six months or more without trial; it has a regime that supports the beating of women and children by its soldiers, and, even when the press reports atrocities, such as killings and beatings not in accordance with army guidelines, the army and the government in most cases cover them up. In another book, currently being written, I am documenting many of these atrocities, and the government responses.

When the breakers of law in Gaza become the makers of law in Jerusalem not only is peace in danger, not only is democracy slowly being eradicated, but also the freedom and dialogue needed for a spiritual existence rapidly erode. Jews justify this erosion as a need for security and economic stability; but as in Burke's time, lust for power, rapacity, and avarice seem to be major reasons Jews choose to exploit, oppress, and physically abuse their Arab neighbors.

Jewish children in Israel are taught the legend of Rabbi Judah Loew of Prague, the famous sixteenth-century rabbi and miracle maker, who, aided by his knowledge of kabbalic mysticism, created a Golem out of the dust of the earth to be his servant. The Golem helped him in his daily tasks and also protected members of the Jewish community from attacks by hostile gentiles. But, after a while the Golem began to rebel against the power of Rabbi Loew and to perform immoral deeds; finally the rabbi was forced to destroy him.

To ensure Jewish existence in Israel establishing the Israel Defense Force was a necessity, as was the building of a viable defense industry. What was not a necessity was allowing the burgeoning military–industrial complex to become a rebellious Golem. But such seems to have occurred. I have already mentioned that around twenty percent of the Jews in Israel are either directly or indirectly employed by this vast military–industrial complex; they have a vested interest in its continual development. Israeli newspapers give much space to details of army life, to the discussions between the representatives of the United States and Israel concerning the U.S. defense contracts Israeli firms will sign, and to the internal developments in firms that work for the Israel Defense Force. Awareness of security issues is rampant; no wonder that cowardly Jews flee their fears and their freedom into a worshiping of the defense Golem. Or, in the terms mentioned above, many Israelis relate to the Israel Defense Force, not as an organization set up to guard freedom, but as a source of values and of inspiration; in short they elevate a preliminary concern to ultimacy.

Perhaps, given the exigencies of security that Jews in Israel face, the worshiping of the Israel Defense Force was inevitable among those Israelis who refuse to live their freedom. Yet this idolatry—which had already begun with the establishment of Israel, in the period of Ben Gurion, and which grew rapidly in subsequent years—has slowly engulfed a great majority of Jews so that today criticizing the Israeli army in public is branded as anti-Zionist or anti-Jewish. This approach is not only prevalent in Israel. Writing in January 1988 in the Israeli daily *Yediot Ahronot*, Elie Wiesel explained that even when he sees Israeli soldiers beating up Arab women and children on television, or reads of the blowing up of homes of Arab suspects, or learns about other manners of oppressing the Arabs of the occupied territories, he refuses to condemn these soldiers, or to criticize the Israel Defense Force, or to judge Israel's policies. This from a Nobel Peace Prize laureate. Wiesel seems never to have understood that the Israel Defense Force was set up and exists not only to guard Jewish existence, but also, and perhaps primarily, to guard an existence worthy of being called Jewish. And many deeds currently performed by soldiers in the Israel Defense Force can in no way be called worthy. In short, Wiesel has joined the worshipers of the Israel Defense Force.

In addition to being idolatry, such a worshiping stands in the way of our pursuing justice and peace. The politicians among these worshipers—who include Yitzchak Shamir, the current prime minister, and his callous supporters—seem to believe that three and a half million Jews can impose peace on a hundred million Arabs. As a century of Arab history has shown, this belief is a folly. Arab nations will not accept an imposed peace, even a peace imposed by nations stronger than Israel. And as the *Intifada* reveals, Israel cannot impose peace on rock-throwing kids, on marching women, on flag-raising teenagers, when they refuse to accept their being oppressed. Yet Israeli right-wing politicians succeed in promoting the unrealistic belief that military force and not political negotiation and compromise can bring peace. They do so by appealing to the fears of Jews and to their greed for additional land. (Nietzsche pointed out: it is the cowards who are greedy, not the courageous!) These idolators of military force do not perceive that our isolation resembles Israel's isolation in Biblical times. Surrounded by idol-worshipers Israel struggled to believe in a God who demanded that they live in freedom. Appealing to this freedom, *Neviim* repeatedly stressed that a life of justice and faith is a key to living in peace with our neighbors. It still is.

Moreover, a repeated message of the Bible is that military strength is not an end in itself. Israel is to sustain military power so as to ensure that its people live in freedom, which is necessary if they are to pursue a life of faith and of justice. If the people of Israel do not realize their freedom to pursue justice and true faith, military strength will not save them from enemy attacks. This message, which, in my reading, need not be combined with the theocratic trends prominent in the Bible, is still true, and apt—even in military terms. As Israeli society becomes more corrupt over the years, the army follows in its wake. And a corrupt army is flabby, inefficient, vulnerable. Here is an example.

According to Israeli military doctrine the chief of staff of the armed forces needs between eight and twelve major generals, subordinate to him. Each major general is in charge of a specific section of the military, say, intelligence, or the navy, or the airforce. Today there are twenty-two major generals in the Israeli army. That means that about half of the generals have no role specified by the official military doctrine. Each such dispensable general endeavors to keep quite busy, but it is a busyness in order to prove that he should not be ignored. He is very much aware that he is superfluous, hence he is very sensitive to criticism and flees confrontation into a false pride. In short, he becomes a pompous ass.

Again, a consensus of stupidity prevails. The dispensable major generals, who have no important role to fulfill in the running of the army, know that they are superfluous; the chief of staff and the defense minister know it also, the press mentions it every so often, but everyone willingly overlooks this fact. Parkinson's law reigns: each superfluous general has a luxurious office and quite a few subordinate officers on his staff, in addition to a high salary and many other benefits. A similar bloatedness spreads to lower levels of the army hierarchy. Of course, bloated, pompous army staffs are not new—in *War and Peace* Tolstoy described the continuous inflating of the staff surrounding Kutuzov, commander-in-chief of the Russian army, and the back-stabbing among the staff officers. But in Israel the bloated defense force has hardly ever been critically scrutinized by legislators, and has only rarely been ridiculed by journalists. A perverse patriotism, encouraged by superficial and myopic politicians, has led many Jews—despite failures in the 1973 war and the Lebanon debacle—to believe that the army is omnipotent, invincible, and almost infallible. No one dares disturb the Golem.

Idolizing the Israel Defense Force is based on a mistaken conception of courage. There is an important difference between the civil courage described above, which emerges when one strives to live in freedom, and courage in time of war. Yishayahu Lebovitz has often pointed out that vile, corrupt, and perverted persons can be very courageous in a war.[8] There were many dedicated and evil Nazis who fervently believed in their Fuhrer and fought valiantly for him. Recently in *True Americanism: Green Berets and War Resisters*, David Mark Mantell has shown that the personalities of the courageous Green Berets in Vietnam were often distorted.[9] These courageous fighters were not at all whole or admirable persons, their way of life was often brutal and callous, utterly divorced from all spirituality. Mantell suggests that their distorted and unwholesome character supported their willingness to fight courageously, and was most probably a result of a vicious and violent upbringing. In short, Mantell's study suggests that such battle heroes will have little inclination to live courageously in freedom and to encourage others to do so.

What is urgently needed in Israel is the courage to pursue peace. Such courage is civil courage, which frequently emerges in the pursuit of justice. In other words, if most Israelis continue to evade pursuing justice in their daily life, and especially in interactions with our Arab neighbors, I doubt that we will be able to establish peaceful relations. I further fear that without civil courage our army will continue to be corrupt, and not strong. Corruption, as thousands of writers have observed, knows no boundaries; once it invades the public realm it infects the army, including a people's army such as the Israel Defense Force.

Here are two examples. Every year in his report, the Israeli state comptroller publishes what he calls "administrative deficiencies" of the government and government-run agencies. A large segment of each yearly report, hundreds of pages, discusses segments of the Israel Defense Force, and shows that within the army certain defects continue for years without much being done to mend them. The report goes into details, like the ways gasoline is "misused" in the army, or the "mistakes" in servicing tanks, or the hiring of too many researchers, or the signing of contracts with companies and not making sure that the companies fulfilled their obligations. Since the comptroller has no legal power to demand changes these "administrative deficiencies" continue unabated. The army, of course, reports that it has initiated changes, but after a few years a new comptroller report reveals that such did not occur.

A second example has to do with drugs. Every Israeli knows that one of the main sources of hard drugs to the Israeli underworld is Lebanon. There is a ten-mile-wide security strip, inside Lebanon, which borders Israel, in which the Israeli army rules with no civilian guidelines or laws. Through this strip all drugs reaching Israel from Lebanon must pass. Furthermore, almost every Israeli soldier who has served in Lebanon knows that there are ways of transferring the drugs from Lebanon to Israel, despite the checks at roadblocks. (I and both my sons served in Lebanon.) Again and again one reads in the press of officers and soldiers indicted for channeling drugs from Lebanese brokers to Israeli dealers, but this seems to be only the tip of an iceberg. The amount of drugs reaching the market seems to indicate that the main transgressors in the army and outside of it are still working peacefully.

Unfortunately, these and other examples are repressed by Israelis. Quite a few Israelis are right-wing fanatics.[10] Others are idolizers of the Israel Defense Force who refuse to see any blemish in the army or in our oppressive policies. And among the nonfanatics, when faced with the challenge of peace, of security without oppression, of seeking manners of relating justly to our Arab neighbors an atmosphere of indecisiveness prevails. The result is a loss of power, especially the power to do good. Machiavelli observed:

Indecisive republics never choose beneficial policies except through force, for when there is doubt their weakness never allows them to arrive at a decision; and if that doubt is not removed by some form of violence which drives them on, they remain forever suspended in a state of indecision.[11]

Thus, it is beneficial for us to be decisive about doing good, because we have no other way to be strong and to hope to live in peace in this area of the world, surrounded by Arab ruthlessness and hostility. Learning from Plato I would like to do good for its own sake. But the widespread Arab hatred that encompasses us, the resurgence of Moslem fundamentalism, fanaticism, and belief in *gihad*, the repeated killing of Arab peacemakers by Arab assassins, suggests that one should also be pragmatic. Therefore, I want Israelis to pursue justice because such a pursuit endows a people with strength, and I want Israel to be militarily strong so as to be able to pursue justice. Such an approach is the only manner to seek and to ensure a lasting peace.

Unfortunately, in dealing with the Palestinians, and in general in initiating peace processes in the Middle East, Israeli politicians have been persistently indecisive. The peace with Egypt, for instance, caught all Israelis by surprise and was initiated solely by Anwar Sadat. Israeli leaders of the two major parties have no suggestions as to how one can initiate peace with other Arab countries. They seem to embrace indecisiveness. Shimon Peres' playing around for two years with the idea of an international peace conference with King Hussein of Jordan is a case in point. He, like most of Israel's myopic leaders, refuses to accept the fact that the Palestinians hold one of the keys to peace with Arab countries, and of course, to the termination of the Palestinian uprising; hence Israel must negotiate with them. To remain indecisive and support their lack of vision Peres and other politicians ignore the fact that for two decades we have been performing a gross injustice: Israel's military rule over a million and a quarter Arabs on the West Bank and in the Gaza Strip, which denies these people all political rights and many civil rights, and often exploits them economically. Until rocks started being thrown at every Israeli car in the occupied territories by young kids, these politicians refused to understand that anyone under twenty years old living in Gaza was born into a world where he or she has no official country, no citizenship, no memories of life without Israeli soldiers guarding their comings and goings, and this is a situation these Arabs resent. And even after the rocks and the burning tires and the continual uprising, Israeli politicians refuse to see the facts, preferring to remain indecisive as to what needs to be done, feeding the Israeli public worn-out cliches, refusing to talk with the Palestinians and with their representatives about terminating the Israeli occupation and oppression. (I know, in Arab countries such as Syria, many Arabs may perhaps suffer worse injustices. But that does not justify our oppression. And, as two decades of Israeli military rule have shown, oppression will not lead to peace.)

I suspect that many Israelis know this; to hoodwink themselves they interpret crime as catastrophe. They discuss what occurs on the West Bank and in the Gaza Strip as if the injustice there were some sort of natural event, like a hurricane or a tornado, something that has nothing to do with our daily decisions. For instance, the Israeli television and radio, which are governmently owned and run, persistently refuse to call the Palestinian uprising an uprising. They ordered their editors and anchormen and women never to use the word *Intifada*, and to call any event tied to the uprising in the occupied territories "disorders." Think about it. For more than a year already Palestinians have been daily marching, throwing rocks, burning tires, raising Palestinian flags, all this with surprising organizations skills, and many Israelis following the government's lead continue to see only "disorders." Thus they interpret the Palestinian uprising as a group of minor events that have nothing to do with our decisions, or with their struggle for freedom. Furthermore, these personally hoodwinked Israelis convince themselves that twenty years of Israeli despotism are merely a result of our inability to solve a few abstruse diplomatic problems with our Arab neighbors. For these self-deluders the daily denying of political and civil rights to more than a million Arabs is no crime; it is an unfortunate catastrophe which occurred to these luckless Arabs.

Of course, there is a risk in evacuating the West Bank and the Gaza Strip. I shall discuss this risk presently. But there is a greater risk, including a grave risk to our military strength and to a lasting peace, in living an insipid, corrupt, superficial, and unjust existence based on lies to oneself and on bad faith.

Don't Israelis see this risk? Many perhaps do. But here is where a new ruse for evading responsibility gains control. Prodded on by myopic indecisive politicans, unthinking Israelis interpret resolving one's anxieties as attaining security.

Colonel Emanuel Wald's report is a case in point.[12] He was appointed by Moshe Levi, chief of staff of the Israeli army after the Lebanon debacle, to examine the Israel Defense Force in its recent wars and to propose a direction for development in the forthcoming decade. The major part of Wald's report reveals that in the past two decades the Israeli army has lost its battle power, mainly as an attacking force, but also as a defense force. This loss is primarily a result of lack of thinking on the strategic level and of the diversion of funds to inflate staffs, who merely interfere with decision-making processes and with the fulfilling of tactical goals in time of battle. Furthermore, the apathy toward thinking embraced by the top generals in the past two decades, Wald holds, has created an army where sycophants thrive, and toadies rise to undeserved military positions.

For instance, Wald points out that the Israeli army botched up the first week of fighting in Lebanon, and that the generals blamed their inability to attain the posited military goals on restraints put on them by the government. By day-to-day analysis of the military decisions made, and the incompetent manner of fulfilling these decisions, he shows that not the government, but the entire structure of the army, the way of reaching tactical decisions at all levels, the way of fulfilling the decisions and organizing the battle, the manner of reporting outcomes of battles and of analyzing results—to mention a few of the deficiencies—were behind the failures of the army during the first week. Therefore, Wald concludes, the Israeli army is weak as a combat force, in its structure, in the quality of its commanders, and in many other areas, and decisive changes should be made immediately.

When Wald submitted his initial findings, Moshe Levi tried to discontinue his work and to file away the report. Wald appealed to Yitzchak Rabin, the defense minister, who requested that Levi discuss the report with the general staff. He didn't. Rabin did not insist. (Here is another example of indecisiveness starting from the minister of defense and including the entire general staff.) Wald responded by leaking the report to three Knesset members, who passed it on to the press. Since then the top military brass and the defense minister have persistently ignored the report; they have spent much time and energy on trying to forcefully suppress Wald, who responded by resigning from the army and publishing his findings in a book.

For some of the military Wald is no more than a bearer of evil tidings who should be silenced; for others he is an iconoclast who is dangerous. By ignoring and disparaging Wald they are resolving their anxieties as to his findings (they refuse to think even in order to criticize these findings). This resolving of anxiety by deliberate ignorance and refusal to think still gives them a deluded sense of security. With the help of the myths surrounding the Israel Defense Force, and the institutionalized idolization of the army for years, they pass this delusion on to Israeli citizens. In short, the chief of staff and his surrounding generals are daily lying to themselves and to the Israeli public.

But Wald's findings like many facts have a stubbornness of their own. The army can ignore them, they can cut off Wald's funding as they did, they can continue to attempt to silence him by backhanded tactics; but the facts he pointed to continue to appear and to assert themselves. Wald, for instance, pointed out that, despite internal army decisions to the contrary, the number of noncombat soldiers continues to rise, which is a burden on the budget and weakens the army. In the past decade the number of combat soldiers has fallen from 35% to 33% of the army. In an army that, including the reserves, can field half a million soldiers even 2% is significant. Wald's point is that this occurred despite decisions to enlarge the percentage of combat soldiers. Most Israeli politicians and many high army officers respond to these unpleasant facts with jingoist pathos. They do not deny the evidence, they refuse to see it.

These deliberately blind politicians—the prime minister, the defense minister, the foreign minister—are sawing off the branch upon which we all sit. Corruption together with a disregarding of facts leads to cynicism; and anyone who speaks with Israeli soldiers knows that in the army widespread cynicism prevails. The cynic, of course, has no dreams for a better future, neither is he or she willing to undertake any responsibilities beyond those specifically designated. In short, as everyone knows, a corrupt, cynical army is a weak army. Furthermore, when flabbiness and corruption are not cut out of an army daily, including in the highest ranks, they grow like a cancer, and this is currently occurring in the Israel Defense Force. The "small head" discussed previously has become the norm; advancement in the ranks is based primarily upon one's belonging to a clique, not on one's merit as a commander; and to explain away its failures the Israel Defense Force relies on myths, not on achievements.

A lasting peace in the Middle East can only be achieved through dialogue, both at the political and on the personal level. (I am not talking about an I–Thou encounter, but about simple, genuine dialogue.) As explained in previous chapters, in order to be able to participate in dialogue a person must feel that he or she has a space in the world in which one is accepted as one is, with all one's idiosyncrasies. A home ground. Hence the statement often repeated by Israeli leaders that we cannot enter into dialogue with the Palestinians, since they engage in terrorism, is a paltry excuse. The truth is that we daily deny the Palestinians living in the Gaza Strip and on the West Bank the right to establish a free state; one of their responses to military oppression is terrorism. A more recent response is the *Intifada*. Israel's oppressive attempts to curb this uprising have revealed to the world that our political leaders are not open to dialogue. Unfortunately, despite these facts the Israeli public and many Jews in the world continue to wrongly believe that Israel is pro-dialogue. It isn't. Being pro-dialogue means giving the Palestinians the right to live as a free people. It means giving them a space in which they can live their freedom. Only then can we hope to initiate dialogue with them. People whom one militarily and economically oppresses, from whom one denies the space needed for them to assert their freedom, cannot become partners to dialogue.

Perhaps despite the pressures one can become such a partner. But to do so one must be a very courageous person, whose belief in dialogue inspires one's existence. During the seven years that I actively worked for Jewish–Arab dialogue, I had the good fortune to encounter two such persons in the Gaza Strip, a man and a woman. Now, with the Gaza Strip erupting in violence and killings, we are still in contact, we still trust each other. But they both are exceptional persons, whose quest to live their freedom, despite abject conditions, is remarkable. (I have documented a few of my encounters with the man from Gaza in my book *Dance, Dialogue, and Despair*.[13])

If our quest is dialogue and peace, our entire approach to Arabs should change. We should view them as fellow sojourners here on earth, with whom we share a portion of the world. Of course we have differences, but these are differences that, to borrow an insight from Protagoras, mutual respect and a sense of justice can bridge. Responding to Arab fanaticism, hatred, and greed with Jewish fanaticism, hatred, and greed, as many right-wing and religious parties in Israel do, is ruining our ability to live a life of dialogue, of justice, and of freedom. Greed, like corruption, knows no borders, as many Israelis who attempted to buy houses from Jewish construction firms who built on the West Bank learned. The managers of some of these firms, who had found semi-legitimate ways of evicting Arabs from their lands, also found ways of not delivering to Jews the houses they had been paid to build.

The above views are not new. Together with other Israelis working for peace, I have been expressing them for some years. The patent response among many Jews in Israel, and not a few persons outside Israel, has been something like the following: It's easy to talk about peace and to interpret our wish for security as greed for additional land. Are you really willing to let Arabs take over the West Bank and set up their artillery within range of Jerusalem or Tel Aviv? Are you willing to let them station their tanks and infantry forty minutes from Tel Aviv and twenty minutes from Jerusalem? Can you really trust the Palestinians, the Arabs? Do you really believe that they won't try to evict or to annihilate you at some later date?

The only way to ensure our life in the Middle East is by working for a lasting peace. Moreover, in the heat of argument many Jews tend to forget that living in the Middle East means living with Arab neighbors, and that means finding ways of living peacefully with them. There has been peace with Egypt for more than ten years, and despite the pressures of other Arab nations, Egypt has made no attempts to act aggressively toward Israel. Yitzchak Rabin, the defense minister, recently announced that a decade had passed without a single shot having been fired along the Israeli–Egyptian border. True, Egyptian statesmen have criticized Israel, often viciously, the Egyptian press has at times published antisemitic slurs, some Egyptians have continued to shun Israelis, but no one has gone beyond verbal criticism.

And, as every Israeli knows, Egyptian soldiers are stationed an hour and a half ride from Tel Aviv.

Someone may ask, is that what you call peace? Yes! I, like many other Israelis of my age, actively participated in four Israeli–Arab wars and have experienced the horrors of war, its nightmares, its fears, its death toll, its terrifying memories which accompany one for years. For me, such a peace of mutual tolerance with the Egyptians is fine. I don't care if they don't like us, much as they don't like many of their Arab brethren. I just don't want to have to kill them and have them kill us.

Jews must grasp that peace with our other Arab neighbors is an opportunity that one must work to realize. Allowing the Palestinians on the West Bank and in the Gaza Strip to set up a nation of their own, with a space where they can realize their freedom, is a manner of working for peace, of building trust with Arab people and nations. If the Palestinians believe that their legitimate representative is the PLO we must be willing to speak with them. *I know* that the Palestinian Covenant has at least two articles which deny the Jews a right to exist in the Middle East. But in negotiations with the PLO these articles can be changed, much as other constitutions and political documents have been altered.[14] *Of course* such an approach entails risks; but living in a perpetual state of war also entails great risks, oppressing millions of people is dangerous militarily and is a manner of breeding corruption and injustice. Furthermore, accepting Jewish oppression of Arabs and war with them as a normal way of life is terrifying; it is also a rejection of our need to pursue justice. With all the hatred encompassing us many Jews tend to forget that the most secure border is a peaceful border.

We dare not give up a dream for peace; not only because it is our only way of ensuring our survival here in the Middle East, and not because it might bring an economic boom if Israel didn't have to spend twenty to thirty percent of its GNP on security. We must continue to dream and work for peace because living a life of dialogue and of freedom are in themselves spiritual challenges, and also ways to pursue other spiritual challenges of Zionism. These challenges, such as the pursuit of justice, have all but disappeared in our continual quest for a larger, more efficient military and during our two decades of oppression of a million and a quarter Arabs. Even after the peace with Egypt, which is the strongest nation in the Arab world, and whose population of fifty-two million includes almost half of the Arabs now living in the world—even after a decade of peace, most Israelis continue to believe that the only key to our existence in the Middle East is military strength.

A dream of peace need not lead to brotherly love, or to profound friendship, although I believe that dialogue with our Arab neighbors can be spritually enhancing. Enough if no shots are fired, no vicious and fanatic hatred is expressed, no oppression is rampant. A correct relationship, with exchange of diplomats and with free movement across borders, would suffice. Such a relationship would, hopefully, slowly eradicate the profound existential mistrust that currently prevails in the entire region. And with less mistrust, dialogue and a life of freedom could begin to emerge. I ask for no more.

NOTES

1. A good overview of the demographic situation in and surrounding Israel in the past century and of the attitudes of Arabs to Zionists can be found in Joan Peters, *From Time Immemorial* (New York: Harper & Row, 1984).

2. There are many important contemporary Arab writings some of which have been translated into English. Here are a few examples: Taha Hussein, *An Egyptian Childhood* (London: Heinemann, 1981); Taha Hussein, *The Stream of Days* (London: Longman's Green, 1948); Naguib Mahfouz, *Miramar* (London: Heinemann, 1978); Naguib Mahfouz, *Midaq Alley* (London: Heinemann, 1975); Naguib Mahfouz, *Children of Gebelawi* (London: Heinemann, 1981); Tayeb Salih, *Season of Migration to the North* (London: Heinemann, 1976); Yusuf Idris, *The Cheapest Nights and Other Stories* (London: Heinemann, 1978). Also, in Hebrew two volumes of Naguib Mahfouz's famous autobiographical trilogy have appeared, which are revealing as to the extent of ruthlessness and enslavement in Egyptian society: *Bayit Bekahir* (Tel Aviv: Sifriyat Poalim, 1981, 1984).

3. T. E. Lawrence, *Seven Pillars of Wisdom* (Middlesex, England: Penguin, 1976), p. 36.

4. Ibid., p. 41.

5. Ibid.

6. Of course, in my description of the rise of the Israeli military I am sketching trends and not describing a detailed history. There were, for instance, some attempts at reducing arms and reaching a peace treaty in Ben Gurion's days, but the Israeli army generals opposed this trend.

7. Edmund Burke, "Reflections on the Revolution in France," in *Edmund Burke* (New York: P. F. Collier, 1937), The Harvard Classics, p. 183.

8. Yishayahu Lebovitz, *Yahadut, Am Yehudi, Umdinat Yisrael* (Tel Aviv: Schocken, 1979), p. 406.

9. David Mark Mantell, *True Americanism: Green Berets and War Resisters* (New York: Teachers College Press, 1974).

10. The Tehiya party and parties to the right of it have six Knesset members all of whom are right-wing fanatics who speak openly of their hatred of Arabs and of the need to oppress them. At least three more religious Knesset members agree with these stated views. Nine Knesset members represent around one hundred seventy thousand voters.

11. Niccolo Machiavelli, "Discourses on the First Ten Books of Titus Livius," in *The Portable Machiavelli*, edited and trans. by Peter Bondanella and Mark Musa (Middlesex, England: Penguin, 1979), pp. 251–252.

12. Emanuel Wald, *Klelat Hacelim Hashvurim* (in Hebrew) (Tel Aviv: Schocken, 1987).

13. Haim Gordon, *Dance, Dialogue, and Despair* (Tuscaloosa, Ala.: University of Alabama Press, 1986), pp. 106–107, also p. 146.

14. See, for instance Y. Harkabi, *The Palestinian Covenant and Its Meaning*. (London: Valentine, Mitchell, 1979), especially articles 20 and 22 of the Covenant.

7

Dialogue: Men and Women as Free Partners

In 1967 Jean Paul Sartre and Simone de Beauvoir visited Israel and spent some time at Kibbutz Merhavia. Beauvoir was very interested in methods of child rearing on the kibbutz and in the "emancipation of women." After being warmly hosted and shown around by proud ultra-socialist kibbutz members, Beauvoir decleared that "she had finally discovered an institution that had come close to establishing equality between men and women" and that "What she had been witnessing in Israel had shown her such an emancipated view of woman that she did not feel she had anything to add to the subject."[1] Simone de Beauvoir's conclusions were not only grossly superficial—they were far from the truth!

Israeli society, which includes the kibbutz, is antifeminist and macho-oriented, albeit the ways that Jewish women are enslaved in Israel are much less violent and demeaning than in Arab, especially Bedouin, society. In a penetrating essay Lesley Hazelton has described three myths that Jewish men and women have embraced since the Zionist return to the land of Israel in order to conceal from themselves women's inequality and their enslavement to men.[2] The first myth was propounded by the early pioneers, who came to Israel fifty to ninety years ago, and declared that they believed in sexual equality; but declarations were set aside when it came to farming the land, or to planting trees, or to paving roads. The vast majority of women were not allowed to participate in these "male" tasks. Instead, they cooked and washed clothes for the men.

In Degania, the first kibbutz, only the men drew a salary from the Palestine Office of the Zionist Movement during the years of establishing the kibbutz. The women members of Degania were told explicitly that they worked for the men. Yet the myth of equality was so dominant that women in the kibbutzim began to believe that their sphere of pioneering was in the kitchen, in the laundry, and later in rearing children. Since those years in all the kibbutzim, including Merhavia, those who cook, launder the clothes, and rear the children are almost always women.

The same was true of the *Haganah*, the volunteer Jewish Defense Force, which was established more than half a century ago and also inscribed sexual equality on its banners. Hazelton points out:

The *Haganah* women knew how to use a gun. But it was generally the men who did the guard duty and the women who welcomed them home and, if necessary, nursed them ... women served as wireless operators, nurses, and quartermasters—exactly as women served in the British Army in World War Two. There were women who actually fought, and died, in battle, but it was solely on these exceptions that the rule of the myth was to be based.[3]

There has been a change in the Israel Defense Force since the period Hazelton describes, but it has been toward less involvement of women in combat roles; of course, there are no women pilots, or naval officers on ships, or tank commanders, but women are also excluded from even partial combat roles. The Israel Defense Force is an army in which males are trained for combat and most of the women perform clerical tasks.

Although the ideal of sexual equality was stated in 1948 in Israel's Declaration of Independence, Hazelton correctly points out that these were empty words "with neither the commitment nor the intention to carry them toward fulfillment."[4] A so-called Women's Equal Rights Law of 1951 followed by a Rabbinical Courts Jurisdiction Law of 1953 reduced many women's rights, by allowing for discriminating laws whose stated intent was "protecting women" and by handing over jurisdiction of marriage and divorce to the patriarchal and woman-demeaning orthodox Jewish courts. Furthermore, in the job market and in leadership roles in Israeli society the myth of equality is a farce. Professions dominated by women, such as teaching and nursing, are considered "second salary jobs" and are grossly underpaid. There are very few women in leading political positions—Golda Meir like Indira Gandhi was an exception, and Golda showed no concern for women's liberation. There are even fewer women in leading economic positions such as top bank executives or directors of firms or corporations. In short, Simone de Beauvoir was being shown a myth of achieved equality that had little to do with reality.

Always His Wife[5] is the name of a recently published autobiography by Leah Rabin, wife of Yitzchak Rabin, who is currently minister of defense. In choosing this name for her book and in presenting herself Leah Rabin accepted two other myths that Hazelton discusses; the myth that it is the male's role to do and the female's role to be, and the myth that biologically the woman, who gives birth to a new generation, has a superiority that men can never attain. Both myths were attacked by Simone de Beauvoir in *The Second Sex*[6] and have been demythicized by feminist writers from Kate Chopin to Doris Lessing. (Already in Tolstoy's *Anna Karenina* one senses the inability to reach genuine dialogue that is a result of embracing these myths.) The fervent adherence to these myths by many Israeli men and women helps them to justify the prevailing chauvinism and inequality.

In addition to permanently excluding women from acting in the political realm, the last two myths create a vicious circle which does not allow for dialogue between men and women to develop. On the one hand, for men as for women it is extremely difficult to develop a dialogical relationship with someone who is believed to be biologically superior. (Note that the myth that women are biologically superior is a mirror image of the prevailing patriarchal myth that men are biologically superior.) And a person whose role is merely to be—to live as an object, which requires that one constantly eradicate one's own freedom—will not endeavor to engage in dialogue with others. On the other hand, when there is no dialogue between men and women they frequently flee their anguish, their disgust with their empty lives, and their chagrin at not being concretely affirmed by other persons into the relieving affirmation of myths.

As I have indicated in the sections dedicated to freedom and courage, the persons who flee dialogue often know that the myths they embrace are a negation of one's freedom. They often know that these myths are a haven of nothingness in which, through bad faith, one can conceal from oneself one's unwillingness to fulfill one's obligation to be free and to establish meaningful relations with other persons. But for these cowards willing nothingness is better than recognizing that they lack the willpower to cope with one's fear of dialogue; or as Nietzsche put it, "man would rather will nothingness than not will."[7]

Given that equality between men and women in Israel does not exist, Jewish women who wish to live in freedom, as equal partners of men, have almost no models from whom they can learn; and there are very few men who are willing to allow women to share their freedom. Hence the dream and the challenge of feminism and of relations of dialogue between men and women poignantly confronts us every day. In seeking to live a life of equality and dialogue, men and women must constantly begin from the assumption that the heritage that nurtured them is antifeminist, including the so-called Zionist socialist pioneering heritage. They must also assume that most men in Israel are chauvinistic, macho-oriented, and will only reluctantly give up power; also, these men are not persons who cherish dialogue, including dialogue with women.

I have already stressed that living a life of dialogue is worthy in itself, hence the lack of dialogue in interpersonal relations in Israel is undoubtedly a bane. Without dialogue one's life is often devoid of freedom, of joy, of love, of creativity. Insipidity, bad faith, and alienation frequently reign. I have also held that many of the challenges described in previous chapters could be better addressed if the relationships between men and women in Israel were drastically altered and were based on freedom, equality, and an openness to dialogue. For instance, I doubt that a man can authentically pursue justice and equality, say, between Jews and Arabs if he accepts as natural and does not question the oppression and degradation of women prevailing in Israel. I also believe that Jewish faith in Israel is suffering from a lack of spirituality, one of the reasons being that it does not encourage equality between men and women.

Furthermore, a man who seeks to establish dialogical relations with women, who begins to relate to each woman's freedom and to encourage her to live that freedom—such a man will soon sense that in the process of relating to the freedom of women he himself attains new strengths, which allow him to live more justly or to seek peace. Of course, his women partners in dialogue will also attain the strength to act in the "between" and the in-between. Frequently a dialectic process will develop by which men and women, through living together in dialogue, will help each other to grow and to live a more meaningful and spiritual existence. In short, dialogue is both worthy in itself and often a key to the dialectic of a life of freedom.

Each person should strive to live a dialogical life. Probably every person has sensed how one's inability to relate dialogically to one's partners in life causes much suffering; and, as Buber noted, where there is pain there is also a possibility of change. But not always. Change will occur only if the pain helps one identify areas in one's life where one was dishonest, where one evaded the responsibility of freedom, and after identifying these areas one is willing to see how they demand change. Consider an instance when I, as a teacher, was enlightened by one of my pupils.

It occurred about ten years ago during a course that I taught at our university on Martin Buber's *I and Thou*. As is known, Buber believes that the I–Thou encounter can lead one to a relationship with God. Well, a group of students in my class questioned this belief. They held, quite vehemently, that they had encountered the Thou, albeit on rare occasions, without such an encounter bringing them any nearer to encountering the eternal Thou, or the Godly, or the holy. I explained and argued but to no avail; they stood firm. Suddenly one of the students, who was not participating in the exchange but was watching quietly, smilingly said: "You know what this discussion resembles. It is as if Haim is standing on a long green lawn, near a fence, and beckoning all of you to jump over the fence and enter a beautiful garden. And you guys are answering, 'But, Haim, there is no fence!'"

In the years that I have been educating Jews and Arabs in Israel to relate dialogically in their personal lives I have often encountered men and women who refuse to see the fence that divides a life of dialogue from living as an alienated object in the It-world. Buber called this refusal a sickness and viewed the educator as a therapist who should assist and encourage the student to heal oneself. I hold that here Buber was evading the issue. When a person refuses to see the fence, therapy—showing a person his or her illness—brings little results, since the sickness is an act of consciously embracing alienation. And as existentialists from Nietzsche to Sartre pointed out, in one's sickness a person may find a meaning that he or she refuses to give up, and which leads the person to cherish that sickness.

In previous chapters I noted that confronting may help persons relate to each other in a manner that leads to dialogue. I should add that Hebrew often helps. It is a confronting language, with little space for politeness or for dillydalling, as any reader of the Bible will note. In the period that I worked intensely for Jewish–Arab dialogue, Arab students often noted that confronting that leads to dialogue is very difficult in Arabic, which is a much more roundabout and poetic language, playing on associations and not encouraging a person to speak in a confronting manner. They often told me: "In Arabic one hints as to one's true intentions. In Hebrew we Arabs speak much more straightforwardly."

Despite the straightforwardness of Hebrew, many Israelis have learned to use Hebrew in order to evade dialogue, or to conceal one's pain, not in order to face it. They use its straightforwardness in order to block all possibilities of opening themselves to other persons or of reaching out to the Other. In short, a confronting language is a two-edged knife that can help one relate dialogically when used with sensitivity, but can also be used to kill any attempt to relate dialogically.

To respond to the challenge of dialogue, one must accept Buber's suggestion that one change one's relations in the interpersonal realm; but that is not enough. One must also work for equality and for freedom in the political realm. Here is an area where I find myself groping to suggest short-term goals that will lead to the ultimate goals of equality and freedom. Feminism, equality between the sexes, is worthy in itself; if men and women learn to live as equal partners our entire existence on earth should be altered; our relations will change on both the personal and the political level. In day-to-day life the challenges of feminism exist from the most mundane to the most spiritual level, from how the chores are divided at home, through how one loves, to how one relates to God. At all levels such challenges confront Jews in Israel. Responding to them requires accepting what may be called the dialectics of change. Here are two examples.

During Israel's Lebanese debacle there arose a strong vocal group of women, entitled "Mothers Against Silence," who vigorously and often vehemently protested against the right-wing government policy of sticking it out in Lebanon. Without in any manner belittling the contribution of these dedicated women to diminishing Israel's imperialistic policies, I feel uncomfortable that only mothers were included. Why were fathers excluded? I suspect, though, that a group entitled "Parents Against Silence" would have been less effective. Why? Because the prevailing myths about women and motherhood, described by Lesley Hazelton, very much guide the perceptions and the actions of politicians.

Locked into these myths, the politicians concluded something like the following, albeit not in philosophical terms: If women, whose role is to be and not to do, angrily enter the realm of politics and zealously start acting, something is rotten in the current situation; one should lend an ear. In short, the fact that women entered the political realm and struggled for an issue was wonderful; the fact that they entered it as mothers was problematic for feminism, since it accepted some of the prevailing conceptions and prejudices concerning women; but these conceptions and prejudices were also a source of power for these struggling women. In short, we have a dialectical situation in which former conceptions and prejudices must be surpassed, but they can only be surpassed by being utilized, which means that they are partially accepted.

A similar dialectic exists with the reading of the Bible and of Jewish sources, which are written in patriarchal language and which degrade and disparage women. Changing the language is not a viable option, since I suspect that much of the force and beauty of these texts will be lost with such alterations. On the other hand, discarding all Jewish sources is an alienating of oneself to one's heritage and will often discourage all striving for spiritual goals. Hence, as suggested previously, one must accept that these are the sources that comprise one's heritage, but one must cut oneself off from those sections which do not allow one to pursue a spiritual existence here and now. I do not only reject, but forcefully cut myself off from all those precepts of Leviticus and other sections of the Bible which enslave women, even while learning from the Bible how to struggle for freedom and to live a life of faith. In short, one should accept the spirit of the text in order to go beyond it.

Here is an example that accords with my discussion of how one should read the Bible. In struggling for feminism, I hold that our situation resembles Jacob's night-long wrestling with the angel at the ford of Jabbok before he entered the Promised Land (Genesis 32, 23–31). In order to enter the "Promised Land" of equality and freedom between Jewish men and women, each Jew and Jewess must leave behind not only certain precepts and customs. Each person must be willing to undergo a painful struggle that will change one's identity, much as Jacob was willing to wrestle all night with an angel even after his thigh was wounded. Jacob was subsequently blessed with a new name, Israel, and with this name his new identity was affirmed. He was no longer the Jacob who had tricked his brother, Esau, out of his birthright and blessing; he was Israel who "hast striven with men and God and hast prevailed" (Genesis 32, 29). As many men and women who have struggled to change prevailing norms and customs have learned, the outcomes of such a wrestling are far from clear; but without it no new identity can emerge.

Concerning this story our rabbis asked. Why did Jacob return to the far side of the Jabbok ford? After all, he had already transferred everything that was dear to him—his wives, his children, his property—to the Promised Land. Why, then, did Jacob return? And they answer: To retrieve small odds and ends. True to the rabbis' thinking, often our unwillingness to let go of small odds and ends leads us to a fateful and painful wrestling; and only if we are determined to prevail in our struggle until dawn can this wrestling help one to attain a new identity.

But while learning the lessons of this text, and delighting in the rabbis vivid insights, I accept neither Jacob's nor the rabbis' way of relating to women, their male chauvinism. Moreover, I will use this text to show again and again the difficult process that each Jewish man and woman must undergo in order to transcend Jewish chauvinism and to live together as free and equal partners. I will proudly cite the rabbis' wisdom; but I will learn from this wisdom how to surpass the enslaving way of life preached and practiced by today's dogmatic rabbis. Only by pursuing such a dialectic can one remain faithful to the spirit of freedom at the core of the Bible.

Thus the need for dialogue, for political equality and full freedom for women is clear, but everything still needs to be done. The prevailing myths about the biological uniqueness of women (or men) and about equality between the sexes in Israel need to be surpassed, through adopting an approach that blends a continual quest for dialogue with a working for real political and economic equality between men and women. In struggling for a life of freedom and equality men and women together should develop a new relationship to the Bible and to the Jewish heritage. This relationship will include a cutting of oneself off from large segments of that heritage, such as the saying from the Jewish Fathers that whoever speaks much with women will inherit Gehenna.[8] Of course some rabbis will argue that the reason one inherits Gehenna is that while speaking with a woman one has stopped studying the Torah. Small consolation. Why, may we ask, did the honorable rabbis decide that women are not permitted to read or to study the Torah? And how do these honorable rabbis know that if one speaks with men, it is always in relation to the Torah? And how do they know that, say, speaking dialogically with a woman is less pleasing to God than the studying of the Torah? I could go on, but it is already clear that these apologists are merely attempting to interpret a degrading sexist saying in a manner that will camouflage their own misogynism.

Yet the new relationship to the Bible and to our Jewish heritage that I envision will not only be based on cutting oneself off from such passages. It will also include a learning from the wisdom of those passages in the Bible and in our heritage that can guide one to live one's freedom responsibly.

There is probably more of a groping in accepting this challenge than in responding to the other challenges that I have discussed. Perhaps because this challenge, of equality between the sexes, is the most visionary and novel at this moment; the intermediary goals of feminism and the means of attaining these goals are revolutionary in senses that we still do not, and perhaps cannot, foresee. But this is a healthy groping which deals with one's entire being and with one's manner of being-in-the-world. As in many other instances of seeking to enlarge the realm of human freedom, this groping may lead to a new emphasis on living as a spiritual being. I suspect, however, that this may only come into being if the concrete changes in men and women, at both the most profound and most superficial levels, open new paths to a life of dialogue and of sharing between the sexes.

NOTES

1. The incident is reported in Annie Cohen-Solal, *Sartre, A Life* (New York: Pantheon, 1987), p. 411.

2. Lesley Hazelton, "Israeli Women, Three Myths," in Susannah Heschel, *On Being a Jewish Feminist* (New York: Schocken, 1983), pp. 65–87.

3. Ibid., p. 69.

4. Ibid., p. 72.

5. Leah Rabin, *Always His Wife* [in Hebrew: *Col Hazman Ishto*] (Tel Aviv: Edanim/Yediot Ahronot, 1988).

6. Simone de Beauvoir, *The Second Sex* (New York: Alfred A. Knopf, 1953). Again and again in the entire book de Beauvoir rejects the idea of the woman as the Other, including the myths suggested above. Here is a passage from the introduction: "Now what peculiarly signalizes the situation of woman is that she—a free and autonomous being like all human creatures— nevertheless finds herself living in a world where men compel her to assume the status of the Other. They propose to stabilize her as object and to doom her to immanence since her transcendence is to be overshadowed and forever transcended by another ego (*conscience*) which is essential and sovereign" (p. xxix). To be an object is of course to be and not to do.

7. Friedrich Nietzsche, *On the Geneology of Morals* (New York: Random House, 1967), p. 163. The flight from freedom with the assistance of an ascetic ideal is one of the topics of Nietzsche's third essay in this study, which is highly relevant for much occurring in Israel.

8. *Sayings of the Jewish Fathers*, Chapter 1, Verse 5.

8

Art: A Gateway to Freedom and Dreaming

For three thousand years and more, due to the second commandment and to the norms prevailing in the diaspora, Jewish art was limited primarily to literature and to poetry. Sculpture, painting, pottery, ceramics, ballet, architecture, and nonreligious music were rarely admitted into the life of Jews. Only with the Jewish Enlightenment, and later with the return to Zion, was a beginning made in many of these arts; but Jews in Israel who wished to be artists had to learn from Masters in Europe and in the United States. Many of them were good students, quite a few were not. Israel has no Marc Chagall who emerged from a Jewish village in Russia to become a great artist. Jewish artists in Israel were not very original, nor have they created the beginnings of a tradition which may be called Israeli art. Given the artistic vacuum of three millennia which these artists are trying to fill, such can be understood. But no similar vacuum can excuse the paltry situation in Hebrew literature today.

Writers in Hebrew, after all, have the Bible, the Midrash, medieval literature, literature of the Enlightenment, Hasidic stories, and many other forms of literature to learn from—if they want to learn. Biblical writing, for instance, is neither an expression of a mood nor a playing around with language. The Biblical writer writes, the Biblical speaker speaks out, because he or she has something important to convey, something that comes from one's stomach, as we say in Hebrew. In the Bible very often words not only express an idea, or tell a story, or convey a message, they express the struggle for a faith based on freedom; again and again the Biblical text reveals that writing is an engagement. And here is where almost all contemporary

144

Hebrew writers are dishonest. They write to flee engagement, to escape the struggle for freedom.

Put bluntly, most Hebrew prose today is written by technicians with a spattering of poetic sensitivity. Israeli writers do not tell a story, they construct it; they do not write an essay, they assemble it. To endow their work with a facade of unity they embroider it with poetic epigrams. Instead of struggling with language so as to make it transparent to a reality which demands change, they poeticize phrases and sentences and surround the reader with complexity so as to better obscure a corrupt reality which sustains them. Worse. They refuse to penetrate into the core of the existential problems that face us; they are masturbators, not lovers. Hebrew for them is a plaything, not a tool that helps one illuminate a vision, a way of life. In short, they use Hebrew in order to play with a reality that they dare not lovingly confront. Enough! Let me prove some of this.

But first, why is this so important? Even if we accept your conclusions concerning the sad state of Israeli art, what does it have to do with making room for dreams? And why this scalding hostility against Hebrew literature? Are you waging a vendetta?

Of course I'm waging a vendetta, if one can call Nietszche's virulent attacks on the priests a vendetta. Many of today's poor writers have replaced—nay, probably they usurped—the priests whom Nietzsche despised. Not in the sense that they strive to arouse among the cowardly and the happily enslaved a recognition of one's sins and a feeling of guilt; but rather in their manner—make no mistakes, here these writers reveal originality!—of finding ways, without embracing the ascetic ideal,

to produce orgies of feeling. ... To wrench the human soul from its moorings, to immerse it in terrors, ice, flames, and raptures to such an extent that it is liberated from all petty displeasure, gloom, and depression as by a flash of lightening.[1]

By arousing orgies of feelings such a writer blinds readers to their sordid, squalid enslavement, to their impotency and insignificance, to their bland boredom in face of both the grandeur and the pettiness which surrounds them. This decadent writing helps such readers flee distress and depression. Its goal, again like the priest's eloquent sermons and vitriolic admonitions, is "to awaken men from their slow melancholy, to hunt away, if only for a time, their dull pain and lingering misery."[2] Of course I'm waging a vendetta! How can anyone who has joy in life, who seeks challenges to undertake, dreams to fulfill, who accepts the responsibility of living in freedom, not wage a vendetta against such writing?

Attacking these writers is important because they are breeders of impotence who, unlike a few Hebrew writers before Israel attained independence, dare not confront their fellow Israelis with challenges, with dreams. Consider Aharon Appelfeld, who recently received the Israel Prize for his contribution to Israeli literature, and who for decades has described the burdens of Jewish existence in the wake of the Holocaust. (The Holocaust is a popular theme in Israel!) The Jews whom he describes are all marked by an inability to overcome the terrible trauma called life. These emasculate persons encounter hollow depressing situations which their past does not let them surpass; they have no future, only sordid and painful memories to relive and suffer through; their sole quest is a respite from distress and misery. In short, true to the priestly tradition attacked by Nietzsche, the world depicted in Appelfeld's books is a vale of tears, devoid of human freedom, populated by nostalgic, feeble-minded, impotent travelers.

Haven't other writers, though, described feeblemindedness, or impotence, or an inability to overcome one's past—say Joyce, or Proust, or at the turn of the century in Israel, Y. H. Brenner? Of course, these writers depicted the mediocre, depressing, debilitating aspects of human existence, but not as an unending maze without the possibility of emerging into the light. Proust's discovery of how remembrance of things past arises through sensory encounters is a moment of elation; Brenner indicated that accepting impotency as a way of life leads to madness, from which one can escape only by learning to live with one's passions and by accepting responsibility for this world in this world; and Joyce, well, Appelfeld's embracing of sterility and impotence would never allow him to write something even faintly resembling the exhilaration of:

and then I asked him with my eyes to ask again yes and then he asked me would I yes to say yes my mountain flower and first I put my arms around him yes and drew him down to me so he could feel my breasts all perfume yes and his heart was going like mad and yes I said yes I will Yes.[3]

While Appelfeld is the high priest of nostalgic impotence, other writers explore the dregs of perversity—Amos Oz, A. B. Yehoshua, and Yoram Kanyuk are examples. The new hit in Israeli literature, David Grossman, is fervently following this trend. Exploring the sewage of human existence can be revealing, it can be an engagement, as Balzac, Zola, and in our century Gunter Grass and Jean Genet have brilliantly shown. What is crucial though is remembering that this sewage is the refuse that appears when human freedom is abused. It is not a determined state. As Sartre showed, persons choose their perversity as a flight from the responsibilities of freedom. But nothing of this flight, and hardly a faint glimmer of the possibility of evading perversity by choosing responsibility appears in the writings of the popular Israeli authors.

Put differently, these writers are already dead. They are writing for critics who will appreciate their ornated Hebrew, their embellished style, their aesthetically constructed plots, not for live readers who have to pick up their daily engagements and face new exigencies after putting down the book. Have they forgotten, or is it cowardice, which leads them to overlook that "In prose aesthetic pleasure is pure only if it is thrown into the bargain"?[4] (And Sartre adds, "I blush at recalling such simple ideas, but it seems that today they have been forgotten.") The fervent dedication of these authors to aesthetically presenting their heroes minute perversities leaves these heroes no freedom; that is why each person who populates their novels is described as a destiny and not a struggle for freedom, as a fate and not a beginning. Such is, of course, much simpler when the person described has already chosen his or her manner of inflicting self-pain so as to evade freedom.

Although some perversity in literature can be enlightening, when it reigns alone it demolishes the transparency of the literary endeavor. Only if, as in the works of Jean Genet or Gunter Grass, perversity is a reflection in a distorted mirror of our cowardly flight from responsibility, of our refusal to see the outcomes of our paltry acts, does it engage us. Only then does it, through our act of reflection, retain its required transparency. But this does not occur in the writings of Israeli authors. Once you step into their novels, you are in the company of abnormality as a norm, you have sunk into a swamp of boring mediocrity, and the reader is required to surrender to opaqueness. But remember, from mediocrity, from abnormality, from self-inflicted sickness, when one surrenders to opaqueness—no glory can emerge. Yes, Oz, Yehoshua, Kanyuk, Grossman, and most Israeli authors are writing books that exclude glory. Small wonder that in them one finds no room for dreams.

Writing about perversity can lead to an embracing of superficiality; but Israeli authors do not learn from Genet and Grass how to cope with this problem. The mirror of a distorted reality which Genet and Grass present is quickly recognized by the reader as a manner of skimming upon the surface of human existence. To ensure such a response they write so as to break down our identification with the persons and situations described—one cannot spontaneously identify with the deliberately retarded Oscar in Grass's *The Tin Drum*; one is forced to reflect upon the distortions that Oscar encounters, to go beyond them, to seek where change needs to be initiated. In Genet's *The Balcony* pervert fantasies lead persons to distorted perceptions of themselves, and to a flight from engaging in the making of history. The fantasies do not flatter us, or help us reach catharsis; they propel us to reflect, to think, to seek their meaning, to go beyond them and from a new perspective perceive the world and our manner of being-in-the-world. In short, they appeal to our freedom, to our ability to speak, to think, to engage in dialogue, to begin anew, to participate in the making of history. They also demand that we unmask the reality that leads persons to cherish such fantasies, to indulge in them, to seek their soothing superficiality.

But Israeli literature appeals specifically to the readers' fantasies, to his or her craving for a soothing superficiality. Hence the authors' dedication to perversity must not, dare not, leave cracks open for reflection, for engagement. A priestly, degrading, creativity flourishes; Oz, Yehoshua,

Kanyuk, and Grossman—and almost all other writers—seek and find ways of diverting the readers attention from the fact that their books continually portray a mediocrity that blocks all glory, a perversity that smothers all thinking. Prevalent among their manners of diversion are the poeticizing of prose, the psychologizing of persons and plots, and miring the reader in complex descriptions of obscenity and degradation. In short, to conceal their unwillingness to write honestly, these authors are best in developing techniques that flatter or indulge the reader.

Here is where the cart comes before the horse. Instead of striving to be published only if one has a story worth telling, a story that, to recall again a phrase from Isak Dinesin, when one finishes reading it the silence speaks—instead of thus questioning one's work, I suspect that these authors publish in order to prove that they have something to say. They do not tell a good story, which, in Buber's terms, relates to the whole being of the reader or, in Sartre's terms, appeals to the freedom of the reader; instead they depict a series of situations that pamper their readers' fantasies. They seem to have forgotten that without being honest, one cannot write a good story, a good essay, good prose. But if one's main concern is to flatter or to indulge the reader, a writer cannot be honest. Here, *I blush* at having to repeat such a simple truth.

Since their writings do not relate to the whole being of their readers, since their prose is opaque and is written so as to *not* be transparent to the world, since these writers do not appeal to the freedom of the reader, it is no surprise that none of the contemporary Israeli authors has attempted to cope with any of the spiritual challenges brought up in the preceding pages. As if the challenges I outlined were camouflaged and were not apparent to anyone who wishes to open his or her eyes. For instance, no contemporary Israeli author has struggled with the problem of women's liberation, or of faith, or of developing the realm of the in-between. Neither in an essay, nor in the manner that Tolstoy struggled with the problem of women's enslavement in *Anna Karenina*, or Dostoyevski struggled with the problem of faith through the trials and travails of Ivan and Alyosha Karamazov, or Sartre struggled with the problem of political freedom in his play *Dirty Hands*. Nor have they poignantly brought up any other spiritual challenges.

No! Don't mention the soap-opera-like novels (or plays) that appear periodically in Israel and depict the difficulties of love, sex, and marriage between a Jewish man and an Arab woman or vice versa. (For instance, A. B. Yehoshuah's novel *Lover* or Yehoshuah Sobol's play *The Palestinian Woman*.[5]) These are sordid attempts to pamper the reader's fantasies, and to blind him or her to the possibility of establishing dialogue and peace between Jews and Arabs in the Middle East. They do it, as mentioned above, by arousing orgies of feelings. In these books no Jew or Arab ever straightforwardly faces the challenge of dialogue as it emerges today in Israel. Desires and feelings are the sole motives for action. Yet perhaps I am asking too much. Perhaps the authors of these sentimental and orgiastic tales have become so committed to their priestly vocation, so engrossed in finding ways to arouse feelings, that they have forgotten what it means to respond to a spiritual challenge.

My vendetta still lacks one detail. I have not yet distinguished between a rebel and a committed writer. The committed writer will passionately take a stance—against the lack of spirituality, against corruption, against exploitation, or bigotry, or prejudice, against any approaches that destroy freedom. He or she will do so by naming things for what they are, and demanding that they be changed—immediately. (The Hebrew prophets exemplify such a commitment.) In contrast, the rebel will merely depict what he or she would call an unfortunate situation. This will arouse our compassion, or our hatred of the villain, or our identification with the misfortunes of the hero. But the situations depicted are closed. They lead nowhere. Unlike Leibnitz's monads they do not even adequately reflect the world beyond. This closedness allows the rebel to compromise with the authority, with the establishment: it permits him or her to not call a spade a spade. In short, the rebel is an accomplice. He or she knows that for one's career to flourish, for one to remain popular, it is better "to keep the forces of negation within a vain aestheticisim, a rebellion with effect."[6]

Outside of a few journalists, Israeli prose written today features no major committed writer. Here and there a rebel head is momentarily lifted, only to sink back into a swamp of listless languor.

With poetry everything is different. As Sartre points out, the poet "considers words as things, not as signs." This does not mean that words "have lost all signification in his [the poet's] eyes."[7] No, it is precisely the multiple significations of words which please and entice the poet, but not because these significations can become tools to change reality. From the poet's perspective the ability to signify aspects of reality is a property of the word, like its rhythm and tone. But unlike other properties which are pretty much fixed, this property has a fluidity that enriches the word, and makes it a fascinating building block for creating a verbal structure that will shimmer with meanings while delighting the ear. Or as Sartre indicated, prose uses words, poetry serves them.

Let me say immediately that there have been great Hebrew poets since the return to Zion and there currently are a few very good poets in Israel; Yehuda Amichai and Dalya Rabikovitch are two examples. In short there is a worthy tradition of Hebrew poetry, which has accompanied Jewish life since the period of the Enlightenment and which features names like Y. L. Gordon, Hayim Nahman Bialik, Zalman Schneur, Nathan Alterman, Avraham Shlonsky, Uri Zvi Greenberg, Leah Goldberg, and many others. But this flourishing of wonderful poetry only emphasizes the problem. Jews have learned to be servants of the word, not utilizers of it.

Some of the reasons are historical. I have repeatedly mentioned the fact that for two millennia political freedom was not a Jewish concern. Without such a concern writers of engaging prose will rarely emerge. What attitudes, then, did encourage the emergence of great poetry?

Central to Jewish life in the diaspora was the study of the Bible, the Talmud, and other texts. This studying was not pursued in order to relate to historical developments in the world; it was often a manner of fleeing from worldly involvement. The words of the holy texts were believed to have emanated from God; the Jew believed that they were divine things worthy of being fervently studied. These word-things were scrutinized and pored over so as to find magical links between them, to disclose their multiple associations, their mutual fitness, their congruity, their nuances. An ideal Jewish male was a scholar who was proud to display his ingenuity at revealing links, proposing associations, discovering congruity, and playing with nuances of words in the Bible. This poetic magical relationship to the words of the Bible, this viewing of the words as things one must serve, was also prominent in the developing of the Kabbalah and other trends of Jewish mysticism. Hence, Jewish poets were hardly breaking with the traditional manner of relating to Hebrew words when they took up their pens and started writing secular poetry.

As mentioned, poetry rarely leads its readers to attempt to act in the in-between. It appeals to one's feelings, to one's delight in rhythm and tone, to one's fascination with the magical association between words. Even when poetry appeals to one's dreams, it is not an explicit call to fulfill them, but rather a delighting in the expression of one's yearnings. Or as Sartre put it:

The writer of prose *speaks* to the reader, attempts to convince him in order to achieve unanimous agreement on one point or other; the poet speaks to himself through the mediation of the other. The writer of prose uses language as a middle term between himself and the Other; the poet makes use of the Other as an intermediary between language and himself.[8]

In other words, as I read the Bible nothing in it is poetry. It is all prose. Whatever aesthetic pleasure one receives from Psalm 23, or Ezekiel's vision of the dry bones, or Jacob's struggling with the angel, is thrown into the bargain. The words of the Bible are not things to be analyzed and played with. They are transparent; they indicate a reality. They describe existential situations in the long history of the encounter between Abraham and his progeny and God. They vividly portray the struggle for freedom that accompanies the quest for a life of faith; but this portrayal is also an appeal to each reader to assume the obligation to be free.

But what about Moses' and Miryam's songs after the crossing of the Red Sea and the drowning of Pharoah and his army (Exodus 15), or Deborah's song of victory (Judges 5), or David's lamenting the death of Jonathan

(Second Samuel 1), or *The Song of Songs?* Aren't these verses poetry? Of course these verses are poetry, but they are a borrowed poetry that exists to serve the prose. Moses', Miryam's, Deborah's, and David's words seemingly emerged spontaneously from the mouths of the speakers or singers when they found themselves in a situation in which a mere exclamation could not describe their feelings. And how can one express being overcome by worldly (or Godly) love except through verses like *The Song of Songs?* Here the Biblical writer, faced with the limitations of prose, borrowed some poetry, so as to convey with maximum transparency the situation that the writer was portraying. Yes, poetry in the Bible never exists in itself, as an independent entity, as a serving of language, as a mere wish to express one's feelings or thoughts. It is always part of the Biblical author's and editor's struggle to convey, with maximum transparency, the trials, travails, failures, and moments of enhancement that emerge when one strives to live a life of freedom which can lead to faith in God.

Contemporary poetry in Israel, unlike the poetry of the Enlightenment, or some of the poetry of Bialik, only very infrequently explicitly expresses a quest for freedom. Thus while Y. L. Gordon and Bialik wrote good poems which partially assumed the role of prose, such rarely occurs today. Still, Israeli poetry, like all good art, is an expression of freedom; as such it is a faint, often indiscernible call to live in dialogue and in freedom. But not much more.

The better architecture emerging in Israel today is a copying of the masters of the Western world. Most architecture, though, is mediocre and many buildings are fascist in style and reek of alienation—a curse for generations. Much building in Israel is government sponsored; hence very often myopic, dense bureaucrats decide on plans for entire neighborhoods, or for public buildings. I have already mentioned some of the outstanding architectural monstrosities built in recent years: the Jewish quarter in the old city of Jerusalem, and the Hebrew university on Mount Scopus (where many students feel trapped like a rat in a maze). But even when a person builds a private villa, the result is usually an eyesore. Jews build fortresses and monuments to reside in, not homes; the aesthetic mingling of form and function does not concern them, neither does the manner in which a building fits in with the surrounding landscape.

These eyesores, these monstrosities express better than a thousand books the fact that the Jew who is building a home, a town, a city, in the land of Israel views him/herself as a ruler, as an exploiter, not as a sojourner. Here is where we could have learned from our Arab neighbors, whose houses blend in with the landscape and do not rape it. And remember, exploiters do not engage in dialogue, they do not seek to establish an in-between and to live in freedom. What is more they assume no responsibility for future generations.

In a city whose buildings are alienating fascist fortresses or bland highrises, such as Beer Sheva where I reside, the encompassing architecture is not congenial to the emergence of dialogue or of political freedom. The boring cubical forms in which we move and live, and to which one cannot relate, demolish spontaneity; they smother one's ability to be a beginner. In short, most architecture in Israel is a blatant and often gaudy expression of the Jew's unwillingness to live in freedom, and as such it chokes off the spontaneity needed for freedom to emerge. This vulgar and alienating architecture also reveals the Jew's refusal to relate to the land as a sojourner, as a partner in dialogue to God and to the land He promised to Abraham and his progeny.

I have already mentioned that there is no tradition of Israeli painting or sculpture. There are Israelis who are painters and sculptors, some of whom have done fine work, none of whom are outstanding. Although some, like Yigal Tomarkin, are famous in Israel and are at times involved in political issues, their contribution as artists to a life of dialogue and to life in the in-between is almost nil. Perhaps such is inevitable, as Sartre pointed out:

The writer can guide you and, if he describes a hovel, make it seem the symbol of social injustice and provoke your indignation. The painter is mute. He presents you with a hovel, that's all. You are free to see in it what you like. ... The bad painter looks for the type. He paints the Arab, the Child, the Woman; the good one knows that neither the Arab nor the proletarian exists either in reality or on his canvas. He offers a workman, a certain workman. And what are we to think about a workman? An infinity of contradictory things. ... It is up to you to choose. Sometimes, high-minded artists try to move us. They paint long lines of workmen waiting in the snow to be hired, the emaciated faces of the unemployed, battlefields. They affect us no more than does Greuze with his "Prodigal Son." And that masterpiece, "The Massacre of Guernica," does anyone think that it won over a single heart to the Spanish cause?[9]

Sartre is exaggerating. It is true that painting and sculpture guide us much less than prose. Still, the masterpieces do guide us, even if by opening our eyes to new manners of perceiving the world. Of course I can choose to see in Degas' paintings and sculptures of dancers whatever I wish. But if I open myself to these works of art I will also sense the struggle of the body to be graceful. The hovel is not a palace; the dancer is not a workman; and it would require much self-deception to see in the hovel a palace or in the dancer a workman.

All this is rather academic in relation to Israeli painting and sculpture, since little of the art now being produced relates to the challenges or to the problems discussed in this book. Worse, one often senses that even the better artists engage in their vocation in order to flee the challenges of the world into the safe haven of their own personal feelings and impressions. Hence, when the artists do try to relate to what is happening they present us with gimmicks, or happenings, or even pranks. As if the true world were confined to their impressions, and the world outside those impressions can only be related to cynically or ludicrously. In such cases, the dialogical element of good art disappears.

One more point should be made. Many, if not most, Israeli artists do not differ from a common trend in contemporary art which seeks technical solutions to what the artist believes to be spiritual problems. Needless to say this trend expresses the widespread alienation that characterizes contemporary life; it has lovingly embraced the accepted belief that technical achievements can lead to a more spiritual existence. This belief is wrong, and, well, rather stupid. As I have repeatedly stressed in this book, a spiritual life is a responding to challenges, it is not a seeking of solutions to problems. Furthermore, I doubt that great art can emerge from steeping oneself in a reality of alienation. Personally, I feel sad to encounter art whose central engagement is a presenting of technical solutions—its creators have joined the enemies of spiritual existence.

There is not much to add concerning the other arts. Classical Israeli music is almost nonexistent. Popular music is greatly influenced by Western and Eastern pop-music. External influences also mold arts such as ceramics, photography, and dance. Drama is an exception. There have been playwrights—for instance, Hanoch Levin and Yehoshuah Sobol—who have written and produced plays that deal with some of the challenges I have described. They have utilized the stage to speak out against Jewish exploitation of Arabs, against dogmatic enslavement of Jews to a corrupt and spiritless religious establishment. But unfortunately they have been poor artists. They have not been able to create drama that is great in itself; it seems that their primary goal is to outrage the spectator or to lead him or her to a catharsis by unmasking an acute problem. Have they forgotten that good drama must have depth? Such depth can be attained by being a bard, as Shakespeare was, or by depicting life in light of a philosophy, as Brecht and Sartre did, or by pointing to the underlying, and often perverse motives of our gallant decisions, as occurs in Ibsen, Strindberg, Tennessee Williams, and Jean Genet, or in other manners. Plays centered around dramatic moments without depth, such as the major Israeli playwrights write, may be entertaining or even engaging; they are not expressions of the spirit.

This very brief survey has merely shown that art in Israel is hardly a gateway to freedom and dreaming.

Wait a minute! All I've read until now is your condemnation of Israeli prose and your critique of most Israeli art! How is art a gateway to freedom and dreaming? You haven't explained.

All right, let's return to the beginning.

Learning from existentialist writers, from Kierkegaard and Nietzsche to
Sartre and Buber, I believe that good art is the result of an act of creativity,
and only a free person can create. Of course some persons who did not enjoy
political freedom wrote good poetry or painted great portraits. That indicates
that the artist, in those conditions, succeeded in creating a "between"
between him- or herself and the work-of-art-being-created, and that he or she
related with his or her entire being to the work being produced. Later, when
others encountered the work of art there was a possibility of it arousing their
entire being, of a new "between" emerging between the spectator or reader
and the portrait or poem.

Prose goes further. It is a manner of engaging oneself in the world. Hence
it transcends Buber's "between" and relates to what occurs in the
in-between. Its readers can be moved to strive to change the world. The
transparency of words, their ability to address a specific situation and
demand a specific response, their capability to guide the reader along a
certain path—in short, the fact that words address the reader directly and
forcefully, as a member of a community that discusses its way of life—is what
makes prose the herald of political freedom.

Thus, art not only addresses one's aesthetic sensitivities. Good art is forged
on the anvil of freedom, and as such it embodies an appeal to the spectator's
or listener's or reader's freedom. Leaders of totalitarian regimes know this.
One of their first decrees is to ban or burn books, magazines, newspapers,
music, and to limit artistic expression. It is not the specific work of art that
perturbs or disturbs the leaders of these regimes; it is the appeal to freedom
embodied in that work.

Good art and especially good prose can also appeal to our capability to
dream of a better future. Such a belief underlies the entire approach of this
book. One lives one's freedom by responding to challenges, not by sitting
back and waiting. And one can only posit worthy challenges if one can dream
of a better future. The arts can complement prose by adding an often
much-needed sensitivity to one's dreams. The gracefulness of a vase or a
dancer, the harmony of a symphony or a painting, the passion and joy in life
expressed in an opera or a statue, the rhythm of a poem or a dance—all these
should guide one's dreams for a better future. Put differently, justice and
peace without harmony are problematic, a faith without passion and joy are
dogmatic, dialogue devoid of gracefulness becomes insipid—and I could go
on.

Hence, the lack of good prose in Israel and the sad state of most arts is
merely another aspect of the fact that few persons in Israel have the courage
to live their freedom. It is a harsh indicator of the fact that few persons are
willing to dream. And since the masturbating prose and the weary art that
one encounters is taken by most educated Israelis as art, as a reflection of
their way of life, it fulfills the degrading role of the priests whom Nietzsche

detested. But in an interesting manner; by masquerading as good art this paltry art promotes what Nietzsche called dishonest lies. The role of these lies is to blur the distinction between truth and falsehood. Yes, the sorry state of art in Israel supports the trend whereby:

Our educated people of today, our "good people," do not tell lies—that is true; but that is *not* to their credit! A real lie, a genuine, resolute, "honest" lie (on whose value one should consult Plato) would be something far too severe and potent for them: it would demand of them what one may not demand of them, that they should open their eyes to themselves, and they should know how to distinguish "true" and "false" in themselves. All they are capable of is a *dishonest* lie; whoever today accounts himself a "good man" is utterly incapable of confronting anything except with *dishonest mendaciousness*—a mendaciousness that is abysmal but innocent, truehearted, blueyed and virtuous. These "good men"—they are one and all moralized to their very depths and ruined and botched to all eternity as far as honesty is concerned: who among them could endure a single *truth* about man?[10]

NOTES

1. Friedrich Nietzsche, *On the Geneology of Morals*, trans. by Walter Kaufmann and R. J. Hollingdale (New York: Random House, 1967), p. 139.

2. Ibid., p. 140.

3. James Joyce, *Ulysses* (New York: Random House, 1961), p. 783.

4. Jean Paul Sartre, *What Is Literature* (New York: Washington Square Press, 1961), p. 16.

5. A. B. Yehoshuah, *Lover* (New York: Dutton, 1985). Yehoshuah Sobol's play *The Palestinian Woman* has not yet been translated into English.

6. Sartre, *What Is Literature*, p. 90.

7. Ibid., p. 5.

8. Jean Paul Sartre, *Saint Genet* (New York: Mentor, 1964), pp. 594–595.

9. Sartre, *What Is Literature*, pp. 3–4.

10. Nietzsche, *On the Geneology of Morals*, pp. 137–138.

SUMMARY

Accepting the Challenges

While I have been writing this book much has become worse in Israel. We are currently facing the *Intifada*, a national uprising of the Palestinian people whom we have been oppressing and exploiting on the West Bank and in the Gaza Strip for more than two decades. This uprising is not accepted for what it is—a national rebellion; government officials call the Arabs kids who throw rocks, wave Palestinian flags, and burn tires in the streets, the Arab women who protest and march, the men who plan the next uprising—lawbreakers. And this distorted view of what is happening in our own backyard is accepted by most Israeli Jews. In the process of dominating and exploiting these Arabs, many, if not most, Jews in Israel have adopted a colonial, apartheid attitude toward the Palestinians. Thus, the children and grandchildren of the persecuted wandering Jew do not mind trampling upon the freedom of almost two million Palestinians. Small wonder that most Jews in Israel ignore the challenges described in this book.

In such a situation one must speak out clearly. One must state forcefully and straightforwardly that our actions and attitudes are evil, and that they are corrupting the Zionist dream and degrading Jewish life in Israel. But make no mistakes. Speaking out for justice and peace today in Israel—especially after the 1988 elections, in which the trends of oppression described in this book received new impact—is like calling out in the desert; much too often one is comforted by the echo of one's own voice.

Thus, the challenges described above have rarely been mentioned or addressed in the past years. There is hardly any pursuit of justice in Israel—the word justice is something Jews refrain from using. The religious establishment is becoming more and more dogmatic, fanatic, and intolerant of human rights. There is little concern in Israel for a just and lasting peace with our Arab neighbors, there is little respect for the Palestinians as a people, and the defense Moloch continues to grow and to be worshiped and idolized. Women are not free, men and most institutions (which are run by males) are very macho-oriented; very few men and women are struggling to change this situation. Need I add that, wherever one turns, a bureaucratic approach to life reigns unmolested, and thinking and acting are forcefully discouraged.

So the question arises: How does one accept the challenges outlined in the preceding chapters? Where does one begin?

It hardly matters where one begins because the challenges are linked, they are merely different perspectives of a way of life. Furthermore, as existentialists have frequently pointed out, it is often wise to begin where one has chances of success, where one senses that one has the strength to change matters. Success or failure where one has strength will often lead one to take on newer, more difficult challenges.

On the abstract level everything seems clear. A person who pursues justice will engage in thinking and not mere problem-solving; he or she will seek peace and dialogue, equality between men and women, and a faith based on human freedom; he or she will also wish that art be an expression of freedom. The same is true of a person who strives to promote equality and dialogue between men and women, between Jews and Arabs. In short, abstractly it seems evident that a person responding to any of the challenges is bound to pursue other challenges. Everything becomes much more complex on the concrete level.

For instance, I suspect that Khomeini believes that he is pursuing a true faith in God, and that he is seeking justice, peace, and the good of the Iranian people and of all Moslems. All this despite the widespread oppression in Iran, despite the millions of victims of the Iran–Iraq war, which was the longest war of the twentieth century, despite the drying up of artistic creativity and even Islamic scholarship under his rule. Even though he has millions of fervent followers, Khomeini is wrong. Because, for persons to be able to respond to the challenges that I have outlined, they need to be able to live in the two spaces of freedom that I have described, Buber's "between" and Arendt's in-between. (Put differently, they need to be able to think, to act courageously on their thoughts, and to engage in dialogue.) Neither of these spaces is allowed to come into being in Khomeini's Iran.

I have repeatedly suggested that the existence of the "between" and the in-between are both criteria for examining whether freedom prevails in a society and a necessary basis for a life of freedom in any society. Hence, the first step in responding to the challenges described in this book requires establishing, through one's deeds, both spaces for freedom. Note, though, that the situation is circular. Because, responding wholeheartedly to any of the challenges is contingent on one's entering the spaces for freedom. One cannot struggle for justice if one does not enter the in-between; one cannot strive for equality between the sexes and disregard the need for dialogue between men and women.

I have made things too easy for myself; because too many people would agree with what I have just written and then go back to business as usual—to accepting prevailing injustices, to embracing our macho culture, to fanaticism in religion, to oppression of Arabs, to degrading women, to lack of thought and of dialogue. They have too much at stake in the present system to fight it, or so they perceive. Other people would counter by saying: Things are still too abstract. What do I do tomorrow? Where do I begin?

My vendetta against Israeli writers here reveals its significance. Because one cannot perceive what need be done if writers, journalists, judges, educators, politicians, and others who influence people through publicly conveying their response to the situation, persist in presenting enslavement as freedom, oppression as peacemaking, rebellion as lawbreaking, or faith as dogma. Still, the writers are those who have the ultimate responsibility of striving for clarity, because their vocation is to use words honestly, in order to see clearly what is happening, in order to demand change. Or, as Sartre put it, "The function of the writer is to call a spade a spade. If words are sick, it is up to us to cure them. Instead of that many writers live off this sickness."[11] In Israel almost all writers live off this sickness.

Thus accepting the challenges requires first of all naming the situation for what it is and perceiving that this situation can be changed by acting. Sartre points out that instead of naming situations and demanding change many writes indulge their readers with lengthy explanations or tantalizing descriptions that may disturb one's conscience, but do not demand action. "Description, even though it be psychological, is pure contemplative enjoyment; explanation is acceptance, it excuses everything."[2] With almost all Israeli writers, journalists, politicians, and educators producing barrages of descriptions and explanations for our debilitating, corrupt, and banal situation, with the Israeli in the street being daily flooded by a torrent of verbiage that never appeals to his or her freedom to act, and which persistently refuses to name the encompassing corruption and banality— with such a dishonest use of language prevailing wherever one turns, it is clear that the challenges outlined above are seldom named, let alone accepted.

Someone may ask, "Why should I accept your naming of the situation in Israel? You have not proved in detail that your naming is correct?" True. I am not holding that I have always named correctly. But, I have attempted to name correctly, honestly. I have not tried to use this naming to my benefit, or to evade naming by clever verbiage as a host of other writers, academicians, and political figures do. Furthermore, I'll be happy if other persons attempt to name correctly, and if they find mistakes in my naming, I'll learn from them and thank them. It should also be clear by now that my naming is only a preface to the dreams that I have been presenting. Hence, even if my naming is problematic, I still believe we should attempt to realize the dreams.

I have written this book because I believe that without courageous writers to depict the degradation of Zionism, without leaders who are willing to dream, the responsibility to name reality and to initiate change falls on the shoulders of each individual. Put differently, today in Israel there are no leaders, there are only followers; Nietzsche's worst nightmares about the rising tide of a feebleminded, sickly, debilitating, cowardly, mediocrity has become a reality in God's Promised Land. In *Thus Spake Zarathustra* Nietzsche indicates that when facing such degradation, one begins to be creative by destroying prevailing values and naming the encompassing cowardice for what it is. For me, such articulation is not enough. I would also demand that each person daily strive to fulfill some of the challenges. When there are no leaders, each person must lead him- or herself; when there are no visionaries, the blind must lead the blind. I firmly believe that even a groping attempt to think and to act, to engage in dialogue and to realize the specific challenges that I have described is a passing through the threshold of creativity, and a step in the direction of realizing a vision.

Of course, I am merely repeating Nietzsche's demands that persons undergo metamorphoses in order to become courageous and creative. No other remedies exist.

Often it is in the details that the response to a challenge is tested. Consider the Patriarch Abraham. According to Jewish tradition he wrote no beautiful resounding psalms to God like David, he did not free an enslaved people and then educate them to live in freedom like Moses, he built no magnificent temple like Solomon. Yet, Jewish lore has it that we are all forgiven our sins because of Abraham, Isaac, and Jacob. Since Abraham began this family of patriarchs we can ask: Why Abraham?

One good answer is that Abraham never overlooked the details. He traveled through the Promised Land, grazed his flocks, met with the residents, built altars, raised his sons, was tested by God—and every endeavor that he undertook he strove to do fully and perfectly. God sends three disguised angels to him; Abraham invites them to a meal, makes sure that they can wash their feet and hands, checks that their food is correctly prepared, and stands above them and waits on them during the entire meal. God tells him about the upcoming destruction of Sodom and Gomorrah; Abraham discusses the details of that decision, slowly bargaining with God, trying to save the cities if they include but ten just people. God tells him to sacrifice Isaac; Abraham says no word, he packs up and goes forth to fulfill the command, but he doesn't forget the wood, the fire, and the knife. In short, the saga of his life is a fulfilling of the popular saying: God is in the details.

Of course some readers may hold that Abraham made some mistakes, as when he lied to Pharaoh that Sarah was his sister. For me, that merely reveals his human dimensions. But his emphasis on the details, without being pedantic or dogmatic, can guide anyone who wishes to respond to challenges that lead to a vision. Belief in justice is a working for justice down to the minute details; striving to relate dialogically is done everywhere, not just in moments of euphoria or elation; struggling for political freedom means speaking up daily, acting daily, never giving up the struggle, even if the results are meagre and hardly encouraging. This is perhaps the main reason that it doesn't matter where one begins, because striving to fulfill the challenges that I have suggested in the details of our everyday existence can probably be done anywhere, every day.

But remember, Abraham was courageous. He cut himself off from the past and from the future, and thus he learned to see. He did not heed the details, as many cowards do, in order to evade the pursuing of a vision or its responsibilities. He heeded the details as a free person, because the details were important in fulfilling a vision, the vision of a people who would not worship idols but the one God, and who would attempt to set up a society according with God's wishes in the Promised Land. His attending to details reeks of the sweat, blood, and tears of a person of faith and vision who is struggling to bring something new and wonderful for all humankind into the world. In short, Abraham, the sojourner and traveler, the courageous struggling person described in Genesis, is a far cry from all the Talmud-regurgitating dogma-loving rabbis.

A very long list of things need to be changed immediately in Israel so as to begin to accept the spiritual goals described above. Such a list includes: Drafting a worthy constitution and a bill of rights which would limit the power of the executive branch of government; changing the electoral system in Israel so as to have Knesset members responsible to their constituents; eliminating all the laws that discriminate against women and Arabs; eliminating the political power of the rabbinate; accepting the fact that the Palestinians on the West Bank and in the Gaza Strip are entitled to a state of their own, if they so wish; cutting the government bureaucracy drastically; initiating broad educational programs that educate how to struggle for matters of principle in a democracy; diminishing the political power of the military by not letting retired generals enter politics for five years after their tenure of office; requiring all government offices and firms working with the government to encourage women to attain top ranks; passing and enforcing laws that would stop the pollution and contamination of the land, the water, and the air; limiting by law the cases for which the security branches can demand that they be judged secretly; not allowing any torture of suspects. I could go on.

Important as these measures may be, they are only a background for living the challenges mentioned above. Because to fully accept the challenges one must live them in one's daily engagements. With Nietzsche's Zarathustra one must know that, "There are a thousand paths that have never yet been trodden, a thousand forms of health and hidden islands of life. Man and man's earth are still unexhausted and undiscovered."[3] Put differently, one must be willing to make room for exciting, unheard of, crazily wonderful dreams.

NOTES

1. Jean Paul Sartre, *What Is Literature* (New York: Washington Square Press, 1961), p. 196.
2. Ibid., p. 201.
3. Nietzsche, *Thus Spake Zarathustra* (Middlesex, England: Penguin, 1961), p. 102.

Room for a New Vision

I can now formulate a basic assumption that has been accompanying everything written in the preceding pages. The only way to make room for dreams, for a new vision is by daily accepting challenges. To refer to Abraham one final time, it was not only his ability to cut himself off from the past and from the future that allowed him to see, it was also his ability to fulfill challenges, including their details. Accepting new challenges opens new vistas of reality for us, and forgoing challenges is a closing in upon oneself, an acceptance of ennui, a nearing of death.

One Biblical figure who repeatedly experienced the difficulties of accepting new challenges was Joseph, the dreamer. This book opened with the verse in which his brothers declare their wish to kill him, and I have not mentioned him again, except as an example of a person undergoing Zarathustra's metamorphoses. Joseph's story belongs here.

Joseph was a dreamer. How does his story differ from fairy tales about persons whose dreams come true?

One difference is that magic plays no role in Joseph's story—everything is human. No less significant is that God does not reveal Himself; Joseph is not a *Navi*, a bringer of God's word, he is a dreamer and an interpreter of dreams. I know he says that God helps him to explain Pharoah's dreams, and the Biblical author says that God blessed everything that Joseph did, but nowhere do we hear God speaking to Joseph directly as he spoke to his predecessors, or to Moses, to Samuel, to Isaiah, to Jonah.

Without magic or direct Godly intervention Joseph is left on his own. All he has are his childhood dreams and the challenges that he daily faces. He learns the depth of his brothers' hatred, the dangers of lust and betrayal through the incident with Potiphar's wife, the ingratitude of being forgotten by persons whom one assisted. Yet, he overcomes his difficulties, continues to accept challenges, and continues to dare to dream.

Daring to dream, that is Joseph's distinction, albeit his dreams did not lead to justice, or to equality, or to a vision of a humane existence. Still, one should learn from his courage: in responding to his enslavement, to his need to start from the bottom in a foreign land, to his being jailed for a crime he never committed, to his being summoned from jail to interpret Pharaoh's dreams. While courageously facing these challenges he never hesitated to dare to dream.

Zionism needs persons like Joseph. Persons who will not wait for external intervention. Persons who dare to make room for dreams in their life and are willing to pursue a vison. Persons with courage to accept the challenges of living justly and spiritually, and who will struggle against all those who daily reject, degrade, and defile our attempts to realize these challenges.

More than anything else, Israel needs persons who make room for dreams.

Selected Bibliography

Agnon, Shmuel Yosef. *In the Heart of Seas*. New York: Schocken, 1948.

———. *Days of Awe*. New York: Schocken, 1965.

———. *Twenty One Stories*. New York: Schocken, 1970.

———. *Two Tales*. Middlesex, England: Penguin, 1971.

Alterman, Nathan. *Shirim Mishecvar* [Poems from the Past]. Tel Aviv: Hakibbutz Hameuchad, 1972.

Altmann, Alexander. *Moses Mendelssohn, A Biographical Study*. Tuscaloosa, Ala.: University of Alabama Press, 1973.

Amichai, Yehuda. *Meahorei Col Ze Mistater Osher Gadol* [Behind All This a Great Happiness Is Hidden]. Tel Aviv: Schocken, 1976.

———. *Love Poems*. New York: Harper, 1981.

———. *Sheat Hahesed* [The Hour of Grace]. Tel Aviv: Schocken, 1983.

Appelfeld, Aharon. *Ashan* [Smoke]. Tel Aviv: Achshav, 1962.

———. *Haor Vehacootonet* [The Skin and the Tunic]. Tel Aviv: Am Oved, 1971.

———. *Michvat Haor* [Lightstroke]. Tel Aviv: Hakibbutz Hameuchad, 1980.

Arendt, Hannah. *The Origins of Totalitarianism*. New York: Harcourt Brace Jovanovich, 1951,

———. *The Human Condition*. Chicago, Ill.: University of Chicago Press, 1958.

———. *Between Past and Future*. New York: Viking, 1961.

———. *Eichmann in Jerusalem*. New York: Viking, 1963.

———. *On Revolution*. New York: Viking, 1963.

———. *Crises of the Republic*. New York: Harcourt Brace Jovanovich, 1969.

———. *Men in Dark Times*. London: Jonathan Cape, 1970.

———. *The Life of the Mind*. New York: Harcourt Brace Jovanovich, 1978.

Beauvoir, Simone de. *The Second Sex*. New York: Knopf, 1953.

Bein, Alex. *Theodore Herzl: A Biography*. Philadelphia, Pa.: Jewish Publication Society of America, 1940.

Benziman, Uzi. *Lo Otzer Beadom* [Sharon: An Israeli Caesar]. Tel Aviv: Adam, 1985.

Berdyaev, Nicolas. *Slavery and Freedom*. New York: Scribner, 1944.

———. *The Fate of Man in the Modern World*. Ann Arbor, Mich.: University of Michigan, 1961.

———. *Dream and Reality*. New York: Collier, 1962.

Boll, Heinrich. *Group Portrait with Lady*. Middlesex, England: Penguin, 1976.

———. *The Train Was on Time*. Middlesex, England: Penguin, 1979.

Brenner, Joseph Hayyim. *Ctavim* [Writings]. Tel Aviv: Hakibbutz Hameuchad, 1978.

———. *Breakdown and Bereavement*. Ithica, N.Y.: Cornell University Press, 1971.

Buber, Martin, *Between Man and Man*. London: Fontana, 1947.

———. *Tales of the Hasidim, Early Masters*. New York: Schocken, 1947.

———. *Tales of the Hasidim, Later Masters*. New York: Schocken, 1947.

———. *Israel and the World*. New York: Schocken, 1948.

———. *Two Types of Faith*. New York: Harper, 1951.

———. *Eclipse of God*. New York: Harper, 1952.

———. *Good and Evil*. New York: Scribner, 1952.

———. *The Tales of Rabbi Nachman*. New York: Avon, 1956.

———. *Pointing the Way*. New York: Harper, 1957.

———. *Hasidism and Modern Man*. New York: Harper, 1958.

———. *Moses*. New York: Harper, 1958.

———. *Paths in Utopia*. Boston: Beacon, 1958.

———. *The Origin and Meaning of Hasidism*. New York: Harper, 1960.

———. *The Prophetic Faith*. New York: Harper, 1960.

———. *I and Thou*. New York: Scribner, 1965.

———. *On Judaism*. New York: Schocken, 1967.

———. *On the Bible*. New York: Schocken, 1968.

———. *The Legend of the Baal Shem*. New York: Schocken, 1969.

Burke, Edmund. *Edmund Burke, The Harvard Classics*. New York: Collier, 1937.

Cohen-Solal, Annie. *Sartre, A Life*. New York: Pantheon, 1987.

Conrad, Joseph. *Lord Jim*. Middlesex, England: Penguin, 1949.

———. *Heart of Darkness & The Secret Sharer*. New York: New American Library, 1980.

Dinesin, Isak. *Last Tales*. Chicago, Ill.: University of Chicago Press, 1957.

———. *Anecdotes of Destiny and Ehrengard*. New York: Vintage, 1985.

Dostoyevski, Fyodor. *The Possessed*. New York: Signet, 1956.

———. *Crime and Punishment*. New York: Signet, 1957.

———. *The Brothers Karamazov*. New York: Signet, 1956.

———. *The Idiot*. New York: Bantam, 1981.

Elon, Amos. *Herzl*. New York: Schocken, 1966.

Faulkner, William. *The Sound and the Fury*. New York: Signet, 1959.

———. *Light in August*. Middlesex, England: Penguin, 1960.

———. *Requiem for a Nun*. Middlesex, England: Penguin, 1960.

Frankl, Viktor E. *Psychotherapy and Existentialism*. Middlesex, England: Penguin, 1967.

Freud, Sigmond. *Psychopathology of Everyday Life*. New York: Norton, 1971.

Frost, Robert. *The Poetry of Robert Frost*. New York: Holt, Rinehart and Winston, 1964.

Genet, Jean. *The Maids*. London: Faber and Faber, 1953.

———. *Deathwatch*. London: Faber and Faber, 1954.

———. *The Balcony*. London: Faber and Faber, 1957.

Gordon, A. D. *Selected Essays*. New York: League for Labor Palestine, 1938.

Gordon, Haim. *Dance, Dialogue, and Despair: Existentialist Philosophy and Education for Peace in Israel*. Tuscaloosa, Ala.: University of Alabama Press, 1986.

————. *The Other Martin Buber, Recollections of His Contemporaries*. Athens, Ohio: Ohio University Press, 1988.

Gordon, Haim, and Grob, Leonard. *Education for Peace: Testimonies from World Religions*. New York: Orbis, 1987.

Grass, Gunter, *The Tin Drum*. Middlesex, England: Penguin, 1965.

————. *Local Anaesthetic*. Middlesex, England: Penguin, 1973.

Greenberg, Uri Zvi. *Rehovot Hanahar* [Streets of the Stream]. Tel Aviv: Schocken, 1978.

Harkabi, Y. *The Palestinian Covenant and Its Meaning*. London: Valentine, Mitchel, 1979.

Hemingway, Ernest. *For Whom the Bells Toll*. Middlesex, England: Penguin, 1955.

————. *The Old Man and the Sea*. Middlesex, England: Penguin, 1966.

Herzl, Theodore. *The Jewish State*. New York: American Zionist Emergency Committee, 1946.

————. *Altneuland*. Haifa: Haifa Publishing, 1960.

Heschel, Susannah. *On Being a Jewish Feminist*. New York: Schocken, 1983.

Hobbes, Thomas. *Leviathan*. Middlesex, England: Penguin, 1968.

Hussein, Taha. *An Egyptian Childhood*. London: Heinemann, 1981.

————. *The Stream of Days*. London: Longman's Green, 1948.

Idris, Yusuf. *The Cheapest Nights and Other Stories*. London: Heinemann, 1978.

Jabotinsky, Ze'ev. *Samson*. New York: Judea Publishing, 1945.

————. *Zichronot Ben Doro* [Memories of a Member of His Generation]. Tel Aviv: Amichai, no date listed.

James, William. *Varieties of Religious Experience*. New York: Macmillan, 1961.

Joyce, James. *Ulysses*. New York: Vintage, 1961.

Kafka, Franz. *The Castle*. New York: Knopf, 1952.

————. *Amerika*. New York: Schocken, 1962.

————. *Letter to His Father*. New York: Schocken, 1962.

————. *The Trial*. New York: Schocken, 1968.

————. *The Complete Stories*. New York: Schocken, 1976.

Kanyuk, Yoram. *Hasipur Al Doda Shlomzion Hagdola* [The Story of the Big Aunt Shlomzion]. Tel Aviv: Hakibbutz Hameuchad, 1976.

————. *Hayehudi Haharon* [The Last Jew]. Tel Aviv: Hakibbutz Hameuchad, 1982.

Kierkegaard, Soren. *Fear and Trembling*. Princeton, N.J.: Princeton University Press, 1941.

————. *Either/Or*. Princeton, N.J.: Princeton University Press, 1949.

————. *Concluding Unscientific Postscript*. Princeton, N.J.: Princeton University Press, 1968.

Kook, Abraham Isaac. *The Lights of Penitence, Lights of Holiness, The Moral Principles, Essays, Letters, and Poems*. New York: Paulist, 1978.

Lawrence, T. E. *Seven Pillars of Wisdom*. Middlesex, England: Penguin, 1962.

Lacquer, Walter. *The Israel–Arab Reader*. New York: Bantam, 1969.

————. *A History of Zionism*. New York: Schocken, 1972.

Lebovitz, Yishayahu. *Yahadut, Am Yehudi, Umdinat Yisrael* [Judaism, Jewish Nation and the State of Israel]. Tel Aviv: Schocken, 1979.

Lukacs, Yehuda. *Documents on the Israeli-Palestinain Conflict 1967–1983.* Cambridge: Cambridge University Press, 1984.

Machiavelli, Niccolo. *The Portable Machiavelli.* Middlesex, England: Penguin, 1979.

Mahfouz, Naguib. *Miramar.* London: Heinemann, 1974.

————. *Midaq Alley.* London: Heinemann, 1976.

————. *Children of Gebelawi.* London: Heinemann, 1981.

Mantell, David Mark. *True Americanism: Green Berets and War Resisters.* New York: Teachers College Press, 1974.

Marcel, Gabriel. *The Mystery of Being* (2 vols.). Chicago: Gateway, 1960.

————. *The Philosophy of Existentialism.* Secaucus, N.J.: Citadel, 1956.

Maslow, Abraham. *Religions, Values, and Peak-Experiences.* Middlesex, England: Penguin, 1976.

Merleau-Ponty, Maurice. *Phenomenology of Perception.* London: Routledge and Kegan Paul, 1962.

————. *Signs.* Evanston, Ill.: Northwestern University Press, 1964.

Montesquieu, Baron de. *The Spirit of the Laws.* New York: Macmillan, 1949.

Nietzsche, Friedrich. *Thus Spake Zarathustra.* Middlesex, England: Penguin, 1961.

————. *Beyond Good and Evil.* New York: Vintage, 1966.

————. *Twilight of the Idols.* Middlesex, England: Penguin, 1968.

————. *On the Geneology of Morals.* New York: Vintage, 1969.

————. *The Gay Science.* New York: Vintage, 1974.

————. *Daybreak.* Cambridge: Cambridge University Press, 1982.

————. *Human All Too Human.* University of Nebraska Press, 1984.

Oz, Amos. *Elsewhere Perhaps.* New York: Harcourt Brace Jovanovich, 1985.

————. *A Perfect Peace.* Middlesex, England: Penguin, 1986.

Peters, Joan. *From Time Immemorial.* New York: Harper & Row, 1984.

Proust, Marcel. *Remembrance of Things Past.* New York: Random House, 1934.

Rabin, Leah. *Col Hazman Ishto* [Always His Wife]. Tel Aviv: Edanim/Yediot Ahronot, 1988.

Rawls, John. *A Theory of Justice.* Cambridge, Mass.: Harvard University Press, 1971.

Rogers, Carl. *Encounter Groups.* Middlesex, England: Penguin, 1969.

Rosenzweig, Franz. *The Star of Redemption.* Boston: Beacon Press, 1964.

Sager, Samuel. *The Parliamentary System of Israel.* Sycaruse, N.Y.: Syracuse University Press, 1985.

Salih, Tayeb. *Season of Migration to the North.* London: Heinemann, 1976.

Sartre, Jean Paul. *No Exit and Three Other Plays.* New York: Vintage, 1949.

————. *Being and Nothingness.* New York: Washington Square Press, 1956.

————. *The Devil and the Good Lord and Other Plays.* New York: Vintage, 1960.

————. *Altona, Men Without Shadows, The Flies.* Middlesex, England: Penguin, 1962.

————. *Antisemite and Jew.* New York: Black Cat, 1962.

————. *Literary and Philosophical Essays.* New York: Collier, 1962.

————. *Saint Genet.* New York: Mentor, 1963.

————. *The Words.* Greenwich, Conn: Fawcet, 1964.

————. *Nausea.* Middlesex, England: Penguin, 1965.

————. *Situations.* Greenwich, Conn.: Fawcett, 1965.

————. *Essays in Aesthetics.* New York: Washington Square Press, 1966.

————. *The Psychology of Imagination.* New York: Washington Square Press, 1966.

————. *What Is Literature?* New York: Washington Square Press, 1966.

————. *Search for a Method*. New York: Vintage, 1968.

————. *Sketch for a Theory of the Emotions*. London: Methuen, 1971.

————. *Existentialism and Humanism*. London: Methuen, 1973.

————. *Critique of Dialectical Reason*. London: NLB, 1976.

————. *Between Existentialism and Marxism*. New York: Morrow Quill, 1979.

Schiff, Zeev, and Ya'ari, Ehud. *Israel's Lebanon War*. New York: Simon and Schuster, 1984.

Shiffer, Shimon. *Cadur Hasheleg* [Snowball: The Story behind the Lebanon War]. Tel Aviv: Yediot Ahronot, 1984.

Smith, Gary, V. *Zionism, The Dream and The Reality*. New York: Barnes and Noble, 1974.

Tolstoy, Leo. *Anna Karenina*. New York: Signet, 1961.

————. *War and Peace*. New York: Signet, 1968.

Wald, Emanuel. *Killat Hacelim Hashvurim* [The Curse of the Broken Tools]. Tel Aviv: Schocken, 1987.

Weizmann, Chaim. *Trial and Error*. New York: Harper, 1949.

Wood, Gordon, S. *The Creation of the American Republic 1776–1787*. New York: Norton, 1972.

Wyschogrod, Michael. *The Body of Faith*. New York: Seabury, 1983.

Yehoshua, A. B. *Late Divorce*. New York: Doubleday, 1984.

————. *Lover*. New York: Dutton, 1985.

Index

Adorno, Theodore, 101
Africa, 25
Agnon, Shmuel Yosef, 10, 53, 58, 79
Aloni, Shulamit, 59, 93
Alterman, Nathan, 149
Amalek, 113
Amichai, Yehuda, 149
Apocrypha, 75
Appelfeld, Aharon, 59, 145, 146
Arendt, Hannah, 2, 11, 15, 18, 23, 26, 28,
    29, 30, 31, 32, 33, 34, 37, 38, 39, 42,
    43, 47, 48, 71, 75, 78, 88, 89, 94, 160
Assad, Hafez, 106
Avneri, Uri, 92

Baal Shem Tov, 108
Babylonians, 105
Balzac, Honoré de, 58, 146
Bank Leumi, 100
Basel, 13
Bashevis Singer, I., 58
Beauvoir, Simone de, 136–38; *The Second
    Sex,* 138
Beer Sheva, 60, 152
Begin, Menachem, 29, 41, 70, 101
Ben Gurion, David, 26, 30, 71, 106, 112,
    126

Ben Gurion University, 48
Berdyaev, Nicolas, 44, 46–49, 53, 64–65,
    91; *Slavery and Freedom,* 46
Bialik, Hayim Nachman, 149, 151
Bible, 3, 11, 14, 18–19, 41, 47–48, 50–51,
    57–58, 64–78, 105–18, 127, 140–43,
    145, 150–51
Bloch, Jochanan, 46
Bnai Brak, 112
Böll, Heinrich, 34
Brecht, Berthold, 153
Brenner, Yosef Hayyim, 10, 58, 146
British Army, 115, 137
Brutus, 17, 58, 68
Buber, Martin, 2–3, 7–9, 11, 18, 23,
    27–29, 32, 39, 44–46, 49, 58, 64–66,
    71, 73, 75, 77–78, 96, 98–99, 116, 118,
    139–40, 148, 154, 160; *I and Thou,* 116,
    139
Burke, Edmund, 124–25

Camp David, 29
Cambodia, 43
Catholicism, 69
Chagall, Marc, 144
China, 25
Chamberlain, Sir Arthur Neville, 39

Christianity, 4
Churchill, Sir Winston, 29
Cohen, Ran, 89
Conrad, Joseph, 117; *Heart of Darkness*,
    117
Crusade, 68

Degania, 136
Degas, Edgar, 153
Diaspora, 5, 8, 14–15, 25, 31, 57–59, 64,
    69, 75, 105, 112, 123
Dinesin, Isak, 56–57, 148; *Anecdotes of
    Destiny*, 56
Dostoyevski, Fyodor, 2, 6, 9, 11, 33, 58,
    69–70, 77, 95, 109, 148; *The Brothers
    Karamazov*, 6, 9, 58, 69, 109; *Crime and
    Punishment*, 33; *The Idiot*, 33
Dreyfus, Alfred

Egypt, 5, 9, 16, 24, 51, 79, 133–34
Eichmann, Adolf, 33–34, 37–39
Eisek of Krakow, Rabbi, 83
England, 124
English Parliament, 26
Ethiopia, 73
Ervin, Sam, 92
Europe, 46, 87, 144

Fackenheim, Emil, 68–69
Fascism, 34, 96
Faulkner, William, 58, 77; *Requiem for a
    Nun*, 58
Feminism, 138–43
Fiji Islands, 25
France, 101, 123
Francis, Saint, 68
Frankfurt, 13
Freud, Sigmund, 28

Galilee, 16, 109
Gandhi, Indira, 137
Gandhi, Mahatma, 39
Gan Shmuel, 89
Gaon, Sadyah, 75
Gaza Strip, 15–16, 35–36, 41, 43, 54, 56,
    71, 96, 124–25, 129–30, 132–34, 159,
    163

Genet, Jean, 146–47, 153; *The Balcony*,
    147
Germany, 34, 39, 40, 45–46, 101
Gide, André, 58
Goethe, Johann Wolfgang von, 77
Golan Heights, 109
Goldberg, Leah, 149
Gomorrah, 77, 113, 162
Gorbachev, Mikhail, 87
Gordon, A. D., 87
Gordon, Y. L., 149, 151
Grass, Günter, 34, 146–47; *The Tin Drum*,
    147
Greece, 35, 43
Greenberg, Uri Zvi, 149
Grossman, David, 146–47
Gur Yeshiva, 109–10

Haaretz, newspaper, 41
Habermas, Jürgen, 101
Hadashot, newspaper, 112
Haganah, 123, 137
Halakhah, 57, 69, 70, 74, 117–18
Hamlet, 33
Hasidism, 75
Hazelton, Lesley, 136–37, 141
Hebrew University, 72
Hebron, 51
Heidegger, Martin, 43
Hemingway, Ernest, 58; *For Whom the
    Bell Tolls*, 58
Herzl, Theodore, 4, 9, 13–14, 26, 43, 47,
    52, 100; *The Jewish State*, 4, 9
Histadrut, 100, 102
Hitler, Adolf, 32, 39, 40, 45, 75, 106, 118;
    Mein Kampf, 55
Hobbes, Thomas, 6, 42, 91, 99; *Leviathan*,
    6, 91
Holocaust, 9, 34, 41, 105–6, 146
Horkheimer, Max, 101
Hungary, 13, 47
Hussein, King, 35, 129

Iago, 33
Ibsen, Henrik, 153
Iceland, 25
India, 25, 124

Intifada, 125–26, 130, 132, 159
Iran, 88, 94, 117, 160
Iraq, 73, 160
Ismaelites, 51
Israel Defense Force, 4–5, 7, 43, 52, 54, 84, 93, 96, 123–33, 137
Israeli Security Service, 92, 93
Israel's Declaration of Independence, 137

Jabotinsky, Ze'ev, 52, 71
James, William, 31
Jerusalem, 16, 33, 41, 60, 72, 109, 115, 124–25, 133, 151
Jesus, 44, 54, 69
Jordan, 129
Jordan River, 15, 109
Joyce, James, 58, 146
Judah Loew, Rabbi, 125
Julius Caesar, 68
Jung, Carl Gustav, 28

Kabbalah, 75, 150
Kadaffi, Muamar, 106
Kafka, Franz, 6, 8, 11–12, 28, 33, 58; *Amerika*, 33; *The Castle*, 8, 33; *The Trial*, 33
Kahane, Meir, 25, 55, 117
Kanyuk, Yoram, 59, 146–48
Keshet, 112
Kibbutz, 4–5, 26, 32–33, 40, 48, 52–53, 84–103, 113, 136–37
Kierkegaard, Soren, 2, 9, 33, 44, 118, 154; "Diary of the Seducer," 33
Khmer Rouge, 43
Khomeini, Ayatullah, 68, 106, 117, 160
King, Martin Luther, 30, 59
Knesset, 26, 30–31, 59, 70–71, 89, 93–94, 98, 100, 102, 118, 131, 163
Kook, Abraham Isaac, 114, 116
Koran, 68, 77
Krakow, 83
Ku Klux Klan, 37
Kupat Holim, 100

Labor Party, 1, 31, 35, 43, 100
Lawrence of Arabia (T. E.), 121–22

Lebanese War, 70, 98
Lebanon, 41, 94, 123, 127–28, 130–31
Lebovitz, Yishayahu, 112, 118, 127
Leibnitz, G. W., 149
Levi, Moshe, 130–31
Levin, Hanoch, 153
Likud party, 31, 35, 43
Livy, 77
Louis Philippe, 15

Maariv, newspaper, 112
Maccabees, Books of, 75
Macbeth, 33
Machiavelli, Nicolo, 129
Mahfouz, Naguib, 68
Maimonedes, Moses, 75
Mantell, David Mark, 128; *True Americanism: Green Berets and War Resisters*, 128
Marcel, Gabriel, 44
Marcuse, Herbert, 101
Marx, Karl, 4–5, 86, 101
Marxism, 47, 86, 90
Masada fortress, 9
Maslow, Abraham, 31
Meir, Golda, 1–2, 4, 6–7, 71, 112, 137
Mendele Mocher Sfarim, 58
Mendelsson, Moses, 15
Merhavia, 136–37
Merleau-Ponty, Maurice, 90, 101
Messiah, 13–14, 48
Mexico, 42
Middle East, 36, 57, 106, 117, 121–22, 124, 129, 132–34, 148
Mirabeau, H. G. V. R., 92
Mohammed, 54
Montesquieu, Baron de, 56
Morocco, 73
Mothers Against War, 140
Mozart, Amadeus, 77; "The Magic Flute," 77
Mrom Hagolan, 85
Mussolini, Benito, 96

Nablus, 60
Napoeon III, 15
Nazis, 34, 41, 45, 69, 128

Nazism, 37
Nebuchadnezzar, 105
Negev, 16
Neve, Kobi, 59
New Testament, 68, 77
Nietzsche, Friedrich, 2, 7, 11, 23, 33, 38,
    44, 50–53, 55, 78, 103, 109–10, 126,
    138, 140, 145–46, 154–55, 162, 164;
    Thus Spake Zarathustra, 7, 50, 78, 162
Nixon, Richard, 94–95
North Korea, 24

Old Testament, 44
Oz, Amos, 1–2, 7, 36–38, 59, 146–47; *In
    the Land of Israel*, 36–37

Palestinian Covenant, 134
Palestinians, 35, 49, 125, 129–30,
    132–34, 159–60, 163
Peres, Shimon, 48, 129
Peretz, Yitzchak, 111
Plato, 10–11, 18, 31, 37–38, 42, 53–54,
    77, 87–88, 93, 103, 124, 129; *Gorgias*,
    37–38, 42; *Protagoras*, 38, 133; *The
    Republic*, 10, 37–38, 42, 53, 87, 103;
    Symposium, 38
PLO, 134
Poland, 41, 73
Polard, Jonathan, 94
Pol Pot, 43
Prague, 83, 125
Proust, Marcel, 41, 48, 58, 77, 146;
    Remembrance of Things Past, 48
Prussia, 92

Rabikovitch, Dalya, 149
Rabin, Leah, 137; *Always His Wife*, 137
Rabin, Yitzchak, 131, 133
Racism, 25, 48, 54–56, 96, 99
Rashi, 75
Rawls, John, 101
Red Sea, 79
Rogers, Carl, 27
Rome, 68, 72
Rosenzweig, Franz, 77; *The Star of
    Redemption*, 77
Rothschilds, 15

Roumania, 73
Russia, 49, 73, 146

Sadat, Anwar, 29, 129
Sadyah Gaon, 75
Sarid, Yossi, 59
Sartre, Jean Paul, 2, 4–5, 7, 9, 24, 28, 33,
    38, 44, 85–86, 88, 89, 90, 101, 136,
    140, 146–50, 152–53, 155, 161; *Altona*,
    33; *Dirty Hands*, 148; *Nausea*, 7; *No
    Exit*, 33; *Search for a Method*, 86
Schneur, Zalman, 149
Scopus, Mount, 72, 151
Security Service, 93, 124
Shakespeare, William, 58, 77, 153; *Julius
    Caesar*, 58
Shamir, Yitzchak, 126
Sharon, Ariel, 70, 98
Shlonsky, Avraham, 149
Sinai, Mount, 13, 68, 73, 79
Sobol, Yehoshuah, 148, 153
Socrates, 17, 34, 37–38, 52, 68
Sodom, 77, 112, 162
Solzhenitsyn, Alexander, 28, 34; *The
    Gulag Archipelago*, 34
Sophocles, 94; *Ajax*, 94
South America, 25
Soviet Union, 16, 24, 73, 87, 123
Spinoza, Baruch, 41–42
Sri Lanka, 25
Strindberg, August, 153
Syria, 24, 130

Talmud, 13, 74–75, 106, 108, 150, 163
Tel Aviv, 15–16, 133
Tel Aviv University, 102
Tillich, Paul, 69
Tolstoy, Leo, 58, 127, 148; *Anna Karenina*,
    58, 148; *War and Peace*, 127
Tomarkin, Yigal, 152
Totalitarianism, 24, 39
Turks, 32, 52

United Nations, 26, 37, 59
United States, 101, 123, 126, 144
Uruguay, 24

Van Gogh, Vincent, 70
Vietnam, 128
Voltaire (François-Marie Arouet), 103

Wald, Emanuel, 130–32
Watergate scandal, 94
Weizman, Chaim, 26, 52
West Bank, 15–16, 35–36, 41, 43, 54, 56,
    71, 96, 124, 129, 130, 132, 134, 159,
    163
Western Europe, 39
Western world, 30
Wiesel, Elie, 126
Williams, Tennessee, 153

Wittgenstein, Ludwig, 95

Yemen, 73
Yediot Ahronot, newspaper, 112, 126
Yehoshua, A. B., 59, 146–48; *The Lover*,
    148

Zionism, 2–3, 7, 10, 14–15, 19, 23, 36, 43,
    47, 52–54, 56, 75, 78, 134, 162, 166
Zionist congress, 13
Zionist movement, 2–3, 26, 52–53, 64,
    74, 136
Zola, Emil, 146

ABOUT THE AUTHOR

HAIM GORDON is Senior Lecturer, Department of Education, Ben Gurion University, Israel. He is the author of numerous books, scholarly papers, and book reviews, and has contributed articles to *Religious Education*, the *Journal of Jewish Studies*, and *Educational Theory*.